The Lives of Jessie Sampter

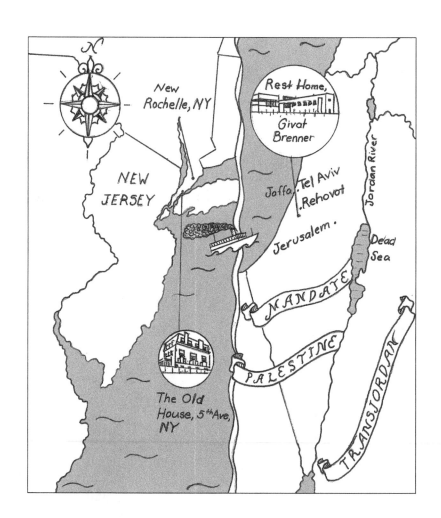

Illustration by Claire Bergen

The Lives of Jessie Sampter

QUEER, DISABLED, ZIONIST

Sarah Imhoff

Duke University Press · Durham and London · 2022

Printed in the United States of America on acid-free paper ∞
Designed by Matthew Tauch
Project editor: Annie Lubinsky
Typeset in Whitman by Westchester Publishing Services

Library of Congress Cataloging-in-Publication Data
Names: Imhoff, Sarah, author.
Title: The lives of Jessie Sampter : queer, disabled, Zionist / Sarah
Imhoff.
Description: Durham : Duke University Press, 2022. | Includes
bibliographical references and index.
Identifiers: LCCN 2021035841 (print) | LCCN 2021035842 (ebook)
ISBN 9781478015437 (hardcover)
ISBN 9781478018063 (paperback)
ISBN 9781478022671 (ebook)
ISBN 9781478092650 (ebook other)
Subjects: LCSH: Sampter, Jessie E. (Jessie Ethel), 1883–1938. |
Authors, American—20th century—Biography. | Zionists—
United States—Biography. | Authors with disabilities—United
States—Biography. | Lesbian authors—United States—Biography. |
BISAC: SOCIAL SCIENCE / Gender Studies | SOCIAL SCIENCE /
People with Disabilities
Classification: LCC PS3537.A567 Z676 2022 (print) | LCC PS3537.
A567 (ebook) | DDC 818/.5209 [B]—dc23/eng/20211206
LC record available at https://lccn.loc.gov/2021035841
LC ebook record available at https://lccn.loc.gov/2021035842

This book is freely available in an open access edition
thanks to TOME (Toward an Open Monograph
Ecosystem)—a collaboration of the Association of
American Universities, the Association of University
Presses, and the Association of Research Libraries—and
the generous support of Indiana University. Learn more
at the TOME website, which can be found at the following
web address: openmonographs.org.

Cover art: Jessie Sampter at Kibbutz Givat Brenner, 1930s.
Courtesy of Givat Brenner Archives, Yesha Sampter
papers.

Contents

Acknowledgments

I have been living with Jessie Sampter for so long that sometimes I wonder if my colleagues and friends feel as though she lives with them too. Winnifred Sullivan would ask me, "How's Jessie?" She's still captivating, Winni.

I could never have come to know so much of Sampter were it not for the generosity and knowledge of archivists and kibbutz members. Dana Herman at the American Jewish Archives, Erin Hess at the Ira and Judith Kaplan Eisenstein Reconstructionist Archives, and everyone at the Central Zionist Archives and the Archives for the History of the Jewish People helped me track down traces of Sampter. I am especially grateful to the members of Kibbutz Givat Brenner who welcomed me when I walked up the hill, sweaty after hiking from the bus stop, trying to find the archives but at first finding only the dentist: Michal, who shared everything she knew that the kibbutz archive held; Danny, who gave me rides to the bus stop in his motorized cart after that first day; and Mimi, who brought me into her home and fed me.

I wish I could do justice to everyone by naming them, but lists are inadequate ways of expressing gratitude. So, a sampling of things for which I am grateful: Jake Beckert read all the way through a weird and sometimes disturbing novel to see what I'd missed about a character based on Jessie. Cooper Harriss has definitely heard me talk about Sampter at least five times, and he always has something productive to say. Winnifred Sullivan has been not only a cheerleader but also a sharp reader. This book owes so much to my graduate student conversation partners: Dale Spicer would pop into my office to talk about disability studies. Mihee Kim-Kort's enthusiasm for our theoretical readings about the body inspired me. Mike Aronson, Jake

Beckert, Jakob Breunig, Steve Kaplin, Dale Spicer, and Eliana Schechter all read an early version and helped me think about the book in the context of American Judaism. Sabina Ali helped me with editing the manuscript.

I've been known to describe the Department of Religious Studies at Indiana University, dryly, as "remarkably functional." And it's true. Faculty and graduate students alike have offered advice and generous critique about so many bits and pieces that made their way into this book. But more than that, my colleagues have made it a wonderful intellectual home. I feel such gratitude for you all.

I have also found a wonderful, supportive corner of the Jewish studies world: S. J. Crasnow shared their insights on queer theory. David Weinfeld sent me correspondence between Horace Kallen and Sampter, and Sharon Musher shared a letter from Hadassah Kaplan to her father, Mordecai, mentioning her visit with Sampter. Esther Carmel-Hakim shared her historical expertise. Gregg Gardner and Dustin Atlas each responded to pleas on social media for photos and pamphlets. Lea Taragin-Zeller helped me think better about kinship. Eli Sacks, Sam Brody, Rachel Gordan, Susannah Heschel, Andrea Cooper, Paul Nahme, Alex Kay, Yonatan Brafman, and Jessica Marglin have inspired me, as conversation partners and as scholars in our little modern Jewish studies writing group.

The field of American religion has been such a source of wisdom and kindness that I hardly know where to begin: the friends and colleagues who made the Taking Exception workshops Cooper Harriss and I hosted into something really special; Samira Mehta, who knows what I'm thinking at conferences just by looking at my face; and the reading group of women who both say smart things and are willing to co-complain in the face of yet another month of a pandemic.

I also want to thank everyone who invited me to speak with them and their students: Ilana Szobel and her colleagues at Brandeis; Seth Perry, Judith Weisenfeld, and the whole Religion in America faculty and graduate student crowd at Princeton; Craig Perry and his colleagues at Cincinnati; Mark Raider, who included me in his conference about World War I; Elizabeth Shakman Hurd and Winnifred Sullivan, who hosted the lively At Home and Abroad project; the wonderful department at the University of North Carolina at Charlotte; Larisa Reznik and her religious studies colleagues at Pomona College; Hillary Kaell at Concordia University; and Melissa Wilcox, Amanda Lucia, Michael Alexander, and their colleagues at the University of California, Riverside. Those talks felt like conversations to me: I learned what students, community members, and faculty thought about Jessie Sampter, and I wondered how I could better answer their questions in the book.

I could not have done this without financial support from Indiana's Borns Jewish Studies Program, the Hadassah Brandeis Institute, New Frontiers at Indiana, and the College Arts and Humanities Institute at Indiana. Several sentences in this book also appear in my contribution to *American Religion at Home and Abroad*, edited by Elizabeth Shakman Hurd and Winnifred Fallers Sullivan, and a small section of chapter 4 is slated to appear as part of my essay in *Over There: American Jews and World War I*, edited by Mark A. Raider and Gary P. Zola.

I especially want to thank Sandra Korn, editor extraordinaire. Right from the beginning, she has been fabulous to work with. She found brilliant and generous readers who renewed my faith in the peer-review process. This is surely a better book because of them.

This book and I both owe so many of the better parts of ourselves to my family, both chosen and more conventional. Eva, your verve and snark and brilliance shaped this from the beginning. Mom and Dad, your support has always been unwavering, and I cannot thank you for that enough. I feel immense gratitude to the nonhuman animals who offered support and a kind ear every time I wanted to talk through some new idea. Jethro (z"l), Moses, and Mr. Meowgi have been the most generous listeners a writer could imagine, even if they will never be readers. And Michael, thank you for listening and loving, and most of all putting up with Jessie and with me.

Introduction

I first met Jessie Sampter in the Central Zionist Archives in Jerusalem. It was cold, and I was fidgeting to keep warm, alternating between sitting on my hands and using them to turn the yellowed, flaking papers. I was looking for early twentieth-century American Zionists, and since Sampter had authored the ninety-five-page *A Course in Zionism*, a primer for understanding support for a Jewish state in Palestine, I requested some of the folders cataloged under her name. I knew that Hadassah, the women's Zionist organization, had published and promoted the first edition in 1915. In 1920 it published Sampter's expanded version, then called *A Guide to Zionism*, and in 1933 a new version called *Modern Palestine: A Symposium*, which tipped the scales at 411 pages and included a foreword by Albert Einstein. I knew that Hadassah approved of her work, even though the books were never great commercial successes.[1] Jessie Sampter, I figured as I wished for my body to warm up, would be a good example of a typical American Zionist.

She turned out to be anything but.

I don't remember thinking about the cold after that first folder in the archive. But I do remember thinking again and again about Jessie's body. Sometimes it felt so present to me, even though all I had were pieces of paper and a few photographs.

As I spent more time with Sampter—with her unpublished autobiographies, with her drafts of later-published poems and essays, with her letters to friends and family, with her published books and poetry—I came to realize that Sampter's own life and body hardly matched typical Zionist ideals: while Zionism celebrated strong and healthy bodies, Sampter spoke of herself as "crippled" from polio and plagued by weakness and sickness her whole life; while Zionism applauded reproductive women's bodies, Sampter never married or bore children. In fact, she wrote of homoerotic longings and had same-sex relationships we would consider queer.

Sampter was also quite complex in other ways, I came to see. In late 1918 she sat with several friends and used a Ouija board to ask her dead mother: Did she approve of Jessie's recent return to Judaism? And how did she feel about Jessie's embrace of Zionism and plan to move to Palestine? These were pressing questions for the thirty-five-year-old. And the more I read about Sampter's life, the more questions I asked myself. The traditional 613 Jewish commandments prohibit trying to contact the dead (no. 64, according to the medieval rabbi Maimonides) and divination (no. 62). So how did Sampter understand Judaism? And the nature of the world and the afterlife? She seemed to be full of paradoxes.

These questions drew me in. I wanted to know more about her ever-developing inner life. I saw her not only as a writer but also as a lover of children, a conflicted pacifist, an adoptive mother, an advocate for the disabled, and an Orientalist who became too comfortable pushing Arabs to the margins of society in Palestine. She also became a puzzle: How did a queer, disabled woman become a voice of American Zionism? And how should I write about the life and embodied experiences of this woman who defied social norms and confounded available categories of sexuality? The more I turned to her, the more she turned me to bigger questions. She became a way for me to think about the relationship between an embodied life and a body of thought—and a way for me to quietly theorize how those two things are entwined in wonderful and complex ways.

To Write Her Life

Why write a life at all? I am an academic, after all, and we generally leave the writing of presidential biographies and celebrity lives to more popular writers. Academic historians can be dubious of biography as a genre. To many, it seems small, amateurish, insufficiently analytic, unworthy. To others, it smacks of the kind of "great man" histories that paint the world as a place where events are driven by a tiny elite, as if the course of history could always be understood by looking closely enough into the lives of these few, usually white, men. Biography rarely serves as a way to rethink the well-trodden paths of established methods.

And yet here I am, writing a book that centers on a single person from the past. It is not primarily because I think Sampter has been neglected, though I do think that is true. During her life she was extremely well connected, and her work was read in both the United States and Palestine. Yet understanding Sampter will not make us see the causes of World War I differently, will not radically change our perspective on the British Empire's dealings in the Middle East, and will not force us to rewrite the history of poetry. I do not think that Sampter transformed the world by the sheer force of her intellect or actions, and so this is not a biography in the "great man" style that claims that its subject is important for making sense of a larger historical narrative. My point is in some ways much smaller and in other ways much bigger: analyzing her life illuminates a sometimes invisible aspect of the human condition—that our embodied selves do not always neatly line up with our religious or political ideals. My point is also a theoretical one, though it lurks beneath the text more often than on its surface: bodies, senses, and feelings are important sources of knowledge.

Maybe this isn't a biography, then. Historian Jill Lepore differentiates between the foundational assumptions and goals of two genres of writing: "If biography is largely founded on a belief in the singularity and significance of an individual's contribution to history, microhistory is founded upon almost the opposite assumption: however singular a person's life may be, the value of examining it lies in how it serves as an allegory for the culture as a whole."[2] Sampter offers this opportunity: her distinctive embodied experience points to the far wider cultural phenomenon of the complex relationship between the body and religious thought. Writing a microhistory about Sampter means staking a theoretical claim that embodiment is a critical piece of even the most intellectual lives. And yet this book is still life-writing, and I identify it with this etymological sense of *biography*. The relationship to biology resonates with attention to physical bodies and embodiment, even as what it means to write a body into textual existence has never been as clear as what it means to write a philosophical analysis or a history. I have come to think of this book as belonging to a slightly off-kilter genre: weird biography.

I wrote this weird biography about Sampter because I am fascinated by her—and also because I believe that historians and other scholars should think more and better about embodiment, and one of the best ways to do this is through a single person. A single body. Of course, even a single body implicates other bodies: familial bodies, social bodies, and the body politic all make significant appearances here. Still, Sampter's body, with all its relationships and permeability and vulnerability, remains the center for my thinking about bodies more generally. When I call for greater attention to embodiment, I think I can best show its importance through one life rather than through the data of many bodies. My first book was largely about American Jewish men and their bodies and why the construction of those gendered bodies matters to our histories of religion, politics, and gender. Though the many men in those pages could illuminate general historical trends, they could not provide the same insight that this intimate look at one woman can: to show us how the body is ever present and fundamentally intertwined with the mind, the soul, religion, politics, and ideology.

An Embodied Method

Many academic books include a self-disclosure: the writers share with their readers that they write "as a middle-class white woman who grew up in upstate New York," "as a gay Black man," or "as an Indian who came to the United States as a child."[3] What is the meaning of these proclamations? Well, if we've learned anything from both physics and literature, it must be that an observer is never outside the system she observes. A chronicler is never objective. These writers seek to acknowledge that for their readers: I am a particular person with a particular identity, and so this book is particular to me.

How would you read this book differently if I told you I was a middle-class white woman? How do you determine which attributes are the ones that matter for understanding the me in this book? Some are clearly germane. For instance, my name and my American accent helped me gain access to materials and forge relationships at the kibbutz that I might not have been able to if I had an obviously Muslim name or an Egyptian passport, say.

And it's true. I *am* a middle-class white woman. I also grow echinacea and roses, I hike, I write sitting cross-legged on the couch, my knee doesn't hurt anymore where I tore my ACL, I scuba dive, I dream of being a migrating whale shark or a tiny cleaner shrimp, I will stop in my tracks to watch a red-tailed hawk fly overhead, I love an afternoon nap, I don't eat meat, I still feel it in the pit of my stomach when I think about holding the lifeless body of my first dog, I can't reach high places but I can do pull-ups, I want to be a runner but I am so. darned. slow. Maybe those are the things you need to know to understand the me in this book. Maybe not.

There are other things you'll find, too, interspersed with my accounts of Jessie Sampter. They are integral parts of my method—an embodied method in which I seek different kinds of knowledge. Not just what she wrote, or what philosophy or history means. That, too, of course. In my research for this book, I explored not only texts and material objects—the things scholars usually interpret through reading and seeing—but also what we apprehend by other senses and feelings: what the air feels like on a hot July day on the top of the hill at the kibbutz, the sting when the soft flesh of my forearm is snagged by a rose thorn while I prune, the taste of fresh dates, the joy of creation when a seed sprouts, and the frustration when leg muscles have nothing left to give. Each of these is its own kind of knowledge.

Take a familiar example about riding a bike: although you could read how-to manuals, learn how the gears work, feel all the parts of a bicycle, and watch all the videos you wanted, you would still know something *more* by learning to ride the bicycle. After riding the bike, you could tell about the feeling of balance, the way something just "clicks" when the bike gets to a certain speed, the contraction of certain muscles, the extra oomph needed to get up a steep hill, and the compelling mix of nervousness, joy, and accomplishment during the first successful ride. (The phrase "It's like riding a bike" partakes in this same shared sense that physical memories can stick with us in ways that differ from cognitive memories.) Some philosophers have explained the difference between "knowing that" and "knowing how." The embodied knowledge in this book includes some "knowing how" and also goes beyond it to include sensations and perceptions. These sensations, perceptions, and physical knowledge matter for the way a person sees the world—in Sampter's case, how she thinks about the relationship of nature and God, how she thinks about the social roles people with disabilities should play, and why she thinks Palestine is a homeland for her people.

I sought all of these kinds of knowledge. And I did so because I learned from it: I saw new things, I asked new questions, and I understood more. This method was the right one for this book. I am convinced that experiential knowledge shapes how we can understand Sampter, her world, and our world. It might not be the right approach for every book, and it certainly has its limitations. I'm quite critical of the idea that you can, for example, wear a blindfold for an hour or two and thereby know what life is like for a person who is blind. In many ways, this is a new approach in religious studies scholarship, but it is hardly sui generis. I have learned from the methods of other scholars who have insisted on going beyond textual and visual evidence, including focusing on bodily senses, affect, and materiality.[4]

Yet the search for embodied knowledge also reminds me of all the things I can't know: I can't smell the streets of Jerusalem in 1919, I can't hear the sound of Jessie's voice, I don't know what it's like to wake up wondering if I will be able to get out of bed or walk beyond the kitchen, and I certainly can't feel the physical pains of polio. I can't experience the past firsthand. And I can't live in someone else's mind and body. But that's not new; that's the challenge for all scholars who write about the past, or about anyone other than themselves, really. I want to get a little closer. And bringing my readers a little closer, strangely, sometimes means bringing them closer to me.

I think that, for all humanistic writers, careful attention to embodiment should be the rule and not the exception. The mind is inherently embodied. As the philosophers George Lakoff and Mark Johnson remind us, contra to Western philosophical assumptions that mind and body are fundamentally different and separate, human thought actually "arises from the nature of our brains, bodies, and bodily experience."[5] Brain science has shown that the neural and cognitive mechanisms that we need to move our bodies are the same ones that we need to think, conceptualize, and reason. The things that make movement possible also make metaphors possible.

It's not just that having a body is necessary for thinking and reasoning—though of course it is—it's also that the material of the body shapes these thought processes. Lakoff and Johnson write, "The very structure of reason itself comes from the details of our embodiment."[6] I propose to take them seriously. By telling Jessie Sampter's life as stories about the body and the mind—and insisting that we cannot tell those stories separately—we see a life more clearly. We do not, of course, see her brain's synapses at work, but we see the profound integration of body and mind. My hope is that my readers, and especially scholars who write about people we call *thinkers*, recognize that this profound integration is not distinctive to Sampter. Having a body is a universal human experience, even though the particulars of that experience are different for each person. Bodies *are* how we experience the world, whether through eyes or fingertips or other senses, as well as shaping how we experience the world, such as through our physical capacities, race, or gender.

Studying the ways minds and bodies work also means seeing that they work imperfectly. Philosopher Jacqueline Rose summarizes the work of trans theorist Susan Stryker: "There is no body without debilitation and pain. We are all made up of endlessly permuting bits and pieces which sometimes do, mostly do not, align with each other."[7] This book, then, is about Sampter, but it's also about the human condition—the condition of having a mind and a body and the condition of imperfection, internal conflict, and debilitation.

Shortly after she moved to Palestine, Sampter momentarily fantasized about being a mind but not a body: "Escape from the body, its pains, shames, and humors, prompted at times a curious disgust of the human life that at other times I idealized. Were not secretion, defecation and even eating revolting as well as troublesome? Were we not physically as noisome as the spider or caterpillar one squashes against the wall?" Yet the flesh, even with its disgust-inducing processes and properties, could not be jettisoned. Despite the appeal of getting rid of the yuckiness of a body, Sampter dismissed the very possibility of a disembodied person. That would be no person at all. She then turned her musings toward having a body without imperfection: "Then I romanced myself into a magic life, in which I would neither eat, drink, sleep, throw off waste, tire nor grow old. I should have golden-red hair and violet-blue eyes and be beautiful; or only be as I was without defect, with unfilled teeth and no deformity. I should go about the world, immortally young, incessantly active, working for the benefit of mankind."[8] But she quickly dismissed this as well. Her mind and her body were one. To think otherwise was to get lost in a reverie.

———

Even stripped down to a handful of facts, Sampter's life was remarkable. Born in New York in 1883, she developed an early interest in religious topics and the craft of writing, both nurtured by her beloved father, Rudolph. When she was twelve, she contracted polio, a poorly understood disease at the time. For the rest of her life, she would live with scoliosis, deformed hands and wrists, weakness, and later what we now call post-polio syndrome.

As she grew to be an adult, her interest in religion deepened, and she published two philosophical books, *The Seekers* and *The Great Adventurer*. Her own seeking brought her to Judaism and Zionism. She joined Hadassah, the American women's Zionist organization, ran their educational department, and wrote *A Course in Zionism*. During World War I, she wrote two more books, the prose-poetry *Sefer ha-Goyim* (*The Book of Nations*) and the poetry collection *The Coming of Peace*.

She settled in Palestine on September 22, 1919. She went as an unmarried woman with no family there but with the blessing of the Zionist Organization of America. In the beginning, she lived in Jerusalem with Leah Berlin, a Russian Zionist who quickly became a central fixture in her life. She later moved to Rehovot, at that time a small town outside of Tel Aviv, where she had a house built for herself and Tamar, the Yemenite Jewish toddler she adopted in 1926. She published essays, poetry, and books—everything from children's fiction to political essays about life in Palestine. Though she visited the United States in 1925 and 1930, she would never again call anywhere but Palestine home.[9] Then, in the winter of 1933–34, she and Leah moved to Kibbutz Givat Brenner, where she used her inheritance to establish a vegetarian rest home for workers. When Tamar wasn't at boarding school in Tel Aviv, she, too, called the kibbutz home. By the end of her life, Sampter had published eleven books, dozens and dozens of poems, and hundreds of articles, including pieces in English and Hebrew. In 1938 Sampter left her room at Givat Brenner to get treatment for an illness and died at the Hadassah hospital.

But lives are about more than a chronicle of events. Sampter not only wrote and participated in political movements but also thought, felt, loved, hurt, despaired, and mourned. How, as a woman living a century later, do I know what I know about Jessie Sampter? Can I ever know what she thought and felt? Not fully, of course. But I have spent a lot of time with Sampter's words, photographs, reading materials, and other things from the world around her. I have read all of the books she wrote, published and unpublished, in all of their editions. She wrote to her sister, Elvie Wachenheim, at least once a week from when she moved to Palestine in 1919 until she died in 1938. These letters were often six or eight pages long, and rarely fewer than four. She praised her niece Jessie (her namesake) when she became one of the first woman airplane pilots in the United States, shared intimate details of her life in Palestine, and declared the errors of the British Empire in its handling of political violence. She wrote to colleagues and friends, including Henrietta Szold, Mordecai Kaplan, and dozens of others. "Letters are the hub of life," she once declared.[10] More than a thousand of her letters survive, and I have read them all (unless I haven't—there could always be one or two or seventeen in another archive or in a trunk in someone's attic). I have read her essays, poems, and articles that were published in the *Palestine Post*, the *Maccabaean*, the Hebrew-language *Davar*, and more than a dozen other newspapers and magazines. I have also studied many of those articles and poems in their infancy since Sampter saved her marked and edited drafts. She was the animating personality behind her kibbutz newsletter and frequently wrote about her reactions and political ideals, discussing everything from day-to-day kibbutz life to world politics in both English and Hebrew. Rarely, such as when she wrote to Albert Einstein, she used German. I read those letters too.

"PS. It seems probable that letters are still being censored," she wrote to her sister in May 1920.[11] The immediate context was the riots earlier that spring, and yet the letter suggests something more fundamental: Sampter's own writing is only part of the story. Although her own voice is central to this book, it is also crucial to listen to other voices around her, and so these stories also rely on the letters and publications of her friends, associates, family, and even intellectual opponents. To see her lives more clearly, I also read what she read: everything from Sigmund Freud to Benedict de Spinoza to the books that inspired *Lawrence of Arabia* to the *Nation* and the monthly magazine *Asia*.

I also pursued other ways of knowing: not only reading but also *doing*. I spent time at her kibbutz, met its schoolchildren, saw some of its agricultural work, and talked to its aging members. As much as I could, I did what she did and used the stuff that she used: I grew nasturtiums, roses, zinnias, and one (very sad) citrus tree. I tried my hand at paper-cut silhouettes. I looked at old ads for Bayer's Compral, and I even tried to get a tube of Kondon's Cattarhal Jelly—not the other brand, as she frequently reminded her sister in her letters requesting the medicinal gel. (No luck.)

These physical bits and pieces, the smell of the roses, the feel of a new Burpee catalog, the natural landscapes, and the built environments shaped her life profoundly. They affected not only her moods but also her religious philosophy and her Zionism.

This method of attending to the body, even when it is not on the surface of the narrative, is part of the critique disability studies makes: it is a privilege to be able to ignore your body, a privilege to pretend that your autonomous thoughts and carefully planned actions are where the real (historical and philosophical) action is at. It is also at least partly an illusion. Nancy Eiesland's groundbreaking book *The Disabled God* puts it this way: "An accessible theological method necessitates that the body be represented as flesh and blood, bones and braces, and not simply the rationalized realm of activity."[12] That method of knowing through the body is reflected in Eiesland's own autobiographical writing, as well as others'. She explains, "Unwilling and unable to take our bodies for granted, we attend to the kinesis of knowledge."[13] And scholars should too. This book shows a woman with a sophisticated set of philosophical ideas that were shaped by her embodied experience as well as her intellect—and also shows the friction among her political, intellectual, and embodied experiences. In writing this way, I also suggest that others' lives, whether they are disabled or not, are more strongly shaped by embodied experiences than historians or scholars of religious thought often presume.

So if I am going to describe what I did in terms of growing nasturtiums, feeling the sun and the hot wind at Kibbutz Givat Brenner, and cutting silhouettes out of paper, it also makes sense to describe what I read. Scholars may take for granted reading as a way of knowing, but I am interested in making it strange again, in a way. Why is it obvious, I ask myself, that a scholar should read everything someone wrote while it is not obvious that they might stand in their house, grow the plants they grew, play the instrument they played, practice their trade, or listen to the sounds of their typewriter?

I cannot say that I always know Sampter's thoughts and feelings, but after years of reading and doing, I know a lot about her. So when I write that Hyman Segal's *The Book of Pain-Struggle, Called: The Prophecy of Fulfillment* resonated with Sampter because of the way it suggested a Zionism in which pain was central, I am not claiming to know all the inner workings of her mind, but I think I do know some. I have in mind two of her books, two letters, two unpublished autobiographies, and three unpublished essays, as well as knowledge of an array of other visions of Zionism of the time. So, while thoughts and emotions may not always be empirically verifiable, the moments where I talk about Sampter's thoughts or feelings are not merely imaginative reconstructions or projections born of overidentification with my subject. In sketching Sampter's inner life, where I can, I have tried never to go beyond reasonable induction based on the sources I have.

How should I tell the story of these facts and feelings? Pursuing these kinds of knowledge also meant that I saw her life and thought from many angles. Sometimes I write about her as *Jessie*, in particular when I discuss her personal and familial relationships. Other times I call her *Sampter*, emphasizing her public and intellectual roles. She was, of course, always both. But I hope that moving between the two can remind us of the fundamentally inseparable nature of a human life. A recent novel's narrator, herself a life-writer, asks, "What if, for once in history, a woman's story could be untethered from what we need it to be in order to feel better about ourselves?"[14] The narrator tells the story of Joan—a postapocalyptic Joan of Arc figure—through a futuristic form of body art akin to tattooing or branding. In a profound act of acknowledging the centrality of the body, she makes the contours of her own body into an artistic rendering of Joan's life. She proclaims, "I will write it. I will tell the truth."[15]

I cannot claim to have told Jessie Sampter's truth in its entirety; that is an impossible task. Nor do I want to paint her as some sort of radical saint. But I can say that Sampter's story here is not meant as an inspirational story tethered to us feeling better about ourselves.[16] At many moments, a sensitive reader might feel it borders on indictment of others ("How could a society treat disabled people that way?") and of Sampter herself ("How can she say that about Arabs?"). Her stories are not, in the end, redemptive. Nor are they cautionary tales or the bearers of moral messages. They are stories of a life.

I am writing these stories in a style uncommon for academics—and, so, uncommon for me. But I have come to see accessibility as a feminist value, not only in physical spaces but also in intellectual ones like this book. Historically, women have been excluded from some conversations because they had been excluded from the kinds of learning that would prepare them to appear as experts there. For example, when women could not get PhDs, they would not be hired as professors. Closer to Jewish tradition, women could not be Talmud scholars until they were allowed to learn the language and discursive style of the Talmud. (Even now, if you happened on an academic conversation among English-speaking Talmud scholars, you would likely find yourself at sea unless you, too, had had a very specific education.) The exclusion wasn't because some official had proclaimed that no woman could become a Talmud scholar, though there are religious traditions that consider it vulgar; rather, rabbinical schools and other experts weren't training women in ways that allowed them that kind of access to the text. The point is that even in the absence of formal exclusion, people have used arcane, technical, or dense language in ways that exclude others from the conversation.

Sometimes scholars do this, and sometimes for good reason. Like baseball fans, communities of scholars have a specialized vocabulary, which might appear as jargon to outsiders. This jargon often refers to a concept whose complexities are well known by the community; a word functions as a shorthand. (Think of "on base plus slugging." If you're a baseball fan, its meaning is self-evident, and you wouldn't think twice using it in conversation with a fellow fan because it's much shorter than describing the whole concept. If you're not a fan, its meaning is lost on you until you get someone to explain it.) If theoretical physicists had to use small, accessible words to describe all of their research to one another, every paper would be six times as long and full of caveats and distinctions—all of which had been worked through before. Humanistic scholarship also has these specialized words. They help us point to concepts without having to rehearse all of the caveats and complexities; they help us think theoretically and discuss exciting new research. Sometimes, too, scholars who want to critique a system find that the best way is to reject the terms of that system. Judith Butler, a frequent target of attacks on "academic writing," argues that it is a scholar's job to "provoke new ways of looking at a familiar world," and that often means questioning "common sense."[17] In short, sometimes complex language is best to show complexity, especially where we might have missed it otherwise.

Yet I have forgone almost all specialized academic vocabulary here, though many times it would have been easier to use it. It doesn't mean that there isn't theory here or that this book makes no academic claims. It does. But they aren't easy: they are about ways of knowing, about the complexity of understanding another person, about the ways religion, politics, and the body are never fully separable. Those are hard ideas, and I am not convinced that dense prose is the best way to investigate them. Instead, I'm doing it through the story of a woman. And I hope that opening the door with accessible writing allows more readers into those deeper questions.

———

Finding women. Making a woman's story accessible, not just to a specialized audience. These are not always easy tasks.

Archives have been predominantly male spaces.[18] The items in archives tend to document the deeds and ideas of those in power, who have largely been men, as well as being oriented toward politics, war, and national movements, spheres often seen as male. Women do appear in archives but sometimes only in relation to men. When I wanted to find out about Julia Dushkin, Sampter's friend and fellow Zionist, I had to go to the Archive for the History of the Jewish People and look at her husband's file. People had saved a few of her papers, mostly ones that related to her husband and some others that related to her philanthropy, and then other people had cataloged those papers under "Alexander Dushkin." Sampter's papers are cataloged under her own name, for the most part. She had no husband whose archives could swallow her own.

Sometimes Jessie's stories contain elements that are not altogether flattering. "The woolen stockings you sent me are a disappointment," she wrote to her sister, Elvie.[19] I laughed when I read this: how entitled she was! Her sister had sent a lovely gift across the ocean at no mean expense, and Jessie didn't have a single nice word to say about it. After she arrived in Palestine, her very first letter to her sister, brother-in-law, and their kids began with a sentence thanking them for letters. The next sentence read, "But even then I was disappointed to find only two from you, dated August 25 and 29, and what bothered me was that there was no copy of the one I received in London. I wish you would number your letters, as I do."[20] Jessie stopped numbering her letters just a few months later. Half a year later, she wrote to her sister, "This is my very busy week for I am moving! I meant to send you a long typewritten letter today, but Leah Berlin came in to help me with my packing—or rather, to do it for me—and I am snatching a moment to scribble, in between directing her."[21] Anyone who has helped a friend move knows that the work is draining, and to have your friend sit and "direct" you cannot have been easy. What a trooper Leah must have been to pack for Jessie and to take her orders. Jessie's letter expressed no gratitude; she merely presented her own task as direction and Leah's as labor. And, no, in case you are wondering: the letter wasn't a tongue-in-cheek description shared between knowing sisters. She rarely wrote anything tongue-in-cheek.

Jessie was a serious woman. She could be demanding, and she had a limited sense of humor. Her cousin wrote to her, "Everyone thinks you are either wonderful or crazy."[22] It was true. Some people also found her difficult. Friends and kibbutz members would often comment about how she and Leah were a bit of an odd couple—the well-heeled, sensitive, entitled New Yorker and the strong and practical Russian. I'm not sure the comparison was always a complimentary one for Jessie.

Sampter was also morally serious and contemplative, and yet despite her deep humanism, she said and did morally unacceptable things. When her cat gave birth to kittens, she drowned them. In early twentieth-century Palestine, this was just what you did with unwanted kittens. But the act is still reprehensible. Sampter also sometimes expressed racism against Arabs and wrestled with what roles she thought they could play in society. Like drowning the kittens, this discriminatory move was typical—in fact, when it came to Arabs, Sampter was better than many of her peers—but typicality does not excuse racism. I will not write these off by saying that Sampter was merely a product of her environment in these respects. She bucked trends in many other circumstances, and so she could have acted differently in these situations. I still see her agency in deciding to drown kittens and exclude Arabs. Her story, then, is not a story of a woman beyond ethical reproach.

Jessie Sampter never became a major Zionist communal leader, nor did her writings enter the canon of Zionist, much less Jewish, philosophy. Her writing about Zionism and Judaism is consistently smart but garnered few followers. I find her poetry interesting because of its political aims, but some of it tends toward the formulaic. Aesthetically, some of it is mediocre. Her correspondents and friends included people well known to history: Mary Antin became famous for her immigrant memoir *The Promised Land*, Henrietta Szold ran Hadassah with seemingly infinite energy, Mordecai Kaplan founded the Reconstructionist movement in Judaism, Louis Brandeis was the first Jew appointed to the US Supreme Court, and Albert Einstein, well, we all know his name. Though she had quite a few famous friends, Sampter herself never became a celebrity. She was neither extraordinarily powerful in her time nor terribly influential after it.

And so it is not my intention here to praise a lost poetic genius, to show ways she profoundly influenced American Judaism, or to hold her up as a saint. Yet I think we would gain something by considering her part of the canon of Jewish thought. And more broadly, writing her life with unflinching attention to embodiment offers us a model of how we can understand religious philosophy and philosophers: not just as fine intellects but as people with inextricably linked bodies and minds. While her life as a queer, disabled Zionist is distinctive—dare I say unique?—it helps us understand something that is shared across humanity.

Far from fame or saintliness, then, it is Sampter's imperfections and incongruities that animate much of this book, and they are a crucial part of what makes her human. I spent a lot of time with Sampter, and I want to root for her (however strange that may be to say about a long-dead woman), but that doesn't mean writing a hagiography. This book is a story about a flawed human with an imperfect body because that is the life she lived. It is the kind of life we all live.

An Unexpected Zionist

The most visible incongruity in Sampter's life was the coexistence of her Zionism with her queerness and disability. Today, if people call themselves Zionists, they mean that they support the existence of Israel as a Jewish state. They might have a variety of reasons for this support: they might see a need for a Jewish safe haven, they might believe that only within a Jewish state can Jews truly achieve self-determination, or they might have Jewish or Christian theological reasons for wanting to support Jewish settlement in the Holy Land. They might celebrate the leadership of the Likud Party, or they might be critical of Israel's treatment of Palestinians; they might support a single state or want, as the saying goes, a "two-state solution"; but in general they support some version of a Jewish state located in and around Jerusalem.

But before the State of Israel was founded in 1948, the options for self-identified Zionists were far broader. Some wanted a Jewish state, and some of those insisted that the Jewish state be in Palestine, whereas others would have been content with a Jewish state located almost anywhere. Others, sometimes called cultural Zionists, were far more invested in Jewish settlement in Palestine as a spiritual and cultural center of Jewish life. They saw a return to the land, the resurgence of the Hebrew language, and greater connection to Judaism as the center of the Zionist project. For example, Ahad Ha'am (literally, "one of the people," the pen name of Asher Ginsburg) wrote essays denouncing the spiritless Zionism of Theodor Herzl and the rush to colonize Palestine "for the Jews" instead of "for Judaism."[23] Cultural Zionists like Ahad Ha'am were often far less interested in pursuing the politics of state creation and inevitable conflicts with both Arabs and colonial powers. Practical Zionists focused on infrastructure, immigration, and settlement. For them, getting Jews to settle on the land and create community there was always the first priority, and other elements like spirituality and culture could follow. Religious Zionists saw the land of Israel as the true home of Jews and so took it as a religious commandment for Jews to settle there.[24] There were yet more: revisionist Zionists, labor Zionists, and various combinations of these groups.

Most Jews, however, were not Zionists at the beginning of the twentieth century. Some were agnostic about the project (non-Zionists), and others voiced their opposition (anti-Zionists), but the majority did not embrace the Zionist cause until later in the century. In the United States, when the future Supreme Court justice Louis Brandeis famously said, "To be good Americans, we must be better Jews, and to be better Jews, we must become Zionists," many of his fellow American Jews disagreed.[25] The anti-Zionist rabbi Isaac Mayer Wise spoke for most Reform Jews when, three decades earlier, he said, "The idea of the Jews returning to Palestine is no part of our creed. We rather believe it is God's will that the habitable world become one holy land and the human family one chosen people."[26] Many acculturated Jews also worried that Zionism would trigger accusations of "dual loyalty" from their fellow Americans. Yet by World War I, the Zionist movement was growing slowly, and, perhaps more important, opposition to it was waning. The Federation of American Zionists grew from about 3,800 dues-paying members in 1898 to almost 150,000 in 1918.[27]

In almost all of its guises, Zionism celebrated the able male body and its potential to reclaim the land of Palestine for the Jewish people.[28] Its most vocal proponents saw weak Jewish bodies as the result of living in exile. Returning to work the land would transform these bodies from their fallen state into proper, healthy, strong Jewish bodies. Or, alternatively, the regeneration of Jewish bodies would enable Zionist national goals.[29] Whichever way the causation went, Zionists saw strong bodies and nation building as intimately connected. *The Guide to Hashomer Leaders*, an eastern European publication for young Zionist leaders, cajoled its audience: we must once again be "whole and healthy men, and whole and healthy Jews."[30] Disabled bodies were nowhere to be seen, except as the negative image to be overcome. Doctor Binyamini, a physician at the first Hebrew school in Tel Aviv, wrote in 1928, "Zionism was accepted only by compatible men and women who were whole-bodied and physically fit. . . . Our people are currently experiencing a natural process of selection."[31] It wasn't true that only healthy or strong people accepted Zionism, but that didn't stop Binyamini from promoting the idea that there was something physically superior about Zionists. Building on the idea of a chosen people, sociologist Meira Weiss calls this whole, able male Jewish body "the chosen body"—a set of ideals that continue to reverberate in the present-day State of Israel.[32]

These idealized strong bodies were also male bodies. Max Nordau, cofounder with Theodor Herzl of the World Zionist Organization, championed what he called "Muscle Jewry." He promoted the establishment of Jewish gymnasiums and sporting clubs; he celebrated the founding of social organizations named after the Maccabees and Bar Kokhba, interpreted as the manly warriors of Jewish history; he declared, "Let us take up our oldest traditions; let us once more become deep-chested, sturdy, sharp-eyed men."[33] These images and ideals extended throughout the Zionist movement. The images in the *Maccabaean*, the American Zionist monthly magazine, were almost always of men or landscapes. Weak yeshiva students with poor posture would be replaced with suntanned young men who could be farmers and fighters.[34] As Daniel Boyarin has quipped, Zionism was, for Herzl and Freud, "a return to Phallustine."[35]

This masculine ideology did not mean that only men were Zionists: both men and women participated in Zionist writing, propaganda, organizing, fundraising, immigration, and settlement. Yet men were more visible both at the time and to later historians. Arthur Hertzberg's classic anthology *The Zionist Idea* collects the writings of thirty-seven important Zionists writing from the mid-nineteenth century to the founding of the State of Israel. All thirty-seven are men. From the United States to eastern Europe, many Zionists held up male thinkers and leaders while also emphasizing the healthy male body as the ideal.[36]

This male-centered story partly results from the fact that relatively few women wrote publicly about Zionist thought. But this scarcity is no accident. Women were actively excluded from the ranks of influencers by

Zionist men. The Federation of American Zionists (FAZ) wanted Hadassah to function as a place for middle-class women to fundraise, not to think or work independently. Historian Mary McCune writes, "Much of the FAZ leadership considered Hadassah a collection agency, a philanthropy, or, worst of all, an insignificant charity, despite the fact that raising funds and distributing them was precisely the role the men had planned for a national women's Zionist organization."[37] Henrietta Szold registered her frustration with this contradiction: "There has been constant criticism because [Hadassah] was not political enough, or because it was too political[;] either it didn't think or it thought too independently." It seemed that the FAZ wanted women "recruits" and their fundraising abilities but "not their minds," she reflected.[38] When historians write about Zionism, however, they need not follow suit. Even if there were fewer women writers, there were some, such as Sampter and her colleagues and friends Henrietta Szold, Lotta Levensohn, and Irma Levy Lindheim. Even if they weren't as widely read as the men, they surely contributed to Zionist discourse and education.

To include some of these women in the canon of Jewish thought, we might have to broaden our ideas of what counts as a thinker—perhaps by including what they wrote in letters, newsletters, or other Hadassah documents and not just books or essays on political ideas. We might even consider positions worked out together, such as the pacifism and politics in Szold and Sampter's correspondence. That Sampter was a woman made her look different from the most familiar Zionist thinkers, but that same fact could make Zionism look different to us.

In other ways, too, Sampter differed from the ideal Zionist. In Palestine many Zionists held ideals of collective living, especially in agriculturally based communities, and these social arrangements clearly valued able-bodied people. The kibbutz, kvutza, and moshav each represented communal ideals of working and living together. Originally, *kvutza* denoted a smaller settlement dedicated to farming, while a kibbutz was often a larger collective settlement that branched out from agriculture to include additional modes of production. Sampter wrote to her sister, "The difference between a kibbutz and a kvutza is that of an organization and its branches. . . . Givat Brenner [where she lived] is a kvutza or group of the kibbutz hameuhad [the United Kibbutz association]."[39] In practice, the labels were flexible, and in time many kvutzot eventually renamed themselves as kibbutzim. Moshavim had a similar ideology of communal living but usually included individual land allotments. All three, however, symbolized the Zionist ideals of the strong working body "making the desert bloom," as the saying went.

In addition to able male bodies and agricultural production, Zionism also promoted Jewish reproduction. "In fulfilling her duty and privilege as a Hebrew mother cherishing the young generation and educating them . . . the Hebrew woman and mother continues the great tradition of the Israeli heroine," as Israeli Knesset proceedings would put it in the early years of the state.[40] Although this trend would become much more visible as the years went on—today we can see the pronatalist policies of the State of Israel as its descendants—the idea that Jewish women should populate Palestine by giving birth to baby Jews existed even in the early twentieth century.[41] Sampter, of course, did not.

Nor did Sampter's Zionism fit easily within the parameters of typical Zionist women's work. Maxa Nordau, Max Nordau's daughter, wrote, "Far from politics, they [the women workers of Palestine] accomplish their real feminine duty by helping the unhappy, the needy, the abandoned, and the children."[42] Nordau was typical in her gendered outlook. Hadassah, the women's Zionist organization, also pursued projects related to motherhood, infants, and early education. Sampter's friend and Hadassah's leader, Henrietta Szold, wrote, "Let us devote ourselves to motherhood work. Our first aim was 'The Healing Daughter of our People,' let our second aim be to make our land 'The Joyful Mother of Children.'"[43] Its social programs matched her rhetoric. For instance, Hadassah created Tipat Halav (A Drop of Milk) to teach mothers preventative medicine for keeping babies healthy. Later it became involved in other "women's work": school lunches, nutritive shopping, and table manners for youngsters. A Hadassah newsletter printed a letter from a Haifa Public Schools official: "Scores of girls—perhaps for the first time in their lives—saw a clean and dainty Jewish kitchen, food tasty and nourishing because it was prepared according to the rules of dietetics, and a table prettily set, all at a low cost."[44]

Scholars often discuss political and theological thought as if the authors had no bodies—or, indeed, sometimes as if people were nothing more than brains and autonomous wills. But Sampter's story refuses this kind of oversight. Moreover, paying attention to women—and especially to a disabled woman—is crucial to a fuller understanding of Zionism in particular. This is especially important because such a significant part of Zionist ideology is focused on the body. But if the vast majority of our histories of Zionism focus on men, how will we know about women's bodies and about women's experiences with the embodied norms promoted by Zionism? Many histories deal with *Muskeljudentum* (muscular Judaism), which focused largely though not exclusively on men, and little of that literature tells us about the embodied experiences of Zionists themselves. Some of it tells us such things as who took up gymnastics, but it rarely reflects on how the people who did experienced their bodies. Even less does it consider the embodied experiences of the Zionists who could not participate in that physical culture.

Sampter's body was not productive (in the sense of working the land), nor was it reproductive (in the sense of producing Jewish children). She didn't even dedicate most of her time to helping mothers and children and working on health issues, as many Hadassah nurses did, though she did take an active interest in the education of Yemenite Jews in Palestine. Sampter's embodied Zionism, then, was a queer one: it did not follow the gender norms prescribed for either the ideal (male) Zionist builder of the nation or the female Zionist nurturer of the nation.

On the Strange Time of This Book

Biography typically begins with a birth and unfolds chronologically. It tells the story of a person, offering a coherent narrative of her life—or more likely his life, since more than 70 percent of recent English-language biographies are about men.[45] As historian Ann Little explains, these narratives are often about "a heroic individual who bends history to his will," marching forward through time.[46] But who among us has a life that follows a single thread?

Writing Sampter's life retrospectively is inevitable; after all, she is dead. I knew the end before I began: I knew she would die in Palestine, a member of a kibbutz, and the parent of a Yemenite Jewish girl. The ability to see the many parts of a life simultaneously is part of the historian's curse. We can see sequence, but it is easy to mistake sequence for causation; knowing later events always colors how we see earlier events. But this simultaneous view can also be a blessing. Biographical writing still tends to be faithful to chronology, but it need not be. Is the best way to tell a life necessarily in a linear order, attending only to the passage of time as marked by the calendar? What if the person lived her life otherwise? What if time hurried and slowed, doubled back on itself, looped and leaped? What if, instead of clocks and calendars, we took cues from the way a body might experience or feel time?

Time, in this book, is less a time*line* than time loops and squiggles. It goes slowly and then quickly. This book marks time by matters of the human body and not necessarily matters of the celestial bodies. Some of these markers, for Sampter, are before, after, and during illnesses: the disease of polio and then post-polio syndrome, which made polio again present and in that way was far more circular than its epithet *post* would lead us to believe; the missed time in hospital beds but also the rich, slow, artistically and intellectually generative time in those same beds.

Theorists of disability and queer theorists have argued that thinking more flexibly about time can help us think better about embodiment. Jack Halberstam discusses "queer time," a way of experiencing time that is not strictly structured by normative families and reproduction, and so its visions of the relationship of past and present to future can be radically different.[47] Queer time has "the potential to open up new life narratives and alternative relations to time and space."[48] José Esteban Muñoz writes, "Queerness should and could be about a desire for another way of being in both the world and time."[49] This queerness need not be limited to gay men and lesbians. "Queer refers to nonnormative logics and organization of community, sexual identity, embodiment, and activity in space and time," Halberstam explains, and so queer time can help us understand all sorts of social and embodied difference.[50]

If queer time is one alternative framework for understanding the time of our lives, then *crip time*—a phrase in which some disabled communities reclaim a short version of *crippled*—is another. Some scholars write about crip time by observing or assuming its existence without defining it; others talk about it in multiple ways.[51] But even when the term is not defined, the general sense is that crip time is extra time—it takes longer to get somewhere if one has a slower gait, if one has to search for an accessible entrance, if one depends on an attendant who is also running late, if one needs additional time to write an exam or read material. As Julia Watts Belser explains, "As a disabled person I spend a lot of time waiting for other people too: waiting for the bus, waiting for the wheelchair man, waiting for appointments, waiting for bureaucracy, just waiting."[52]

Other scholars suggest crip time is about being outside of time or excluded from it. Petra Kuppers calls these times of slowness, these moments of pain or immobility that overwhelm the possibility of "normal" physical activity, "moments out of time."[53] Joshua St. Pierre does something similar in his discussion of people who stutter: "The noninstrumental(izable) 'speaking speech' of the stutterer is cast out of time."[54] These metaphors of exclusion from time are fascinating and poetic, but in my view they miss the mark. Perhaps time haunts these moments of pain, immobility, or stuttering. Perhaps it's *extra*-present. But these moments are not "out of time"—not for a disabled person, nor for the others with them.

What if crip time were more than extra time waiting for elevators, extra time for completing a college exam, "lost" time because of pain, or the time it takes for a stutterer to express himself in words? Paying attention to the abilities and disabilities of our bodies might lead us to think about time differently. When a boy with trachoma complained in the doctor's office, "It's terrible to wait so long! It's awf'ly annoying!" Jessie Sampter said to him that she found waiting interesting. There was "much to hear and see."[55] Belser explains her own experience: "The question of how you wait is something that I've come to understand differently in part from my religious practice. . . . What I *can* do sometimes is to transform the way I am experiencing the waiting."[56] But what might this transformed experience look like? Theorist Alison Kafer suggests one model: using the corporate idea of flex time as a reference point, she tells her readers, "Crip time is flex time not just expanded but exploded." She writes, "Rather than bend disabled bodies and minds to meet the clock, crip time bends the clock to meet disabled bodies and minds."[57] But even in Kafer's description, time always moves forward, sometimes faster, sometimes slower, often with different attitudes and perceptions about the past and the future. Time seems to have only one direction.

Sampter's stories can push this idea of crip time further: it's not just a speeding up and a slowing down—though it is certainly those things. It's not just an adjustment of how we think about the past and the future, though it is that too. It is expanding these notions to see how time moves in many directions. In this vision, time is neither one-dimensional nor unidirectional but can move in several dimensions and directions. Here I think about crip time as something other than a one-way progression: the past intrudes into the present, the future shapes the present, and some moments cluster together while others recede. This view of crip time is not as radical as it may seem; in fact, it resonates with much of the language we use when we talk about recurring illness and pain. *Recurrence, relapse, remission*—these words suggest a return, even circularity, in the experiences of a body.

Crip time also reflects the way a researcher sees a life. Although this nonlinear, nonuniform time may seem odd to readers, it's far closer to the way historians and biographers encounter materials from the past. Biographers often take materials and construct a linear model. But that's not how they find materials. And, as Jessie Sampter has showed me, it's not the way their subjects always experienced life. Even the cohabitation of her written materials collapses time: the dozens of boxes at the Central Zionist Archives refuse to heed chronology. Here is a brief and incomplete overview, just to give a sense of what you might experience if you went to look: a collection of essays from different years comes first, then an autobiographical novel from the 1930s, then more essays and clippings, then an autobiography from 1921, then Sampter's obituaries and others' reflections on her life, printed in 1938 and 1939, and later the letters she wrote her sister from 1919 until the end of her life.

Even these letters and essays themselves are shot through with recollections of her past selves. The first draft of "The Speaking Heart," for instance, first identified all the characters by their proper names. Later, Sampter took a black pen to the typewritten pages, crossed out these names, and replaced them with pseudonyms. Mary Antin became Sarah. For Josephine Lazarus: "I shall call her Judith."[58] She also changed, deleted, and added to the prose. Her neat handwriting would appear on each page, adjusting the precise way she told the story of her life. Later she added partial typewritten pages, neatly trimmed to the size of the text, never a whole page where six inches of paper were sufficient. And then another layer of sparse editing, this time in blue pen. Occasionally a new section was pasted over previous writing. Even published writings were not sacred: she sometimes scribbled deletions, additions, and adjustments on magazine and newspaper clippings of her articles and poems.[59] Writing a life was always also rewriting it. Each piece existed as a product of multiple times in her life.

Crip time, if we think about it hard enough, also informs the way we all live our lives. Time spent in pain seems to take forever. Sickness throws us back to childhood days of being cared for—or throws us forward into old age when we may require that care again. Even positive experiences of the body can bend time: most of us know how the smell of a certain food can bring childhood rushing back. The expectation of future things can overwhelm our present. The past recurs, the future intrudes, time slows, it speeds up, it circles back or jumps forward.

When I say that all people might see crip time in their own lives, I don't mean to say that everyone is disabled. But I am implying that disability is not some *thing* experienced by a separate group of people who are essentially different from a normal "us."

The way I write about disability frames it not as a given fact in the world but rather as an experience created through the built environment, relationships, and social norms. (Chapter 2 discusses the models for thinking about disability more fully.) Sidewalks without curb cuts or fire alarms without visual signals create a disability for wheelchair users or Deaf people. Moreover, what we think of as a disability is culturally conditioned. For example, why is someone who uses a hearing aid often categorized as disabled when someone who uses eyeglasses isn't? Many people with disabilities affirm this social model and declare that there is nothing lesser about their lives and bodies—that they wouldn't change them if they could. Yet this does not apply to everyone with a disability, especially for those who consider chronic pain to be a disability. It is much harder to argue that physical pain is fully socially constructed, though it is surely exacerbated or eased by built environments and social norms. And people with chronic pain are far less likely to say that they wouldn't change their disability if they could. Sampter's life has both of these elements—a disability that is shaped by the world around her, as well as chronic pain. Each also shaped her sense of time.

I think of noncrip time as "regular" time: regularized, regulated, rule bound. Yes, there are good arguments for regular time. It is good to have a shared knowledge of when class begins. It is generally helpful if airplanes leave on time. But regular time often does not match our life experiences. Was time moving regularly the night your daughter was born? How does time move when you hear a song your mother loved? What is time like when you have insomnia? The philosopher Maurice Merleau-Ponty wrote that the body "secretes time."[60] Time is not some wholly objective feature of the world—something we might learn from Einstein's theory of relativity or our own embodied sense of time's movement. Our bodies are not so regular, and so the time of our lives is not so regular either.

―――――

Unlike a traditional biography, this book does not begin at the beginning of Sampter's life, and it ends long after her death. In fact, it begins several times and suggests that any ending is not really the end. Sampter dies at the end of chapter 2 and again at the beginning of chapter 5. Her stories, here in this book, entwine and loop back on themselves, thwarting any expectations that lives follow a single, chronological path.

Chapter 1 tells Jessie Sampter's story as a story about religion. It considers Sampter's early years of religious experimentation and interest in theology, including her most significant early book, *The Seekers*. It contextualizes Sampter as part of a vibrant landscape of American religion and challenges the idea that people had one single religious identity to the exclusion of all others. People drew on many kinds of metaphysics as well as ritual but did not think of themselves as engaging in a shallow "cafeteria approach" to religion.

Then the second chapter begins again. It tells Sampter's story as a story about disability, beginning with her childhood polio and moving to her adult body and body of thought. It bridges Sampter's years in the United States with those in Palestine and explores the relationship between Sampter's Zionism and her bodily experiences. She was, in her own eyes, both "a cripple" and a pioneer. She was a Zionist who could neither provide productive labor nor reproduce. Although the chapter is at times chronological, it also makes two intertwining moves: the first part uses disability studies to illuminate Sampter's story, and the second part shows how her story can speak back to disability studies.

The third chapter presents Sampter's life as a story about queer kinship and queer desire. Though she certainly wouldn't have used the term *queer* to describe herself, and it is an anachronism, the current theoretical concept of queerness helps interpret Sampter's embodied experience in a way that is both legible and relevant for our understanding of history. Like other women of her time, she left little direct evidence of her sexual practices, so we must remain agnostic about what happened when she and Leah Berlin lived together and shared a bed. Yet queerness is a helpful category precisely because it is not strictly limited to sexual practices but rather encompasses desire, gender, relation, and kinship.

The fourth chapter tells Sampter's story as a story about politics and theology. It explores what seem like a series of paradoxes: How could she simultaneously advocate for both nationalism and internationalism? How could she be a pacifist and support Jewish armed defense in Palestine? How could Zionism and democracy go together? And how could she make sense of the gendered ideals of her political movement and the reality of inequality?

The final chapter thinks about Sampter's various afterlives and considers the way things after her death shaped her life. Here time often runs backward: it intervenes in moments, it shapes narratives, and it makes a life, even though that life was over. Or was it? From her childhood, Sampter pondered human immortality, and she always held that human minds and bodies do not live on in any material sense. But she toyed with the idea that something of the spirit could be reborn. In her 1910 book, she wrote, "I, for one, believed, yes, knew, that I had been forever, that I was not 'made' in these few years. . . . If we believe in the vast Self of life, and if we are a part of that awakening Self, how can we die?"[61] That final chapter considers Sampter's various rebirths: as a suffering saint of labor Zionism (in the years following her death), as a children's poet and songwriter for Reform Jews in the United States (in the 1950s), and as a quotable philosopher appearing in Weight Watchers inspirational books, on websites, and on a road sign in India (in the 1990s); and as a figure who grew to be part of my own life.[62]

This book highlights what scholars already know but the form of our work does not always acknowledge: the worldview of the scholar shapes the data she interprets, and there is never only one true story. Sampter's stories refuse the idea that life-writing should be a single coherent whole or a continuous narrative and instead insists that this life—like all lives— has many threads, stops and starts, contradictions, and loops and should be written that way. Yet the book also shows how these stories intertwine: Sampter did not experience her disability as separate from her queerness or her religion, and so we, too, should see them as intertwined. To do so illuminates how Sampter's Zionism was a crip Zionism and, to a lesser extent, a queer one.

CHAPTER ONE

A Religious Life

As a child, Jessie Sampter was fascinated by religion. One evening, after overhearing adults talk about Christian theology in the kitchen, she spent hours wondering how religions started. "I used to think how interesting it might be, when I grew up, to start a new religion like that man Jesus Christ," she wrote.[1]

Her fascination never went away.

I can sympathize. Though I never wanted to start a religion, I find it endlessly interesting. Because of Sampter's interest, aided by mine, here I tell Sampter's life as a story about American religion.[2] I tell about her religious and theological experiments, whose most public forms included her published poetry and earliest books, *The Great Adventurer* (1909) and *The Seekers* (1910). I tell how religious innovation—especially the question of how religion could speak to a modern person—captivated her thought. I also tell how Sampter and many of her friends and intellectual colleagues might change the way we think about religious diversity or pluralism. They make me wonder if it is less helpful to think about exclusive categories of religion—Episcopalian or Hindu or agnostic—than to think about how and where people make religious meaning, even and especially when it crosses those categories. They inspire me to write less about religious identity (what religion we say someone *is*) and more about how many sources shape people's religious lives.

Sampter read voraciously, led a religiously diverse group of young adults in salon-like theological conversations, discussed metaphysical ideas with people such as philosopher Josiah Royce and rabbi Mordecai Kaplan, and visited palmists for readings. The story has twists and turns: She had visions. She embraced a Judaism her parents had rejected. And all the while she reflected on and participated in Theosophy, the teachings of Jiddu Krishnamurti, occult practices like the Ouija board, and what she saw as the wisdom of "Eastern" religions. How could she do this? Was she a heretic? Confused? A bizarre anomaly in the landscape of American religion? And how and why should a body matter in a story that so often seems to be about religious philosophy?

As an acculturated American-born Jew, she was in the minority of the minority. Around the turn of the twentieth century, Jews made up only a small percentage of the US population (between 2 and 3 percent). Sampter's background—born into an English-speaking household to acculturated parents—meant that as immigration increased, even American Jewry would look less and less like her. There were about a quarter of a million Jews living in the United States when Sampter was born in 1883, and then more than three million by the time she left for Palestine in 1919.[3] Immigrants from eastern Europe made up the vast majority of this increase. So Sampter was an outlier.

Or was she?

Even though, demographically, Sampter represented just a small sliver of the American pie, I see her religious reflections as anything but idiosyncratic. Adapting and adopting characterized her whole religious life, even when she firmly identified with Judaism. Although she never turned away from her Jewishness once she discovered it, we would be mistaken if we saw the story of her religious life as some sort of inexorable intellectual path to Judaism, or as one involving one shining moment of conversion that changed everything. She incorporated religious wisdom from any place she could find it. Though people often associate "seeking" with a post-1960s United States, the tale of Sampter's life shows us that drawing on many religious sources—what I think of as *religious recombination*—is far older than that. Her story also shows us how these seemingly unorthodox approaches to religion can go hand in hand with a single, strong religious identity—and ultimately that these combinations and recombinations aren't all that unusual.

The Early Life of a Seeker

One way to tell a life is to begin at the beginning. For Jessie Sampter, like for many people, the earliest important characters were her parents. She adored her father. Page after page of her unpublished autobiographical writings recount her memories of him. She loved both her parents, Rudolph and Virginia (Kohlberg) Sampter, but her father held a special place in young Jessie's heart and mind. As she wrote in an autobiographical novel about her early life, she "loved him just a little bit more, because he understood."[4] He understood Jessie's inquisitive nature, her quest to make sense of the world, and her love of writing. A lawyer by profession and lover of literature and philosophy by disposition, he nurtured Jessie through language. From just a few years after Jessie's birth in 1883, she would make up poems, and as she learned to write, her father would help her hone her craft. The poems he deemed extraordinary, he would preserve in cardboard; the maudlin and overly sentimental ones he would read aloud in a dramatic—and often silly—voice. "Father makes fun of my 'poem' about the 'Soldier boy who dies with joy' and recites it with melodramatic gestures that are killing," she recalled fondly.[5] Her narration of a family trip to the countryside grounded him as her reference point, even as it foreshadowed his death: "That we had come for my father's broken health, I did not realize, even though I knew him as the center of the universe, the cause of all things."[6] She revered him and wanted to be like him, even with his physical limitations and ill health.

Rudolph's approach to philosophy, writing, and religion set the tone for the Sampter household. Like Virginia's parents, his parents had immigrated from Germany in the mid-nineteenth century and raised their children in New York. For the first years of her life, Jessie lived with her parents, her sister Elvie, her aunt and uncle, and her fraternal grandparents in a stately three-story house with a manicured lawn on Fifth Avenue in Harlem.

I visited the spot. Courtney Callender playground, with its park benches and twisty slide, is now where the Sampter house stood. The built environment of the neighborhood has changed, too: instead of individual houses separated by green spaces, there are brick buildings one next to the other, playgrounds, little groceries and cafés, individual trees muscling their way into small spaces between the concrete, and cars lining every street. For me, being there was an important reminder of the power of place, of the way senses and feelings shape our lives at least as much as thoughts. But my visit also reminded me of the distances that a scholar can never overcome, how we can never fully know or experience the past. I knew more about Jessie's life, but I was also reminded of things I could never know: the sound of the oak leaves rustling without the ubiquitous noise of traffic, the feel of opening the heavy front door, the hubbub of a house full of Sampters, or the smell of Virginia's cooking. Walking those streets also drew my attention to other things that are missing from Sampter's own accounts and those of her peers. Race—especially Blackness—goes almost unremarked, in spite of the ways it mattered for Sampter's life and her intellectual interests. Yet the street names hearken to a history that included her contemporaries: Marcus Garvey Park, named after another nationalist thinker who was born the year before Sampter. A public school named for Fred R. Moore, the influential editor and publisher. Harlem wasn't yet the center of Black culture it would become, but there was important Black intellectual life around Sampter. She didn't seem to notice.

Her community in Harlem was white. Immigrants and acculturated Americans mixed, and so did religious observances. Though both her parents were raised in Jewish households, they celebrated Christmas and hid Easter eggs. One childhood year, Jessie recalled the holidays: "Aunt Billie, whose husband is friends with a reform rabbi and with the editor of a Jewish weekly, has a Jewish Christmas tree this year. She has it on Hanukkah, the Jewish festival, instead of on Christmas, so the rabbi's children may come. I go too. I have two Christmases."[7] When Jessie and Elvie were small, the girls and their mother said prayers in German before bedtime, but when Jessie told her story, she often claimed that there was almost no talk of God or religious ritual in her childhood home.[8]

And yet life at the Sampter home was steeped in philosophical and ethical reflection. Before Jessie was born, her parents had joined the Ethical Culture Society, led by Felix Adler, and they grew to call him a friend. Adler himself had quite a story: his father was a famous Reform rabbi who came to the United States to head New York's Temple Emanu-El, the flagship of Reform Judaism. The younger Adler, following in his father's footsteps, had been ordained as a Reform rabbi. But when he was offered his father's pulpit, he dramatically declined, declaring that he did not see an important place for God in the future of Judaism. After a brief stint teaching at Cornell—instead of renewing him, the college turned down the grant funding his position rather than retain an alleged atheist on the faculty—he founded his own movement for like-minded humanists invested in ethics and human betterment but not necessarily committed to the existence of a god. When the Sampters found Adler's teaching and regular Sunday lectures appealing, they joined many other acculturated American Jews in the seats.

Jessie's childhood "religion," then, had elements of Judaism, Christianity, and Ethical Culture. Yet no one in the household imagined that it was a mishmash, or that it was incoherent, or that it was heretical, or that it was syncretism. To the contrary, having a sound and coherent ethical outlook on the world was important to Rudolph and became so for Jessie from her earliest reflective years. This kind of religious worldview—one that drew on different traditions, rituals, and philosophies but nevertheless felt whole—was hardly unique to the Sampters.

Before her father died, Jessie and her cousin had played make-believe. She wrote in one of her unpublished autobiographies, typed and then hand-edited, "I invent all our games, dramas of terror and death, and Anita and I take dozens of parts, one after the other, and die dozens of times." Then one night Anita had a nightmare, and her mother (Rudolph's sister Jane) put to an end Anita's play with Jessie, whom she called "a morbid child."[9] Her harsh decree lasted less than a week. Henceforth the two could play together, only no more make-believe about dying. When the girls recommenced playtime, their solution was to enact the same tragedies and just make sure to stop them before the final death scenes.

This death play was not merely about some melancholic disposition. It was an embodied experience that allowed for theological reflection, and thinking about the workings of the cosmos in the context of her own life:

> I read in the paper that a prophet has said the world is coming to an end in three days. Well, let it! Anita and I, at least, will be prepared. We discuss, in awed whispers, God and death and immortality. The world will disappear—what is beyond? We are pitched to high stoicism. If it doesn't come to an end now, Anita, when our minds are made up, how shall we bear it?
>
> And it doesn't.
>
> What if somebody real should die, somebody I love? That is impossible, incredible. And yet—everyone dies. I imagine how ~~people~~ mother or sister would look dead; sometimes if they sleep long in the morning, I fear they may be dead.
>
> Father often speaks of death. He likes to joke. He quotes from some book: "Life is a disease from which all die save those who were never born."[10]

The end is nigh! a prophet had said, not for the first time in American history. Young Jessie and her cousin Anita contemplated what that would be like: Would there be life after death? What was the nature of God? They were almost excited about the possibility. And yet when it came to imagining a death that was real and imminent, Jessie's imagination had its limits: her father could joke about death, and she could imagine her mother or sister dead, but imagining her father dead was a step too far.

When Rudolph Sampter died of tuberculosis in 1895, Jessie was crushed. He was forty-four years old, and Jessie was twelve. She knew he had been sick, and so his death did not come as an intellectual surprise. But emotionally, it was shocking: he had been her role model, her inspiration, and her beloved father. After his death Jessie began her own form of religious practice: "I prayed, I began to pray without words, with an overwhelming emotion that carried me out of myself into a Presence I could not see nor understand. These religious emotions came unbidden; they surprised me and filled me with joy."[11] Jessie began physically engaging in wordless prayer and having religious experiences without an institutional framework. But her practices were, of course, not without religious context. Jessie grew up in a world where religion happened around her, and even with her. In the wake of her father's death, praying to a power beyond herself made sense to her because it was modeled by others but also because when she did it, it made experiential sense to her. That is, praying was a kind of survival mechanism—it was just what you did in the face of this kind of devastation—and so she continued to do it.

If Jessie's reactions to her father's death pointed inward toward a personal religiosity, his *New York Times* obituary subtly pointed outward to the broader American religious scene. It read, "Sampter was a member of the Ethical Culture Society. In the workings of this society he took a deep interest, and, as far as his health permitted, took an active part. He was connected with no other religious body. The funeral will be held at 1,238 Fifth Avenue, at 10 o'clock to-morrow morning. The body will be cremated."[12]

As Rudolph's obituary intimated, Ethical Culture looked like a religion—a "religious body"—in many ways, but in other ways it did not. So was it a religion? Most of us think we know what religions are. Perhaps we could make a list: Buddhism, Christianity, Hinduism, Daoism, Zoroastrianism, and so on. The list is flexible in some ways; for example, new religious movements can be added. But religious identification is less flexible in other ways: in particular, we tend to think of religions as exclusive. You are either a Methodist or a Muslim, a Hindu or a Hasid, but not both. This assumption is one reason for the recurring kerfuffle over religious intermarriage: The children will be neither fish nor fowl! detractors cry. But of course, in real people's lives, they can and do have multiple religious identities and theologies.

At an institutional level, Ethical Culture represents another challenge to these assumptions about religions as discrete and exclusive. Some members of the Ethical Culture Society also identified themselves with other religions (for most, Judaism or one of the various forms of liberal Protestant Christianity), while other members, including the Sampter parents, did not. Ethical Culture's intentional nonexclusivity meant it did not fit the standard model for a religion. If one could be both an Ethical Culture member and a member of any other religion, was Ethical Culture a religion? It also didn't fit into a denominational mold because it did not fit under the wider umbrella of a single identifiable religion, as Baptism, Congregationalism, and Catholicism fit under the broad category of Christianity. Nor did it fit the mold of an interreligious organization, like the early twentieth-century Men and Religion Forward Movement, which sought to bring Protestants, Catholics, and Jews together *as* Protestants, Catholics, and Jews.

What's more, Ethical Culture professed to have no rituals or dogma. "Deed not creed," a riff on the title of one of Adler's books, was one of the society's mottoes.[13] Despite denying the profession of creed and the practice of ritual, however, both members and observers tended to imagine it as a religion. A 1906 observer wrote, "[An] organization which does not lend itself so well to the classification of a religious organization is the downtown Society for Ethical Culture; however, the seriousness of the movement permits of its classification under this head. The latest utterances of Dr. Felix Adler on the subject of symbols, ceremonies, and religion, allow for the prophecy that this society will have much to do in a positive religious line of work in the near future."[14] The Ethical Culture Society bent the boundaries of the concept of a religion. It defied the concept of a singular, definite religious identity marked by shared creed or ritual. It could not be a clear column on a tally sheet of religious diversity. Jessie, then, grew up in a household with the writings of Charles Darwin and the atheist Robert Ingersoll far more than the rabbis or Revelation, but the ethos of Ethical Culture and her father's reflection on the place of ethics and moral behavior infused her young life.

Long after her father's death, Jessie still saw herself in his image. Though her sister Elvie had remained active in Ethical Culture circles, Jessie claimed that her own path was truer to their father's legacy: "[Elvie] felt herself Father's true heir; but he had speculated and then renounced, and I considered my searchings as a more dynamic continuation of his intellectual honesty and fearlessness."[15] Like her childhood death plays, Sampter's lifelong intellectual searching came with and through her embodied experiences of the world.

Religion, Ethnicity, and the Impossibility of Separation

The picture of religion, metaphysical worldview, and self-identification in the Sampter home was complex, and the role of Jewishness in that picture made it all the more so. Though neither Jewish religious observance nor ritual played a major role in their lives, Rudolph and Virginia still thought of themselves and their daughters as Jewish. A year before Jessie's death, she dramatized a childhood incident in the *Reconstructionist*: "When I was seven years old, some children in the street told me I was Jewish, which impressed me exactly as if they had told me I was a rag-picker, a gypsy, or an idiot. I denied it hotly. I went home to be enlightened, to pass through the fire of indignation into a defender of my race, but to continue to hang up my Christmas stocking and paint my Easter eggs."[16] In an earlier recollection, Jessie recounted it less dramatically, and not for a Zionist audience: when Jessie was young, she asked her mother if she was Jewish. Her mother said yes—Jessie was Jewish, but why did she ask? Jessie explained that her playmates had asked if she were Jewish, and she had said no. So she had better go back out and tell them that she was![17] In an unpublished semi-autobiographical novel, her main character, Evelyn, had a similar experience: she was at a summer resort when another girl said to her, "I suppose you are Jewish." Evelyn denied it. "A few times she had heard the word 'Jew' used by strange children as an epithet of scorn or shame, never directed against herself. She was not Jewish, she could not be." But she spoke with her parents and discovered that it was true.[18]

When I first read these recollections, I wondered how it actually happened. Was she truly insulted to be called Jewish, or was she just surprised? Memory is such a slippery thing; how could I know? How could she? But as I thought about it, I discovered that what interested me more than the details of her reaction at the time was understanding how she told this story later in life. Adult author Jessie saw the child Jessie as Jewish, whether the child knew it or not. How can a person have a religious identity without knowing it? One apparent explanation is that Jessie saw Jewishness as racial or ethnic. She was Jewish, whether or not she knew it, because she was born to a Jewish mother, who was also born to a Jewish mother. Jewishness, in this view, is heritable and has little to do with religious beliefs, practices, or worldview. But Sampter's later reflections suggest that Jewishness had elements of both religion and heritage. Her autobiography also recalled the same incident as a turning point: "And yet from that moment I was Jewish."[19] This recollection suggests that some sort of conscious knowledge, not only heredity or ethnicity, is necessary for Jewishness. And in this sense, it aligns with ideas about religious identification. These were two understandings of Jewishness: in one, the child Jessie could be Jewish without knowing it and without espousing any of its doctrines or performing any rituals. But in the other, the adult Jessie saw religious ideas and self-knowledge as central to her Jewishness.

To oversimplify for a moment: is Jewishness ethnic, or it is religious? At first, this may seem to be a distinctive dilemma in thinking about what people today often call *Jewish identity*. There are a lot of opinions and no easy answer. In 2013, 22 percent of Americans who identified as Jewish said they had no religion, just as Jessie Sampter's parents might have answered had they been asked. Most of the others polled said their religion was Judaism, though some chose others such as Buddhism. Sixty-two percent agreed that Jewishness is "mainly a matter of ancestry and culture," while 15 percent said it's "mainly a matter of religion."[20] Jewishness in America, then, is sometimes ethnic, sometimes religious, and sometimes both.

Although this dilemma may be more pronounced in Jewish communities, the fraught question of heritage versus choice haunts American religion more generally. To assume that all religion is purely voluntary, or entirely a matter of choice, is naive. To think about religion solely as a matter of personal faith and belief and not simultaneously a matter of family, ancestry, and the body is a mistake. The role of heritage in forming the religious worldviews and practices of contemporary religious people is particularly evident in some religious practices: it is on display in Native American life, African American religious practices, Hindu and Sikh communities where religion and ethnicity are closely tied, ethnic Catholic communities, Christian spirituals with roots in slave societies, and even investment in genealogical research and personal DNA testing.[21] Yet embodiment and heritage play significant roles even for those people and practices where they are less obvious. The culture, the time, the family you are raised in, and even the body you inhabit also play central roles in religious formation. Would you be the same religion you are (or aren't) if you had been born in a different body to a different family? We cannot isolate heritage, race, and ethnicity from religion, nor can we reduce any of these categories to another. Judith Weisenfeld, in her writing on African American religious movements, uses the term *religio-racial identity*, precisely because of the inextricability of the two categories.[22]

The muddiness of race and religion also reminds us that religion is not always purely an individual choice. Communities make claims on people, often from birth; other people can make assumptions about your religion because of the way you look. Some religious communities are more accepting of newcomers than others. Both your appearance and the people you know can determine what access you have to religious spaces, conversations, and relationships. Jessie Sampter participated in Jewish, Unitarian, liberal Protestant, transcendentalist, and other religious spaces that would have been much less accepting of a fellow New Yorker who was Black, South Asian, or Chinese. So twinned religio-racial perceptions or even self-identifications aren't uniform in their weight. For some people in some eras, racial constructions are more powerful and more prominent, whereas others may be able to downplay them. Other moments may see religious difference as weightier. (Think about what it meant to be Muslim after 9/11, and then think of how Arabs—even those who were Christian or another religion—were also caught up in that overwhelming scrutiny.) Black Americans have often felt the weight of religious and racial difference, which makes them a crucial example for understanding the ways that race and religion intertwine.

Although Sampter's whiteness allowed her more opportunities for self-definition than her Black contemporaries had, Weisenfeld's insight also helps us understand Sampter. Jewishness, as her case shows, can also foreground the impossibility of separation. She was both a child who could be Jewish without knowing it (a model that fits well with ideas about heritage, race, and ethnicity but does not fit well with American ideas about religion) and an adult who saw Judaism as the foundation of Jewishness (a model in which Jewishness is primarily—though not exclusively—about religion).

What was young Jessie Sampter's "identity," then? At first, I imagined that she felt pulled in many directions: thinking of her Jewishness as racial but also thinking that Jewishness in the wider world had something to do with religion; thinking of her family as sort of religious and yet not really religious; doing Christian things like having Christmas trees and Easter eggs and learning about Jesus, and doing Jewish things like praying a Jewish prayer at bedtime. But in time, I realized that what I saw as friction between these categories didn't seem to trouble Jessie. She wrote about many kinds of religious problems—doubt and theodicy were regular topics for her—but when she wrote about drawing on different religions, she never framed it as a problem. It was not for lack of introspection, nor for lack of understanding the social world around her (though she certainly downplayed any structural, economic, or racial barriers). Rather, when Jessie wrote about her religious worldview, she explained it as internally coherent and in concert with her own experience of the world. Not only did she not see herself fitting neatly into one religious box (Judaism, Christianity,

Hinduism, or none)—she refused to acknowledge them as separate boxes. You might think that she was simply young and naive and that these distinct religious categories would come to structure the way she saw the world as she got older. But that never came to pass.

Transcendentalism, Spiritualism, and Other Cases of Religion/Not-Religion

The same year her father died, twelve-year-old Jessie fell ill with polio—but that is another story. (In fact, it is part of the story of the next chapter.) The disease left her isolated from other children and often from the birds and plants and trees and meadows and mountains she loved. But it gave her a lot of time to think and to write. When Jessie thought about polio and its physical effects, she reflected on the social world and its relation to God. She grappled with theodicy, how suffering could exist if God were good. She contemplated death a lot. Jessie did not have a strong sense of religious identity, if that means which religion-related label to apply to herself, but she had a strong and well-developed sense of how she saw the world and God theologically and what she found meaningful (or not) ritually.

Americans often talk about organized religion as one thing and spirituality as another thing, but the lines between the two are very blurry. The popularity of spirituality today suggests that the spaces of organized religion—houses of worship, Bible studies, prayer meetings—aren't the only place that religion actually happens. People buy crystals in health food stores to cure what ails them. Yoga classes sometimes include recitation of mantras that invoke deities or are steeped in Hindu religious ideals. Dream catchers, appropriated from Native American traditions, decorate Americans' households and rearview mirrors. Even when religion does take place in the familiar spaces of institutionalized religion, the people participating do not always believe or do everything associated with their denomination. Many self-described Christians believe wholly in reincarnation. Other American churchgoers practice Buddhist meditation.

In the nineteenth and early twentieth centuries, too, people encountered religious ideas and even practices outside of church walls. Transcendentalism, for example, drew on Christian philosophy. The Upanishads and the Bhagavad Gita (largely in translation) gained popularity not as scripture or creed but as literature and poetry. Spiritualism, a new religious movement, purported to put people in contact with the spirits of dead people. Palm readers claimed the future was knowable and for a price could provide a glimpse to their customers. Dozens of other examples like this exist—each of these might seem not to be religion but in fact profoundly shaped people's religious lives and ideas.

Transcendentalism had a strong formative effect on young Sampter. In addition to contemplating theology, theodicy, and the nature of her place in society and the material world, during Sampter's many months indoors after her polio diagnosis, she nurtured her habit of writing reflectively. She particularly honed the poetic talents her father had supported. The editor of the children's magazine *St. Nicholas* was so impressed by a poem she submitted that he not only published it but also paid her a visit. In another poem she published in the magazine, Jessie described herself as "the sickly child" who could not attend school but instead got her education through nature: "And all unheeded by my side, I saw a lily spring, it taught me of the Love and Law that guideth everything."[23]

I, too, did a lot of sitting in nature as I learned about Sampter. It wasn't a new practice for me, but I took particular notice of the birds (a new hobby of Jessie's in her early life and also a new one for me). I listened closely, and I thought about what it would mean to see and hear a god primarily through the birds and flowers and trees that flourished around me. The monarchs and the milkweed, the red-tailed hawks and the rabbits, the ajuga and the bees, the spent echinacea spikes and the hungry goldfinches. They were Sampter's teachers, so I learned from them too. This might sound airy-fairy, but bear with me. Observing nature—immersing yourself in its sights and sounds and feelings—means experiencing beauty. It also means experiencing death. Cycles. Relationships. Intertwined and dependent lives. Those lessons extend to humanity, too.

Many years later, Sampter still saw nature as a religious teacher, as she wrote in a poem for Jewish children:

My prayer book open on my knee,
Another prayer is taught to me,
  A Torah without words:
I hear it sung by swinging leaves,
By every breeze that sighs and heaves,
  By all the choirs of birds.[24]

Sampter characterized her own learning as a theological education at the hands of nature, and she hoped the same for other children. This was a theology that came through and resonated with her own senses.

Without Rudolph, finances were tighter, and the Sampter family would move several times in fairly quick succession. For six weeks, they boarded with a woman who "took us to a séance, an exciting and adventurous experience."[25] Attending a séance wasn't quite the out-there activity it might sound: the woman was an upper-class New Yorker, and for the early twentieth century, this wasn't an absurd way to spend an evening. Jessie explained, "I went skeptical, but I did not look it, for my delicate and spiritual appearance deceived the medium into thinking me an easy subject. So messages began coming to me. We sat in the dark around a table, and counted rappings, and once I managed to get my hand under the table, where I touched a very big co[a]rse hand, no doubt a spirit's. I received a message from a sister of Mother's who had died in childhood, and who said I ought to sit at séances for I was psychic and should get important messages."[26] The idea of feeling a hand beneath the table or hearing knocking on wood was not so odd in the early twentieth century as it might sound to some of us today. American audiences flocked to public demonstrations of "rapping," knocking sounds on wood. The Fox sisters, to take the most famous example, acted as mediums who communicated with the spirits of dead people. Sometimes people asked for mundane things, like a prediction of railway stock's prices (as Arthur Conan Doyle wrote in his history of Spiritualism).[27] But most often, people asked after dead loved ones. Spirit communications may have been frivolous entertainment for some, but they also demonstrated something more profound: people's beliefs about the nature of the body and the soul.

Although attending a séance might not count as organized religion, it was nevertheless undeniably religious. Catherine Albanese explains that Spiritualism in particular helped people make sense of both death and the world around them, all the while managing to be both religion and not religion: "It bequeathed a piety that tread softly between the Bible and a fully scientific world."[28] Séances facilitated communication with spirits; they presumed theologies of the afterlife and even theologies of the self. Though spirit communication of this Spiritualist sort fit with neither Jewish nor mainstream Christian theologies, séances still attracted believing Christians and Jews who wanted to talk to the dead. Jews, Christians, and other Americans from all walks of life were captivated by the idea that science (or was it religion?) could help them communicate with the dead.

Sampter remained agnostic about whether the communications were real. But she certainly believed there was *something* to the spirit world. "My skepticism worked both ways: I was almost sure deception had been practised, but I could not be certain. To this day I do not consider the data on spiritualism sufficiently clear to be convincing one way or the other. It was a subject on which one can have opinions, not convictions. At that time I came to no conclusion, but I decided—with the consenting advice of Mother and Sister—that I was far too psychic to make it safe for me to attempt sittings, and so my interest remained lukewarm, despite the fascination of the subject."[29]

For Sampter, a séance was not something other than religion. It was another route into haunting religious questions. "Did I not long to solve the supreme problem, the meaning of life?" she asked.

> And cannot the understanding of death alone solve it? If we are not immortal, what are we? I wanted God more than immortality. A personal immortality, such as, from the books, I gathered that spiritualism might reveal, would only prolong the problem beyond life. I wanted God. I sought him in this world, in the stars, the living things, the love of man to man, the changes of nature that converted one life into another. I wanted to melt, to find God not in the continuance of myself but in the absorption of myself. I was becoming a pantheist. Having shut the gate to God in my heart, the gate of prayer and personal communion, I sought him and caught glimpses of him in the outer world.[30]

As she wrote this reflection a decade later, Sampter saw the séance not as heresy but as yet another way to gather information about the world and about God. She hoped to gain theological knowledge through the sights, sounds, and maybe even goosebumps of her séance experience.

Sampter's idea of the "outer world" included both transcendentalist interests in the natural world around her and also interaction with people, especially people from other walks of life. So as Sampter became more interested in Judaism, she moved into a settlement house associated with the Ethical Culture movement.[31] She relocated from her swankier neighborhood to the Lower East Side, the home of many thousands of Jewish immigrants. She would encounter God through encountering the world.

Settlement houses, in some ways like séances and Spiritualism, were places of religious formation even when they weren't explicitly affiliated with organized religion. A hallmark of Progressive Era American city life, settlement houses sought to use "scientific philanthropy" to help the urban poor, especially immigrants. Settlement house workers were overwhelmingly religious—mostly Protestant young men intent on changing their world for the better. Even if settlements and Christian missions seemed similar, settlement workers insisted, the former was surely not a religious institution or project. But they protested too much: marketing themselves as nonreligious could help settlement houses reach the many immigrant populations in the city, but underneath that, the movement was bound up with Protestant postmillennial theologies, and most settlements actively promoted religion in general. "Our influence is distinctly *for religion* but not for any denomination or creed," explained the head of the Philadelphia College Settlement.[32] Even the Jewish settlement houses sought to help their mostly immigrant Jewish clientele "adjust" to religious life in America.[33]

As Sampter became interested in serving in a settlement house, not coincidentally, she was also becoming more interested in Judaism and the Jewish life around her in New York. She began learning Hebrew, studying alongside Alice Seligsberg, who had also been raised in an Ethical Culture household but came to Hadassah and Zionism as an adult. Around the same time, Sampter went to a gathering at the house of Albert Bigelow Paine, the editor of *St. Nicholas*.[34] He had invited both Sampter and another young Jewish writer to his home. "She had read my poems, and I her little book, and we expressed a desire to meet," Sampter remembered.[35] And so they did. Sampter and Mary Antin became fast friends. They would sit together on the floor, talking for hours about religion, about immigration, about social issues. Sampter referred to meeting Antin as her "second great event"—her first was her earlier connection with her friend Nora (whom we will meet again in chapter 3). Antin, who would later write the best-selling memoir *The Promised Land*, came from different circumstances than Sampter. She had immigrated from Polotzk, Belarus, to the United States when she was fourteen. Antin and her family had lived in a crowded, working-class Boston neighborhood, and she had attended public school. She had Americanized quickly and enthusiastically, and by the time Jessie met her, she was already honing the skills that would make her a best-selling writer. Despite their different upbringings, they had much in common. Both loved Ralph Waldo Emerson and looked to the natural world to form their metaphysical views. Both Antin and Sampter were published poets by their early teens, and both grew to become outspoken educated women. They both attended Columbia University, though Sampter's formal coursework was short-lived. Antin adored Sampter, and she also felt protective of her. She once wrote to Horace Kallen, when the two were scheming with Henrietta Szold to get a book of Sampter's poems published without Sampter's knowledge: "Jessie Sampter is one of the most delicate things I know. I'm a brute compared to her. . . . Please return these letters, and do see that no harm comes of my meddling."[36] In the end, Antin and Szold decided that they should not pursue any publication without Sampter's full knowledge. Sampter and Antin remained close friends, exchanging letters and visits, until Sampter's death.

If you know a little about American Jewish history, you probably recognize Antin's name. Theodore Roosevelt praised her as an ideal American, and she campaigned on his behalf. Today children learn about her in Hebrew school, and college students read *The Promised Land* as the example of American Judaism and even immigration more generally. She has become an icon of American Jewish history. And yet Antin was not so unambiguously and exclusively attached to Judaism as these presentations of her imply. She, too, was a religious recombiner.

Antin, like Sampter, has an intriguing religious biography. Until her early teens, she lived in an observant Jewish household. "When I came to lie on my mother's breast, she sang me lullabies on lofty themes," she wrote. "I heard the names of Rebecca, Rachel and Leah as early as the names of father, mother, and nurse. My baby soul was enthralled by sad and noble cadences, as my mother sang of my ancient home in Palestine, or mourned over the desolation of Zion. With the first rattle that was placed in my hand a prayer was pronounced over me, a petition that a pious man might take me to wife, and a messiah be among my sons."[37] After coming to the United States, she and her family jettisoned Jewish religious practice. Twenty-year-old Antin married a Christian man, Amadeus Grabau, who was a professor at Columbia University. The two separated soon after World War I, in part because of political differences—she supported the Allies, and he the Germans. Though Antin always thought of herself as Jewish, she found a compelling view of the world in the metaphysicals, especially Henry David Thoreau and Emerson. Like Rudolph Sampter, she found Darwin captivating.[38] In Antin's later life, she was attracted to Christian mysticism. From 1922 until her death in 1949, she spent much of her time at Gould Farm, a Christian restorative community for the mentally ill in Monterey, Massachusetts. There the married couple "Brother Will" and Agnes Gould spread their philosophy of Christian love. As historian Joyce Antler explains:

> Even at the Christian home, where Antin was both patient and sometime secretary, she turned "Jew on occasion," describing herself as a "Jewish member of the staff" and showing sensitivity to references to Jews. For Antin, there was no inconsistency between affiliating herself with Will Gould's philosophy of Christian brotherhood and identifying herself, when necessary, as a Jew. "One current of continuity runs underneath

all the abortive phases of my life," she explained while in her fifties. "From childhood on I have been obliged to drop anything I was doing to run after any man who seemed to know a little more than I did about God . . . I most want to write about: how a modern woman has sought the face of God—not the name nor the fame but the face of God—and what adventures came to meet her on this most ancient human path."[39]

Antin also spent some of her final years as a disciple of Rudolf Steiner, a proponent of "spiritual science" and anthroposophy, a European metaphysical tradition.[40] For a time, Antin followed Meher Baba, who claimed to be the Avatar, or God in human form. (Jessie did not always approve of this phase of her friend's spiritual life. She harbored both theological disagreements and deep personal concern for Mary, especially during the Meher Baba years.) And yet, despite all of Antin's different religious traditions, she did not feel herself to be engaging in syncretism or approaching religions as a buffet from which she took whatever appealed to her from each separate religious tradition. She saw herself as seeking a unified religious truth, where the particular sources of that religious truth were beside the point. She, too, sought to gain theological knowledge by doing, whether it was by following a guru or living on a farm where even daily acts could have religious significance. Identity was never central to her religiosity; understanding God and the world around her in a way that made sense to her was.

Not long after the two met, Antin also introduced Sampter to a woman who would become her intellectual, religious, and political guide. Today Josephine Lazarus's claim to fame is her family connection: she was the older sister of the poet Emma Lazarus, whose "New Colossus" appears on the Statue of Liberty. But she was also an intellectual and a writer in her own right. Her 1895 *The Spirit of Judaism* argued that Judaism's emphasis on duty and justice could benefit from incorporating the Christian emphasis on love—something we might see as a call for religious recombination on broad theological and institutional levels. "The Jewish idea, broaden it as we may, straighten it as we might, does not contain all the truth," she wrote.[41] Josephine was thirty-seven years older than Jessie, who saw her as both friend and mentor. From a well-heeled Sephardi-American family, Lazarus celebrated Christmas, had mainly Christian friends, and yet held a strong sense of connection to other Jews.[42] Her sister Emma is celebrated as an exemplar of the American Jewish community. And yet Emma, too, was not as unambiguously identified with Judaism as her place in the pantheon of American Jewish history suggests. Upon her death, a fellow intellectual remembered, "She died, as she lived, as much a Christian as a Jewess—perhaps it would be better to say neither one or the other."[43] The seeming religious promiscuousness of the Lazarus family was not, however, a sign of wishy-washy temperaments or sycophantic desire to fit into Christian social circles. It was a sign of their sense of the relevance of religious philosophy and reflection, from whichever tradition it came. Sampter recalled of Josephine Lazarus that she "was a seeker for God, on the great adventure of modern times, when God has hidden himself behind the veil that is to melt in a new revelation. She saw in me a fellow seeker, a child with a vision, or at least eyes strained for vision."[44]

The two discussed religion, theology, politics, and writing. Lazarus taught Sampter to read the Bible—to *really* read it for the first time, though Sampter had encountered it before—and the two discussed both Hebrew Bible and Christian New Testament books. Together they pondered what Jewishness was, whether Jews could be religiously Orthodox, Reform, or "fasten upon a race tradition," in Lazarus's words.[45] Sampter came to think of her as kin, calling Lazarus her "spiritual mother." Sampter's own mother died just a decade later than her father, leaving twenty-three-year-old Jessie without biological parents. When Sampter published *The Great Adventurer* in 1909, she dedicated it to "J. L.," Josephine Lazarus.

Sampter had other famous patrons as well. On a trip to England with her mother and sister, sixteen-year-old Jessie wanted to meet Israel Zangwill, the Jewish playwright and Zionist. At the time Jessie visited, he was already known for his Jewish-themed plays, such as *Children of the Ghetto*. Zangwill would later write a popular, sappy play about Americanization called *The Melting-Pot*, which popularized the metaphor for the United States as a society comprising people from different geographic backgrounds. Zangwill, too, was a religious recombiner. He was an ardent Zionist, but he also championed culturally and religiously mixed marriages; his play's protagonists were a star-crossed Catholic and Jew who had far happier fates than Romeo and Juliet. The young writer Jessie admired Zangwill and kept in touch with him as the years went on.

The religion of Josephine and Emma Lazarus, Mary Antin, Israel Zangwill, and Jessie Sampter might at first seem obvious: it was Judaism, of course. And history has represented them in this way. And yet, as it turns out, their religious lives included many other religious things, from Christianity and Hinduism to Spiritualism and transcendentalism. Since they also drew on other religious ideas, texts, communities, and bodily experiences, one response might be to demote them from paragons of American

Jewishness and search for "purer" examples of Jewishness. While we might be able to find such historical figures who never entertained a religious thought or participated in a religious ritual outside of Judaism, it would still not tell us why so many Jews did, and when they did, they rarely saw it as apostasy or even religious border crossing.

In American Jewish history, Jewishness is most often figured as exceptional in some way: Jews are an ethnic minority; Jews are religious outsiders; Judaism is a minority religion in a nation where the very idea of religion takes Protestant Christianity as a model. But what might we be able to see if we put aside the insistence on Jewish difference and instead framed Jewish lives as typical, as at the center of American life, or as illuminating dominant trends? Here, instead of beginning with the assumption that Jewishness is otherness, that Jews are always in some way cultural outsiders, and that there is such a thing as "the Jewish experience" that is necessarily distinct from non-Jews' experiences, I am telling Jessie Sampter's story as a story about religion in the United States—not as a story about a religious outsider but as a story of the widespread and dominant trend of religious recombination.

Adventurers, Seekers, and the Creation of Religious Worlds

In 1909 Sampter published a slim, genre-defying book. The *New York Times* reviewer wrote that in it "one catches notes of Whitman, of the Vedic hymns, and of the Psalms, but through it all an individual note not surrendered."[46] Sampter herself could hardly have written a better advertisement. The book would be an unlikely best seller today; the prose is sometimes overwrought, and ironically there is little plot development from the beginning to the end of the "adventure." Overall, it puts an awful lot of faith in a person's ability to shape her own life, with little attention to external constraints. And yet it is a fascinating and sometimes beautiful insight into Sampter's worldview. A series of short philosophical and poetic vignettes, *The Great Adventurer* suggestively described a human's place in the world. The "great adventurer," a protagonist of sorts, was the author herself, but it was also each and every person. And each person's great adventure was living an embodied and philosophically reflective life.

The great adventure of life, as Sampter saw it, was about experience and understanding—two things that should be mutually supporting. From the beginning, Sampter emphasized the harmony of sensory experience and religious worldview: "I behold a green hill, and I believe that the upheaved rock is beneath it; I see the surface of a lake, and I believe there is a depth below. Such is my faith. I behold the surface and believe in the depth."[47] The material world and embodied experience work in concert with belief. She built on this concept to claim the need for religious ideas to resonate in a personal, even embodied way: "If the voice of creation were to speak to me, saying, 'I am,' I could not understand the word unless it were spoken within myself, unless I myself experienced the universe."[48] She both quoted scripture—the "I am" alludes to God's speech to Moses in Genesis 3:14—and also insisted that institutional religion and scriptures work only if they are verifiable experientially. Religious understanding of the world could take place only alongside experience of the world.

But the religious self created through these experiences of the world was not always a simple self; Sampter recognized the multiple nature of her experience of the world. In *The Great Adventurer*, she referred to the universe as a self that, like human selves, sometimes felt multiple but was in actuality unified: "I feel the universe as a self, a myriad of selves in endless relation, that clash and seem to destroy one another, and know not that they are the same, even as the waves of the sea. I am a wave of the sea. . . . But I am one with that boundless, multitudinous sea, with that whole existence, that prolific self, which is also within me."[49] Sampter saw people's minds, bodies, and selves as part of a unified material and spiritual world. In this sense, she espoused a kind of pantheism, in which God is not separate from the natural world but rather coincident with the cosmos and its workings. Though the world was unified, however, that did not mean that people always experienced it in the same way. Part of each person's challenge was to understand a universe that seemed diverse but was actually whole.

Sampter also wrote that humanity was going through a similar set of sequential "selves" that did not yet know they were one:

> The fruit of reason, no less than the fruit of feeling, is faith. In one age men get for their questions this answer: Jehovah; in another age this answer: Christ; in a third age, this answer: Nature. Each is an act of faith. Different are the fruits of reason and feeling for each man. But their root is one. Though the scientist believes that lightning is an electric flash, and the savage believes that it is a sign of the anger of gods, and though both may be wrong, yet both have seen and known the flash of lightning. Every man who knows the wonder of life within him . . . knows the truth. His act of faith is a living thing; his form of faith is a dress.[50]

Here she argued that embodied experience connects a person to the real thing—the truth—and the tradition through which one can explain it is merely the "dress." Reason and feeling could both gesture toward truth, or inspire reflection on it, but they alone could not reveal it. Sampter thought that Judaism, Christianity, Islam, Hinduism, and other religious traditions were valid in that they provided philosophical and affective means of accessing the divine/nature. In another way, they were all equally invalid because none was precisely true. Rather, one's own experience led to self-knowledge, which should help confirm knowledge of the divine/nature.

If different religious traditions provided different answers for different people, which answers did Sampter espouse? From the previous passage, we might assume that she saw progress throughout the ages and saw nature as the most sophisticated answer. Though it would be more accurate to characterize her view as one in which each age has something valuable to contribute, Jessie did think of the transcendentalist Ralph Waldo Emerson as a kind of patron saint—she even visited his grave three times during her young life. Emerson's ideas meshed with (and surely influenced) her own: humans could find the truth about God and the universe not through revelation but through nature. Matter and spirit were not separate but rather parts of a unified whole. Like Sampter, Emerson did not fit easily into a religious category. Once asked to define his religious position, he said "with greater deliberateness, and longer pauses between his words than usual, 'I am more of a Quaker than anything else. I believe in the still, small voice, and that voice is Christ within us.'"[51] And yet to label him a Quaker would obscure so much else: he was the son of a Unitarian minister, he served briefly as a Unitarian minister himself, his ideas caused a rift with even his theologically liberal alma mater Harvard Divinity School, he never was a regular attender of a Quaker meeting, and others have identified the indebtedness of his thought to Plato and Neoplatonists, Buddhism, Emanuel Swedenborg, Johann Wolfgang von Goethe, and others.

Emerson, along with other transcendentalists such as Henry David Thoreau, is often labeled a freethinker. He was a paradigmatic recombiner of religious ideas and experiences. But beyond these celebrated figures are a multitude of less famous people who do something structurally very similar. Sampter's religious recombinations, for instance, may not have inspired many thousands of other people, but she, too, worked out her religious views in conversation with her own experience of the world and the various ideas around her.

Sampter developed her religious ideas in a more systematic way in *The Seekers*, published in 1910. The book chronicled a weekly course she had conducted with six teenagers, in which they inquired about the nature of the world, truth, God, and religion. "It is a philosophic adventure, an experiment," she explained.[52] But this book was not about religious seekers in the way we sometimes use the term now. They were not searching for a religious community. They were not traveling from spiritual place to spiritual place. They were not trying out various religious traditions in turn, like Goldilocks seeking the right fit. Sampter and the members of her group were quite grounded in their principles—and, more important for our purposes, they were not seeking religious identities or trying to find the "right" religion. They were seeking in the sense that they were seeking to understand more of the deep truths about the world, divinity, and humanity.

The book provided summary versions of the meetings in which Sampter led the teenagers in conversations about theology and philosophy. Quite unlike *The Great Adventurer* with its single poetic voice, the words and personalities of the six teenagers as well as Sampter herself drive *The Seekers*. Sampter positioned the book as educational, both as a model for others to follow and as a model for readers to reflect on their own religious ideas. From the outset, she presented her questions and quest for religious understanding as typical. She referred to "our modern faith," a sense of religion shared with her audience. The book, she wrote, contained "my thought. Not mine alone, but yours and every man's."[53]

She also expounded on her earlier claims that all well-considered religions offered relationships with the truth but that none contained absolute truth. She told the teenagers and her readers, "I am convinced that to-day all thoughtful men believe the same, where vital questions arise, and that each man sees a different angle of the same truth, which grows and grows in our vision, with the growing knowledge of man. All our ministers with their different churches, and our congregations with their sectarian prejudices, have at heart a common goal."[54] The young members of the Seekers club, too, were typical, she maintained. Each was between fourteen and sixteen, and they came from relatively affluent New York homes. There were more girls (four) than boys (two), which she attributed to philosophical issues piquing boys' interest at the age of eighteen or nineteen, rather than fifteen or sixteen. Though they were educated—all had attended some high school—they weren't above average mentally, she assessed. Most had grown up with some religion but were "free from those clogging superstitions" of dogmatic creeds.[55] They came from homes with a variety of backgrounds: Alfred, her cousin, had "a good knowledge of evolution, and no religious training of any sort"; Virginia, also a cousin, had "no definite religious training, but much sound religious philosophy at home"; Florence came from a "home of mixed and uncertain piety"; Henry, Florence's cousin, came "from a conventional home" of some Protestant denomination; Marian's "parents belong to the Ethical Culture Society, and have given her no religious education"; and Ruth, Marian's friend, had a Christian mother, a Jewish father, "and their religion is Christian Science."[56]

Were they typical? In one sense, no. They were from the relative upper crust in a city that had many working-class immigrants. There were no Catholics. They were all white. But in another sense, yes. They each had exposure to a variety of religious ideas. Some had mixed families. They all saw religious reflection as an important part of life, though they had (and continued to develop) individualized notions of what exactly that should look like.

Josiah Royce, an eminent philosopher and Harvard professor, wrote the introduction to *The Seekers*. Royce had made a name for himself writing about religious aspects of philosophy and spent much of his career thinking about the nature of God, immortality, and nature. He was an idealist who later also described himself as a pragmatist. He gave the Gifford Lectures the year before his friend, colleague, and longtime intellectual sparring partner, William James. He taught T. S. Eliot, George Santayana, and W. E. B. Du Bois. As a Harvard philosopher, Royce was a member of an American intellectual elite, and he deemed Sampter articulate and insightful about religion. He didn't know Sampter well, but the two had met, and he agreed to write an introduction to *The Seekers* because he had been impressed by her writing.

In his introduction, Royce called the book "a successful experiment in non-sectarian religion, in moral and aesthetic enquiry, with young people in new ways, in search of the Meaning of Things." Royce used the phrase "non-sectarian religion" as if to say that the available categories of religious thought were not adequate to the book, but it nevertheless was religious. Royce, too, saw himself and his task as a philosophy professor in a similar way: he was teaching a theological philosophy that defied any neat boundaries of religious tradition, and he wanted to propel his students toward what he called "spiritual independence" rather than doctrine or faith.[57]

Royce praised Sampter for educating her young charges rather than inculcating them with religious dogma. They would emerge from her course as self-critical independent thinkers:

If one undertakes to consider such topics with a class as youthful and at the same time as enlightened as the "Seekers," the dilemma is obvious. One must indeed be more or less dogmatic in tone about at least some central interest; one must make use of the persuasive power of a teacher's personal influence; or else one will lead to no definite results. On the other hand, if one propounds one's dogmas merely as the traditional teacher of religion has always done by saying: "This is our faith. This is what you should believe,"—one is then in no case teaching philosophy, and one is hardly helping the young people to "seek."[58]

Sampter dealt with this dilemma well, Royce wrote. And yet if one pushed either Royce or Sampter, both would have said that this dilemma was only apparent: religion is always already about seeking and changing and developing. Religious thought needn't be dogmatic.

Furthermore, Royce suggested that *The Seekers* was ideal preparation for students because of the way it would help them understand their future experiences: "They are thus prepared for a variety of future religious and philosophical experiences, and yet they are kept in touch with that love and hope of unity which alone can justify the existence of our very doubts, of our philosophical disputes, and of our modern complications of life."[59] In spite of all the modern complexities in the world they would encounter, they would be able to keep in mind "our sense of the great common values of the spiritual world."[60] This, Royce wrote, upping the ante, would be the foundation of the American nation.

Sampter did not make such politicized statements—at least not this early in her career as a writer. Yet to get her students to consider big philosophical questions, she frequently asked them to reflect on the social and religious world around them. In fact, she began the book by asking, "Now, are we all agreed that there is very little religion—true religious belief—at present?" Each student reflected on this, and five of them agreed. Henry, however, disagreed, saying that he thought that people today were just as religious as ever. "'I think,' said Florence to Henry, 'that you are confusing religion and creed. People belong to churches and temples, and think they are religious, but they don't know what they believe.'"[61] Sampter greeted Florence's comment with approval: merely participating in the forms of religion was not being truly religious. Metaphysical and theological reflection was the cornerstone of "true religious belief," which was the sign of real religion. And so she sought to help her students cultivate the practice of these philosophical reflections.

As it replayed Sampter's weekly meetings with the six students, *The Seekers* continued its focused theological inquiry: How could the students understand the world around them and the relationships of humans to God and the cosmos? Though the conversation often reached a high level of abstraction, Sampter brought the conversation back to two main things: the participants' experience of themselves and the world, and traditional religious (almost always textual) articulations of metaphysical relationships. Like the creation of Sampter's own religious worldview, this moving among traditions was not a process of conversion, or of religious switching. Their intellectual and religious movement was not discrete in its steps but combined and recombined religious ideas, philosophical ideals, and their own experience of the world.

Building on her thoughts in *The Great Adventurer*, Sampter explained to her students how she saw the relationship between God and the cosmos. To do so, she drew on a textual tradition of Hinduism:

> "I believe God to be in each of us, to be the self within us, and within all others, and within the universe; to be the knowledge, the light and the understanding. I can explain to you what I mean by reading a passage from the Indian Vedas [*sic*: Upanishads], which seems to me so true, and so exactly what I want to say, that I could not explain it so well myself." Then I read the following: "In the beginning was Self alone. Atman Is the Self in all our selves—the Divine Self concealed by his own qualities. This Self they sometimes call the Undeveloped. . . . The generation of Brahma was before all ages, unfolding himself evermore in a beautiful glory; everything which is highest and everything which is deepest belongs to him. Being and not being are unveiled through Brahma."[62]

Sampter did not read Sanskrit, and yet she had read some Hindu theological texts. In this, she followed an American trend of the late nineteenth and early twentieth centuries. The leading figure of this popular dissemination of Hinduism for an American audience was Swami Vivekananda, who first visited the United States as part of the World Parliament of Religions in Chicago in 1893. Vivekananda preached a version of Advaita Vedanta—or a nondualistic Hindu theology—which sees God, the human self, and the universe as one.[63] Sampter used the text from the Upanishads because it was "exactly what" she wanted to say, and she "could not explain it so well herself." It was both a description and a shaping of her own religious worldview, and she hoped it would similarly resonate with her students' experiences and theological stances.

Geographically closer to home, the American-centered New Thought movement also harmonized with much of Sampter's theology. New Thought, like Spiritualism, made metaphysical claims about the human and the cosmos, but it did not have clear institutional bounds. This loose movement of diverse people and communities tended to agree that mind, body, and nature were one.[64] Sin and sickness were the result of faulty perceptions. For many Americans associated with New Thought, this meant that physical healing, for instance, could be effected through mental or spiritual processes. Sampter was unconvinced by the claim that sickness was merely a perceptual error and by the tales of healing by "right thinking," but she saw the basic claim of the oneness of mind, body, and nature as a fundamental metaphysical insight.

Sampter also wrote a hundred-page novella from the perspective of Asoka, the Indian emperor traditionally credited with the spread of Buddhism. *King Asoka* philosophized about the relationship of nature and the divine, the role of human suffering, and the ways seemingly finite humans might experience infinity.[65] Even as a child, Asoka learned from the golden bees and red poppies and pointed out the errors of the "masters."[66] Sampter was intentional in her choice of religious ideas. Every movement had errors, she thought, and one could discern what was truth and what was an error only by a combination of experience and contemplation.

———

Eight years after the publication of *The Seekers*, in late 1918, Jessie Sampter sat with her friends and asked a Ouija board, Did her deceased mother approve of her recent return to Judaism? And how did she feel about Jessie's embrace of Zionism? These were pressing questions for the thirty-five-year-old Sampter. She sought her mother's approval in part because she was second-guessing her own life: "Had I accomplished anything?" she had wondered when she thought she might be dying of pneumonia earlier in the year.[67] She also wanted her mother's endorsement because she had embarked on an unlikely religious path for someone of her social position—she was incorporating more Orthodox Jewish practice, and she supported a Jewish society in Palestine. Her mother might have found observant Judaism and Zionism surprising; after all, statistically very few American Jews moved from nonobservance to significant halakhic observance in the early twentieth century. But in another way, perhaps her daughter's philosophical plight would not have been so surprising: she had always been fascinated by religion, and she had always sought out new ways of seeing the world.

The Ouija board belonged to a friend she called Evelyn, also an accul-turated American Jew, who was interested in Spiritualism and had been using the board to communicate with her dead father. The first day yielded no messages for Jessie, but "my presence and my touch seemed to accel-erate the messages" for Evelyn. The second day, however, was a different story. "At last! A message for me! I thrilled. I am afraid I was wholly con-verted. From Mother!" Jessie sat with her hands on the pointer as it moved and Evelyn looked on. "Are you pleased with me?" Jessie wanted to know. "No," the pointer indicated. Her mother's displeasure was not because she planned to go to Palestine but rather because she was not taking care of herself. "It was dangerous for me to use the board; in doing so, I was not taking care of myself." She resolved never to use the board again.[68]

I recall playing with a Ouija board (manufactured by Parker Brothers) at sleepovers in middle school. None of us thought it was remotely religious—nor, if we were honest, that it was remotely effective. It was the equivalent of telling ghost stories, which, in fact, often followed once we grew tired of saying, "You're moving it! We know you're moving the pointer!" and put the board away. Our parents thought it was harmless too, and if any of them had religious objections, we never heard them. White suburban families in late twentieth-century New Jersey mostly didn't see any connection be-tween religion and Ouija boards, it seems.

But maybe early twentieth-century New Yorkers knew better. When I read this episode, I wondered, If she had become so committed to Judaism, what was Sampter doing with a Ouija board? The two systems of thought met neither epistemologically nor in their view of the cosmos. American Jewish theology in the early twentieth century put little stock in the spirit world. Some Christians saw their religion as compatible with Spiritual-ism, and many Spiritualists claimed Christianity. The *American Spiritual Magazine* explained in 1877, "We have nothing to gain by setting ourselves up in opposition to the Bible or Christ. That book has more evidences of Spiritualism than any other in existence, and we have more reasons to ac-cept Christ as the founder of our philosophy, and the head of our church, than any other religion."[69] Few Jews, however, claimed that Spiritualism and Judaism coincided. And yet Sampter's approach to the Ouija board was sincere. She didn't participate merely as a parlor game. In fact, she reported that the experience had been successful, though it had left her spiritually exhausted. She was pleased to have connected with her mother, but she felt she could not do it again without risking her mental and spiritual health in a permanent way. Nor was this her only experience with the mystical or the occult. She also consulted palm readers—and communicated with the spirit world in other ways.

In 1918 Sampter had a vision. To be precise, she had several visions, and she also heard voices. Though her sister and friends feared she had had a mental breakdown, and she, too, admitted that her vision "culminated in twelve hours of actual insanity," Sampter still found the visions and voices meaningful years later.[70] She explained how it was possible that she had heard voices, even the voice of God. It was revealed to her that "the consciousness melts into the All-consciousness, and the deep streams of the unconscious well up from the world of all-being. We are one."[71] Then she had a dream-vision of Jesus: "Outlined in stars appeared the image of the dead Christ. . . . Why should I dream of Jesus? Yet I know it had some other significance, it had something to do with my people."[72] Although many early twentieth-century American Jews read or heard sermons about Jesus, they saw him as an admirable historical figure but never a divine one.[73] Why, Sampter wondered, would she, a Jew, see images of Jesus? The answer was revealed to her: "Now I understood interpreted in verse that strange dream of the crucifix of stars. It was Easter Sunday. My people had been crucified, but my people were resurrected."[74] Sampter saw Christian images in her vision about the Jewish people! Even her mystical experiences reinforced the idea that religious truth drew on many images and traditions.

These visions and voices did not change her theology, but they gave it images—ones she would return to for the rest of her life. When she wrote a poem about the 1920 Jerusalem riots, Jesus as a metaphor for the Jews formed its central image:

Easter Sunday. And there is the one crucified.
A thousand times upon the cross he died,
A thousand times, until the world of stars
Blazons upon the heavens his galaxy of scars.
A thousand times—and still he has not risen—
Crowned with bleeding rags, cast into prison. . . .
We have smeared our doors with blood, we are waiting the pascal sign.
We are the sacrificial lamb, the crucified divine.[75]

Though it was Passover—a holiday celebrating the sparing of Jewish firstborn children from death—the poem also marked the religious time of Easter. By including both Jesus and the sacrificial lamb, Sampter alluded to a Christian theological interpretation in which Jesus becomes the lamb and sacrifices himself for the sake of all humanity. Despite the clarity and depth of her vision, however, throughout her life she would still consider paths not taken: "Had I not become a Jew, I should have become a Quaker," she would later muse.[76]

Even later in life, she still saw religious recombination as the best religious path. Rabbi Mordecai Kaplan had been an early influence—he tutored her in 1914–15, and she came to his home for salon-like discussions about Jewish philosophy—but when he visited her in 1938, the student became the teacher: "My discussions with her interested me greatly," he wrote in his diary. "I marveled at her Hebrew poems and especially over her thoughts, expressed in fragments over various matters. She gave me *The Discussions of Krishnamurthi*, which I read with great pleasure. Even though I do not agree with all his thoughts, he directed my mind to the practical side, which I tend to overlook."[77] Kaplan wrote in his diary that he had gone to say blessing before the meal for the holiday of Shavuot but changed his mind about the wording: "I had in mind to say in the Festival Kiddush 'Who has sent us prophets of truth and bestowed upon us lofty aspirations' in place of 'who has chosen us, etc.,' but after reading *The Discussions of Krishnamurthi*, I became convinced that it is not right to glory in ideals. I phrased the beginning of the blessing thus: 'who redeems us from slavery and makes us rejoice in His salvation.'"[78] Sampter herself had translated the Krishnamurti volume into Hebrew, though she had given Kaplan the English version. Kaplan appreciated Sampter's insistence on the serious contemplation of religious wisdom, whatever its source. As he created Reconstructionist Judaism, he, too, engaged in religious recombination.[79]

In addition to writing deeply theological poetry and having heady conversations, Sampter saw religious openness as important in daily life. She was critical of Orthodox Judaism in Palestine: she saw merely empty forms without true understanding or experience of the natural world. The other option—atheism or antireligion—was equally unappealing.[80] "In Jerusalem one has to choose between anti-religious and fossilized religious. But does one have to choose? Is there not a third choice, a new way?" she wrote in 1922.[81] In her unpublished autobiographical novel, she described Evelyn, a character clearly modeled on herself, as follows: "Not having been educated in orthodoxy, she chose for herself in every day life those customs that captured her personal sense of beauty and her personal reason; and living with Rivka, the revolutionist with an orthodox background, she directed the household along traditional lines . . . but she yielded to Rivka's laxities and enjoyed it. Why should one not sing Sabbath songs all week? She enjoyed the paradox of turning laws back into customs."[82] In those early years in Palestine, Sampter tried to gather a group of like-minded Jews, including Henrietta Szold, Julia and Alexander Dushkin, and Helen and Norman Bentwich, to have gender-inclusive services without unappealing theological content (no mention of renewing temple sacrifice, for example), but it never quite gained momentum.

After seeing dire poverty and a dead child in the aftermath of a Jerusalem snowstorm, Evelyn cried and then prayed the traditional Sabbath prayer over candlelighting. Joseph asked her, "What makes you go through that comedy?" and she replied, "I didn't say anything I don't believe." Joseph asked her if she believed in "God, in a big kind old gentleman," and she got annoyed. "She could not answer Joseph's logic, and she knew it to be both unanswerable and false. Hours of talk might have proved her case to her own satisfaction, but it could not have made him know ~~that inwardness of which she could not speak, that faith embedded in life itself which harmonizes any smallest action at the propitious moment with the pulses of feeling and being~~."[83] Sampter crossed out the description of Evelyn's religious experience, perhaps to show that Evelyn could not quite talk about it. Though Sampter's character could not articulate her religious worldview, the author herself had a clearer sense of her own. It must match experience and feeling in the world with metaphysical ideas. But that hardly meant she had it all figured out; religion was an ongoing process for Sampter. "We are all groping," said her character Evelyn, as she agonized about how to make a religiously meaningful life that was also intellectually palatable.[84] It was never an easy task.

Sampter and the Study of American Religion

My interest in Jessie Sampter is not just about telling the story of a woman neglected by history. Her wide-ranging religious interests were more than capriciousness or an idiosyncratic theological quest. Her life and thought have convinced me that we need to reorient the analytic categories of American religious history.

In particular, Sampter's story has convinced me that the category of "diversity" is not the best way to frame the American religious landscape, especially when we view it from the perspective of individuals rather than institutions. Much of the scholarship on religion in the United States uses the category of religious diversity to think about the early twentieth century. It is easy to assume that the religious seeking and blurry lines between religions that we see today are contemporary phenomena, born of the 1960s or postmodernism. But Sampter's life shows us the ways that a person could have a strong sense of religious identity and yet appropriate, incorporate, and adapt other religious ideas and practices.

Here Sampter's story illuminates part of a vibrant landscape of American religion. Scholars such as Courtney Bender, writing on theosophy and metaphysics, and Ann Braude, writing on Spiritualism, have challenged the idea that people had one single religious identity to the exclusion of all others. People drew on many kinds of metaphysics, theologies, and rituals but did not think of themselves as arbitrary or syncretistic. As I spent more time with Sampter's thought, writings, family, and friends, I developed a broader conviction about American religious life: that religious diversity and its conceptual confrere religious pluralism are not the most useful models for understanding religion in the early twentieth-century United States.

Despite what sounds like an utterly unique story, Sampter's life illustrates these broader themes in American religion. As a queer, disabled American Zionist woman, she was hardly the typical Jew, let alone the typical American in a demographic sense. But Jessie was born to Jewish parents involved in the Ethical Culture movement, became what we might call a religious seeker for a time, and then embraced Judaism, all the while developing her own particular metaphysics informed by other religions, Theosophy, and even the occult. In this sense, her life and thought were representative of American religion: she had an ascribed religious identity (Jew) that she took as true, but she also interacted with ideas and ideals from other religions without imagining that they destabilized her own religion. And in this she helps show the utility of—as well as the messiness and imprecision of—the categories we use to think about religion.

As I read through Sampter's reflections and imagined her world, I could not help but think about what religion looked like. What religion looked like for Sampter, of course, but also what religion looked like to others in her world. Religion was a general category, a genus encompassing the available species Christianity, Judaism, Hinduism, Islam, and the like. But religion also constituted an essential sphere of society, as well as forming a component piece of the self. Sampter didn't thoughtlessly reproduce general ideas about religion, nor did she simply choose one of the species of religion to embrace as her own. She formed her thought in a fiercely individual way, but she yearned for community; she philosophically eschewed what she saw as empty ritual and still insisted on ritual's social value; she recognized religious difference while maintaining an omnivorous approach to religious learning. How should we imagine religion in the world around her, and how should we make sense of her own religiosity? Though Sampter's story is distinctive, the two questions converge.

When Americans describe religion today, one of the most common categories we use is religious pluralism. This concept of pluralism implies different and distinct religious groups within a geographic area, such as a nation-state. Politicians, clergy, journalists, parents, and educators use it to talk about national demographics, schools and neighborhoods, social justice, immigration, and a vast array of other social issues. We see it on television; we read it in newspapers. But it isn't merely popular or feel-good jargon: pluralism also remains a popular scholarly way to think about American religion. Harvard University, for instance, runs the Pluralism Project, whose mission is to "help Americans engage with the realities of religious diversity through research, outreach, and the active dissemination of resources."[85] A project like this crosses the bounds from scholarly to social and uses the idea of religious pluralism to do it.

Pluralism's conceptual sister diversity also appears in both popular and scholarly conversation. Sometimes *diversity* functions as a synonym for *religious pluralism* and sometimes as a related concept, where diversity means the presence of many religions, and pluralism signals the acceptance and valuing of religious diversity. When we talk about biological diversity, for example, we are talking about the existence of multiple, discrete species. It is less a spectrum, with many varying shades between species, than an intricate set of either-ors: an organism is either an oak or a pine, and it could be a northern red oak or an eastern white pine but not its own singular combination of oakness and pineness. Religious diversity, then, suggests discrete religious identities. One could be a Christian or a Jew, or a Free Will Baptist or a Reconstructionist Zionist or even an atheist.

Both diversity and pluralism also play major roles in the way scholars conceive of American religious history, including Jessie Sampter's time.[86] Classics in the scholarly annals of American religious history, such as Sydney Ahlstrom's and Catherine Albanese's one-volume histories of religion in America, have different takes on the desirability of religious diversity (Ahlstrom is uneasy, Albanese more optimistic), but they see it as a fundamental feature of American history.[87] These concepts of religious diversity and pluralism appear across disciplines (history, sociology, anthropology, political science) and across methods (quantitative and qualitative; intellectual history, cultural history, ethnography, rational choice theory).[88]

Historian William Hutchison, for instance, argues that diversity happened to the American religious landscape in the nineteenth century, and pluralism happened in the twentieth. Hutchison sees pluralism as having three sequential modes, each better than the last—pluralism as toleration, pluralism as inclusion, and pluralism as participation. Throughout, his historical account takes religious diversity as a fact, and his tale implies that Americans have made progress in dealing with that diversity.[89]

Over the past two decades, some scholars have critiqued the concept of pluralism as a scholarly category, arguing that it is ideologically freighted toward sympathetic, positive, and harmonious visions of religion.[90] "Religious pluralism is more than the acknowledgement that religious diversity exists; it is an idealized view of how religions should coexist," religious studies scholar Amanda Porterfield writes.[91]

Diversity, in contrast, has held its own because it is a more descriptive category, noting the presence but not the quality or value of multiple religions.[92] Diversity may be more acceptable as a category for defining American religion because it comes with less ideological baggage, but Jessie Sampter's story suggests that it does not always do helpful analytic work.

What diversity and pluralism have in common is the assumption that there are discrete religions and that dividing up religions is a useful way to organize the map of American religion. Although religious pluralism and diversity imply that there are many religions to choose from, and account for religious switching, or conversion, they do not call attention to the ways that religious people often defy religious boundaries in much subtler ways. It is easy to sneer at the Baptist who believes in reincarnation, the Anglican with a dream catcher dangling from the rearview mirror, or the Reform Jew who devoutly reads her horoscope. It is easy to pooh-pooh the "cafeteria approach," in which a person puts together beliefs and practices from different religions. It is easy to call someone who picks and chooses elements of a tradition a hypocrite. But it would be a mistake to think that these people are insincere or that there are just a few outliers.

Perhaps when scholars look at the religious landscape from a bird's-eye view, diversity retains some utility. If we want to count butts in pews, assuming that there are discrete, nonoverlapping religions may aid our work. But if we want to study people as individuals, as family members, and even as communities, pluralism and diversity don't really work to describe the landscape accurately. Scholarly work on "lived religion," for instance, can throw a wrench into the works on pluralism: it shows the ways that individuals' religious practice, thoughts, and experience often do not fit neatly into one category.

Jessie Sampter's life and thought suggest some of the ways that the category of diversity oversimplifies and misleads us in thinking about the American religious landscape. While she could identify different religions, such as Judaism, Christianity, and Hinduism, as well as religious movements such as Spiritualism, New Thought, and transcendentalism, she did not think they had mutually exclusive claims to reality. Even less did they have mutually exclusive claims to individual people. In the lives of people like Sampter, her parents, her friends, her intellectual heroes, and many others in her world, diversity can only poorly describe their religious sensibilities, or the religious landscape as they saw it. If we looked deeper, we might even find the same to be true for many of the characters in classic books that use religious pluralism and diversity as categories.

Sampter has pushed me to imagine a new model for the process we see in this religious landscape: religious recombination. Recombination is a metaphor borrowed from a naturally occurring genetic process. When human cells make new reproductive cells, for example, the chromosomes line up next to one another. When they are aligned, they exchange information. This process can occur by one chromosome snipping out a section of itself and inserting it into the analogous section of the other chromosome. But it more commonly occurs without such a removal. Instead, one section can be copied and given to the other chromosome without the source chromosome losing a part of itself. It's more a kind of sharing. The process can happen many times, with either chromosome acting as the source of the information and either acting as the receiver of the information.

Applying this metaphor to American religious life, we have a model in which a person (one chromosome) acts both as a source of religious ideas, rituals, and worldviews and as the receiver of religious ideas, rituals, and worldviews. Sometimes they receive, sometimes they give, and sometimes they give up ideas. But throughout the process, the person retains a sense of intactness (analogous to the chromosome's completeness, in that it has the correct number of alleles). The person need not feel that she is incomplete, or that he has become a different person, just as the genetic recombination does not result in an incomplete or wholly new chromosome. Moreover, which ideas they will pick up from their environment is not predetermined. This give-and-take happens organically but not mechanically. Though their particular religious ideas, rituals, and worldview change and adjust as they come in contact with the various religious ideas, rituals, and worldviews around them, they continue to feel that they have a set of religious ideas and practices that go together.

How, then, should we think about religions within communities, and religions within a single person? And how should we think about religion in Jessie Sampter's world? We should not give too much credence to diversity and its attendant temptation to fit people into distinct religious boxes. Sometimes recombination happens even at the level of institutional belonging. A small but significant number of American Jews, for example, embraced Christian Science while continuing to attend synagogues or belong to Jewish fraternal organizations such as B'nai B'rith. A Reform rabbi in Minnesota noted a "peculiar" situation in which several of his synagogue's members claimed that they had not only not abandoned Judaism but had in fact become better Jews since embracing Mary Baker Eddy's Christian Science teachings.[93]

Some American religious historians' work also offers examples of how people engaged in religious recombination at the individual level. In her work on Spiritualism, Ann Braude shows that plenty of self-identified Christians engaged in Spiritualist practices, such as séances, and espoused Spiritualist beliefs, such as those about the afterlife.[94] Who, exactly, was a Spiritualist? It was hard to say. How would they fit into a picture of American religious diversity? Not very clearly—as Braude points out, it gave rise to no permanent institutions, demanded no exclusive loyalty, and was characterized by people's movement into, out of, and around Spiritualist beliefs and practices during the course of their lives. Many of Spiritualism's sometime-participants were mainstream Christians. Braude traces the history of several families of Quakers who followed the Fox sisters and their Spiritualist rappings, for example. The popularity of mid-nineteenth-century Spiritualist novels, such as those of Elizabeth Stuart Phelps, further suggests the widespread appeal of the religious ideas of Spiritualism across traditional denominations and affiliations.[95] Phelps's novels challenged traditional Protestant notions of the afterlife when they depicted heaven as a place for reuniting with loved ones more than uniting with God. Even though they did not comport with much Christian doctrine, many Christians bought them: her first, *The Gates Ajar*, sold more than 100,000 copies.

Similarly, in her work on Boston's religious past and present (including the nineteenth and early twentieth century), Courtney Bender shows how many Bostonians, some of whom considered themselves Christian, while others who did not, shaped their spirituality. One shamanic "soul singer" explained how shamanism increased his connection to Christianity through the Holy Spirit. A New Thought writer encouraged Christians to read the Bible better, for there they would find the truths of reincarnation and human liberation.[96] Bender's historical subjects variously participated in transcendentalism, Theosophy, Swedenborgianism, and other metaphysical movements, but they did not see themselves as cobbling together a worldview from disparate pieces. They felt they were creating a whole, unified picture of the world and their place in it—one that fit with their own experiences. Bender's characters were not lone wolves, or a handful of religious outliers, but rather were part of religious communities and networks that were themselves informed by religious traditions. "While my respondents tended to reject broad labels," Bender writes, "they nevertheless recognized that others were fellow travelers, and that a number of groups and institutions promoted similar interests."[97] Even the people we might expect to be the most individualistic about religion, then, draw on its social aspects.

For another unlikely example, take missionary work: it seems obviously suited to thinking about religions as single, exclusive categories. After all, missionaries think that their religion is the true or right one, and they seek to convert people—a way of thinking that relies on the singularity and distinctiveness of their religion. If there were ever a context to see religions as separate and distinct, this would be it. And yet missionizing, too, can be a practice of recombination. Matthew Cressler writes, "The missionary-missionized encounter is less about the imposition of a monolithic religious system on a passive people and more about the creation of new religious worlds through the encounters between missionaries and missioned."[98] These new religious worlds are recombined worlds.

We can see very similar developments today. From where I sit, almost everyone who uses the phrase *spiritual but not religious* to describe themselves is, in fact, religious. (According to recent polls, they now make up between 18 and 30 percent of US residents.[99]) These SBNRs, as the abbreviation goes, sometimes don't identify with a single religious tradition, and they usually see themselves as rejecting so-called organized religion, but they engage in religious practices and think about religious ideas. Scholars have noticed this too, using phrases like "spiritual *and* religious."[100] If we began to look at the US religious landscape not with an exclusive list (Judaism, Christianity, Islam, etc.) but instead with an idea like religious recombination, we would see how these SBNRs have a lot in common with people who are more comfortable with traditional religious labels.

It's not just those outside institutional frameworks. Samira Mehta writes about Christian-Jewish marriages and shows how families make sense of religion; the concern that multiple religious ideas and practices will confuse the children is misplaced. She also demonstrates how interfaith families where one parent is a person of color find different sets of expectations, choices, and limitations. While synagogue leaders were often more accommodating of non-Jewish traditions in these families, the families also often found that they had to be more intentional and outspoken to register as Jewish to others. These families also demonstrate how religion overlaps with other social categories, particularly race. One family, for example, wanted their son to be "comfortable in his grandmother's Black Baptist Church. . . . [A]t least in their family, the church is a large part of what Blackness means."[101] Andrea Jain writes about how US Americans who identify with various religions (and none at all) use yoga as a way of shaping themselves but also as a way of shaping others. She points out the use of postural yoga in US prisons, for example, where it is designed to mold prisoners into calm, well-disciplined citizens.[102] Jain and Mehta each give examples of the ways people incorporate aspects of different religions into their lives and of the ways that social forces such as race and economics can determine what is available for adopting, how religious recombination is received by others, and how other people and institutions push some religious ideas or practices over others. Religious recombination exists in a world of many forces.

Diversity might be one way to understand the religious landscape, then, but it misses something important in all these phenomena, past and present. Jessie Sampter, many of her friends and family, the Quakers who followed the Fox sisters, the New Thought writer who found reincarnation in the Bible, and a host of others do not fit neatly under an exclusive religious label. If we began with the category of American religious diversity with its discrete labels, these people would not fit. Perhaps, if pushed, we could say that each one of these individual people was also diverse or had diversity within their own religious thought. But they don't see it that way at all. As Bender's work suggests, they think of their own religious or spiritual selves in a similar way to many contemporary Americans. When Presbyterians do yoga at church, when Protestant churches hold Passover seders, when Jews follow the "Kirtan rabbi" who uses Hindu devotional chanting, these practitioners don't think of themselves as dabbling in some other person's religion over there. They see these practices as contributing to an integrated religious worldview, a coherent spirituality.[103]

Something similar to recombination happens even at communal levels. In the nineteenth and early twentieth centuries, Jews went to churches to socialize, hear lectures, and meet people—and far more often than you might expect. Shari Rabin explains, "It is impossible to prove but entirely conceivable that there were weeks in the nineteenth century when more Jews attended church than synagogue."[104] Christians would likewise attend synagogue, especially for special events like synagogue openings and lectures.[105] More widely, nineteenth- and early twentieth-century Reform Jews talked about Jesus as a Jew and as a moral exemplar, almost as much as their Christian counterparts.[106] They emphasized the Bible but downplayed rabbinic literature, in a way that often made them part of the same religious conversations as their Christian neighbors. Communal-level recombination is not merely individual recombination on a larger scale, but its presence suggests that the category of diversity and its attendant assumptions about clear boundaries between religious groups may also need rethinking at the level of larger communities and institutions.

If, instead of Sampter, we looked at a child living in her Harlem neighborhood a generation or so later, we would see a very different picture—but not wholly different with respect to the ways that people "did" religion. During the late 1910s and 1920s, Harlem became a predominantly Black neighborhood and one of the centers of African American cultural life. It also became a fascinating place to see religion. Like Sampter, though not always in identical ways, many Harlem residents saw theology and the body as intimately related. Women playwrights of the Harlem Renaissance used themes of magic and religion where those ideas were hardly separate, including African-originated religions, conjure, Yoruba, Islam, and Christianity.[107] Even Langston Hughes, whose religious work centered on Christianity, attended different churches on different days, refusing to choose membership in a single one.[108] African American men and women embraced religious movements that helped them understand their own bodies as well as the racial order of society differently. These people, as well as the movements they joined, practiced recombination. Marcus Garvey's United Negro Improvement Association was structurally similar to Ethical Culture: you could belong to it, find meaning in the religious language it sometimes used, and also belong to any one of a variety of other churches and religious bodies. Members of Father Divine's Peace Mission—which proclaimed that the only real race was the human race—could also identify with other churches. The Moorish Science Temple promoted a worldview in which so-called Negroes were actually Moorish Americans whose ancestral religion was Islam. It recognized Buddha, Jesus, Confucius, and Muhammad as prophets, and its central text, presented as a lost section of the Qur'an, drew from Rosicrucianism and an esoteric Christian text (one that has more recently become important to New Age spiritual groups).

Ethiopian Hebrews came to an understanding of the world through theologies, texts, and rituals from Judaism, Christianity, and African religions.[109] This is not to say that the Peace Mission, Moorish Science Temple, and Ethiopian Hebrew movement were derivative or syncretic but rather that engaging with other religious texts and practices played a central role creating their understanding of the world.

Farther away from Harlem, though also during Jessie Sampter's life, we can see another scene of religious recombination: that of Native American struggles for religio-racial protection. To convince Bureau of Indian Affairs agents to allow ceremonial practices, Native American tribes often had to describe them in Christian terms—or, more often, include explicitly Christian elements. For example, a Kiowa leader explained that the Ghost Dance was "worship," different in form but not in meaning from forms of Christian worship. Pawnee tribal leaders found their requests to hold a Ghost Dance denied until they invited Methodist and Baptist pastors to preach as part of the gathering.[110] These moves were strategic, but that does not mean they were disingenuous. Many of these Native American movements explicitly and intentionally included Christian theological concepts such as the trinity, which white settlers had introduced to them and their ancestors but which they believed.

These glimpses into other stories of recombination show that not all people shared Sampter's relative freedom to choose. The possibilities of recombination are always in part determined by context: which religious ideas and forms you encounter and which religious language you use to present your own ideas are not always of your own choosing. Some will be more available, and some may be more advantageous than others for working within your own legal or social system. Some may even be thrust upon you. Recombination, unlike the cafeteria model, does not assume consumers who can simply survey the religious options and freely choose whichever are to their liking in the absence of power or coercion.

Here I am telling a story of how religious recombination works as a model for individuals and communities in the United States, but we could also tell it about people in Israel, India, Canada, Japan, England, Germany, and every other nation I have encountered. The US case may sometimes be easier to see, in part because of disestablishment and the particulars of church-state arrangements, but I don't mean to suggest that the model of religious recombination is uniquely American.

Jessie Sampter's story is my inspiration for conceptualizing this religious recombination—a process of incorporating religious ideas and practices from the world around her in harmony with her own experiences. But religious recombination is not just her story. It is the story of Jessie's parents, friends, mentors, students, and others beyond her small circle, as well as the people at the edges of the narrative, such as the Jews in churches, the Christians in synagogues, New Thought enthusiasts, Ethical Culture participants, and even Jews who talked about the moral example of Jesus. If we expanded our view, we would also see it in the thousands of attendees at the 1893 World Parliament of Religions, in many Americans who converted from one religion to another, and in the members of new religious movements.

It's also the story of countless people I know today: the family who wished us a "Merry Christmas from our Hindu/aesthetics household," my yoga teacher who talks about chakras and crystals and church, my tiny neighbor who is equally invested in the miracles of Santa and Hanukkah, and the people who attend the midday mindfulness meditation classes in the union at my university. It's the story of many intermarried families, the neo-Hasidic people who came to Judaism through New Age and hippie movements, and the people who go to transformational festivals like Burning Man.[111] It's also the story of Ralph Waldo Emerson and Alain Locke. Maybe, depending on your theological orientation, you can even see it as the story of Joseph Smith, the founder of Mormonism, or Mary Baker Eddy, the founder of Christian Science. Sampter's story is the story of how recombination worked for one person, and it hints at how it may have worked for the people around her. But their religious lives radiate out beyond them, shining light on patterns of religiosity past and present.

Conclusion

Perhaps Jessie Sampter, her parents, her cousin Anita, her friend Nora, Mary Antin, Josephine Lazarus, Ralph Waldo Emerson, Josiah Royce, Mordecai Kaplan, the six teenagers Sampter taught, and the other characters here were no more than curiosities of history, outliers on the American religious map. Perhaps Ethical Culture's position of challenging the idea of separate, distinct religions was also quirky. If it was, then Spiritualism, Theosophy, and various other metaphysical systems were too. But all of these things together, as well as a close-up look at Sampter's own religious life and thought, suggest that American religious life is not always best characterized by religious diversity—that many people, maybe even most people, do not fit clearly into one of the discrete religious categories to the exclusion of the others. If we take seriously Sampter's emphasis on the harmony of one's own embodied life experience with one's religious understanding of the world, then we should not expect a landscape full of people who fit into discrete religious boxes. We would expect something that looked messier. We would expect people exchanging ideas and philosophies, inheriting some practices and adopting others, and crafting religious worldviews in dialogue with the friends, family, and social world around them. In short, we would expect religious recombination.

So Jessie Sampter's story is a story about religion.

But it's also a story about disability, the body, and the mind. Years after she had gone to a palm reader, she wrote in a letter to herself, "It is funny, that thing the palmist told you. She said you were morally weak, because of the depression in your thumb due to paralysis. Perhaps it is so."[112] Sampter was not utterly convinced by the palm reader's interpretation, but neither was she dismissive. Sometimes she felt that it matched her embodied experience: "If you had the courage to exercise your thumbs until they became strong, perhaps you would have the courage to live properly," she told herself. And, as we see in the next chapter, Sampter herself thought the physical world and the moral and spiritual world were all of a piece, but she also ruminated on how to understand her own disabled body in the world. Especially as she came to espouse Zionism, with its emphasis on physical health and strength, how could she understand her embodied experience and her physical role in the world?

CHAPTER TWO

A Life with Disability

The genesis of Jessie Sampter's story—or at least one of its creation myths—began in her early adolescence. Like a creation myth, it served as a controlling narrative for what came before and what came after, and even sometimes called into question the very categories of before and after. And, like a creation myth, this part of her story both seemed "out of time" and marked the beginning.[1]

Less than a year after her father died, twelve-year-old Jessie Sampter suddenly fell ill. Months earlier, she had begun to attend the Horace Mann School—her first introduction to regular schooling, which she loved. One day Jessie came down with a blistering fever; she recalled, "A violent nosebleed was accompanied by pains in my head and neck. I moaned and whimpered."[2] But no one knew what was wrong. Because the symptoms mimicked other illnesses, because the disease often struck younger children, and because it was considered rare in the United States before the turn of the century, the doctors did not immediately diagnose Jessie's "infantile paralysis"—or, in today's terms, polio.

Jessie's mother initially assumed it was just a routine childhood cold and called her "fussy and troublesome," but the day after her fever set in, doctors and nurses confirmed she was very ill.[3] The symptoms worsened and multiplied. Paralytic polio—the kind Jessie had—began to cause excruciating pain in her lower back and limbs, as well as paralysis in some muscles. Unlike in most other types of paralysis, polio patients can feel their limbs, so even people who can't move an arm, a leg, or several limbs can feel burning pain there.

How could Jessie make sense of all this pain? Many young polio patients tried to escape their bodies by dissociating—what another polio survivor described as choosing to "not be there."[4] Yet Jessie rejected this move to separate her sense of self from her body. Though she grew up to become an intellectual and even at this young age was a poet and amateur philosopher, she never wrote about herself as if the real Jessie was the mind, and the body merely a vessel. "I am my body, and much more than my body," her sagely King Asoka character had said.[5] The body and soul and mind were all of a piece for her—not only for her but for every human—which meant that her physical pain and weakness were an integral part of her self-conception.

As her illness went on, Jessie's pains became excruciating, her fever remained high, and on one day she experienced hallucinations—a "delirious dream" in which the rules of logic did not hold. Two plus two could equal five in this state, she thought with dread. Her body was in pain, and she could no longer trust her mind. Both her body and her mind were working improperly, abnormally, seemingly out of her control. Even in these moments when she might most want to divide herself or reject the parts that did not seem to work right, Jessie still narrated an integrated self: a body, a mind, and a soul without visible seams.[6]

And yet Jessie Sampter would become a renowned Zionist writer. She would join a cause that celebrated the strong and healthy body, but she spoke of herself as "crippled" from polio and plagued by weakness and sickness her whole life. While Zionists elevated productive bodies that worked, built, and farmed, Sampter could rarely work with her hands apart from tending flowers and writing; while Zionism applauded reproductive (women's) bodies, Sampter never married or bore children—in fact, she wrote of homoerotic longings and had same-sex relationships we would consider queer. How can we make sense of a person whose embodied experiences did not conform to her religious and political ideals? What story did she tell herself? And what stories do we tell ourselves when our embodied lives don't fit seamlessly with our own deeply held ideologies?

This might at first seem like a story about a disabled person, without much import for able-bodied people. But, as Susan Wendell points out, "Unless we die suddenly, we are all disabled eventually. Most of us will live part of our lives with bodies that hurt, that move with difficulty or not at all, that deprive us of activities we once took for granted, or that others take for granted."[7] What's more, none of us has a body that is fully under our own control at all times; none of our bodies always works the way we want it to. We may not be disabled, but these insights about time and about the mismatch between our embodied lives and our ideals have something to say to all humans.

This mismatch between our bodies and the normative, and the even more obvious distance between our bodies and ideals, applies not only to Sampter or even to disability more generally. The artist Johanna Hedva has written about Sick Woman Theory, which uses chronic illness to re-think what it means to be human: the theory "*redefines* existence itself as something that is primarily and always vulnerable. It insists that a body is defined by its vulnerability, not temporarily affected by it. And so we need to reshape the world around this fact."[8] And as Alexis Shotwell explains, there is no pure and uncontaminated body, "no Eden we have desecrated, no pretoxic body we might discover through eating enough chia seeds and kombucha."[9] All bodies are always already limited, at least partially out of control, and contaminated.

Sampter's story also has something to contribute to the growing conver-sation of disability studies: it pushes us to consider the problem of chronic pain more fully, to reconsider the relationship of medical and social mod-els of disability, and to take religion seriously. Although many—perhaps most—memoirs about disability address religious belief, practice, or com-munal belonging, scholarship about disability studies tends to pay it little attention. Apart from theologically informed medical ethics and a growing scholarly literature that attends to religious texts with disability at the cen-ter, books and articles that analyze disability give almost no consideration to religion.[10] For example, Wendell argues at length for including the idea of transcendence—in particular, transcendence of the body—as part of a theory of disability.[11] Yet despite the centrality of this fundamentally theo-logical concept, she does not mention religion or theology.

Religion can sometimes seem to be a force for good, sometimes a force for ill, and it is often a source for making sense of the world, whether in ways we approve of or ways we do not. Disability studies needs to pay atten-tion to religion not because religion is good, ameliorative, or progressive but rather because it is a central way that many people make sense of pain, suffering, and "abnormal" bodies. To ignore religion or push it into the dustbin of irrelevance is to miss out on a significant way that both disabled and able-bodied people see and make sense of disability.

The first half of this chapter uses disability studies to illuminate Samp-ter's story, and the second part continues by showing how Jessie's story can reflect back on disability studies. Overall, it offers a new take on disability studies by narrating religion not merely as a site of ableist oppression but also as a source for making sense of embodiment.

Writing about disability while also using embodied methods of research can be complex. In writing much of this chapter, I used my own experiences with pain and limitation; I did not try to replicate Jessie's. I did not spend a day using a wheelchair. That strikes me, and many wheelchair users, as a condescending exercise, not to mention an ineffectual one. I did, however, think about the weeks that I was in pain, could hobble only short distances, and felt exhausted when I did. That was temporary, and I knew it at the time, so it's hardly identical. But it was a time of pain, frustration, and stark experience of my own body's limitations. During that time, and ever since, I have paid much closer attention to the conditions of sidewalks, the presence of stairs or elevators, and the times I walk over uneven ground. I also made it a point to plan my days with my physical capacity in mind. How much walking would I need to do? How long would I have between opportunities to sit? Although my physical limitations differ from Sampter's, these habits drew my attention to my body in ways that were similar to how Sampter talked about hers.

I drew on experiences I had not planned—admittedly, an unlikely approach to scholarly method but nevertheless one that generated insight. While I wrote, back pain appeared, lingered, disappeared, and then came back again. A terrible toothache plagued me for weeks. Sampter wrote about the ways toothaches made deep concentration difficult. I had a new appreciation for that kind of distraction, as well as a new way to see the connection of my own mind and body.

A woman with an autoimmune disease relayed a conversation with her friend: "I don't know if I can take this anymore. . . . I just want to get better. I want to go for a day without *thinking* about my body."[12] One of the values of telling Sampter's story is that it does what able-bodied people can avoid: it does not waver from its attention to the body. It does not allow the body to be a mere shell or an unremarkable material object. The body is always present, sometimes foregrounding itself, like a toothache, and sometimes more quietly reminding us that it acts as the grounds of possibility.

———

The doctors did not diagnose Jessie until a year after that terrible fever, but an earlier diagnosis would have made little difference for her physical prognosis.[13] There is no cure for polio, and some of the treatments used in the late nineteenth and early twentieth century may have done more harm than good. Doctors often immobilized patients, sometimes putting their limbs in casts or stretching out their arms and legs and securing them with straps. These treatments aimed at decreasing later deformity, but they only sometimes met with success and clearly traumatized many patients. Jessie did not have the kind of polio that attacks the nerves in the brain stem that help control breathing and swallowing, so she was never in an iron lung. In fact, since doctors began to use iron lungs only in the late 1920s, she never even saw the device that would become emblematic of polio. When the initial phase of polio passed, her body was profoundly changed: "The fever subsided and left me helpless, a mass of pains. My hands could hold nothing; I could move only my elbows and my knees." Jessie, who had already been cast as the fragile child of her family (Elvie called her a "very delicate, nervous child"), spent the better part of a year in bed and in pain.[14] The recovery, including physical therapy and massage, caused pains like a "wild beast [tearing] into the torn, sore muscles. . . . I yelled. I made no pretense at endurance."[15] *Recovery*, then, might not be the best word. Even after the initial fever and pains passed, Jessie could not recover a body that was lost.

In the months after the fever, the adult Sampter reflected, she saw her body differently than she had before: "Gauntly thin and deformed, I saw myself as a cripple. The muscles of my upper back and my upper left arm and of my thumbs had been destroyed, I had a curvature—I held my head to the left side—and my thumbs were deformed."[16] Polio commonly affects arms, legs, feet, hands, and spines, though the particular combination differs from person to person. The virus does not attack the muscles directly but instead the nerves that communicate with the muscles. Without that communication, muscles shrink. Eventually other nerves may sometimes grow to do the job of the destroyed ones, giving the person some of her movement back, but even for those who recover, the process is long and arduous. And the disease often left people's bodies profoundly changed: limps, braces, and wheelchairs became part of the embodied lives of many polio survivors.

Sampter's experience would have been fundamentally different if she had not been born into a white, relatively affluent, urban family.[17] Her family could afford doctors and rehabilitation, and they didn't depend on her to bring in money as part of the family economy, as many African Americans and immigrant families also living in New York during this time did. Potential immigrants with disabilities were often kept out of the country all together; officials turned people away at Ellis Island because they were deemed unable to support themselves, "likely to become a public charge," or simply "freaks."[18] Sampter's family could also care for her at home rather than giving her up to institutionalization—which might have been the only choice for a family that could not afford to care for a disabled teenager. Yet her family's affluence and whiteness could not insulate her from many of the other effects of polio.

In the immediate aftermath of her illness, Jessie's disabilities violated the way she wanted to see herself. They made her abnormal. "As I could not walk more than a few steps, the physician proposed that I go out on a rolling chair. Vehemently I protested. A rolling chair, a cripple! (Memories of the idiotic girl.) Above all things, I wanted to be normal, to be ordinary. I became acutely self-conscious and ashamed about my body."[19] A wheelchair, a shrunken arm, and weak legs made Jessie feel the weight of normalcy. How different her body was from the bodies she—and the rest of society—saw as normal. How fragmented her body felt. How its parts did not coordinate. How little control she had over it.

She wrote in her memoir, "I was awkward, deformed. Sister kept criticizing. My wrists still dropped. She would say: don't stand with your hands like a rabbit's paws. You have snaky hands, like Uriah Heep. Don't touch me with your clammy hands. This was when I tried to caress her. I winced. But her tortures drove and drove me on to the striving for normality. I conquered the wrist drop; I attempted to keep my hands from trembling." Then Jessie's own handwriting added, "*I tried to overcome the lethargic heaviness and weariness that made me dawdle over the simplest actions and that she dubbed willful helplessness. 'You don't want to do it.'*"[20] But, of course, she did.

Poliomyelitis can be an unpredictable disease, and little was known about exactly how it functioned in the late nineteenth century. It wasn't until 1908 that scientists discovered it was caused by a virus and not a bacterium. Polio destroys the motor neurons that send messages to muscles. For some patients, the virus destroys the nerves that communicate with the limbs; for others, it destroys the brain stem nerves that communicate with the muscles used in swallowing, speaking, and breathing. At first, people thought that the disease must be affecting the muscles—after all, they were the parts of the body that didn't work and that wasted away during the disease. But the truth was more complicated: the muscles were just fine. Instead, polio damaged communication within the body. The virus, then, made human bodies into otherwise healthy parts that couldn't communicate with each other, that existed together but couldn't work together. Even though a person would have all her limbs, and the muscle cells in them were fine, life after polio meant her body would struggle to feel whole. And this became

Sampter as a young woman, in a posed studio photograph. She is turned at an angle that hides the curvature of her spine, but some of the changes in her hands are visible. Courtesy of Givat Brenner Archives, Yesha Sampter Papers.

the challenge for Jessie and other polio patients: how to have all your parts work together and communicate, how to exist as an integrated whole.

In one sense, then, there was no life *after* polio; there was only life *with* polio. It didn't come and then go. Polio lived with and in Jessie. And it also shaped young Jessie's life in the time before she caught it—she talked about that young Jessie as sickly and weak, in a way that gestured toward her disabled body even in her earliest years. Yes, the fever and nosebleed stopped, and on most days of the rest of her life, she could move her body well enough to write letters and tend to the flowers in her garden. But her disabled body was how she experienced everyday life.

Her everyday life seemed to be marked by loss and by obstacles. Jessie had loved playing the violin both because she loved music and because she shared that love with her father. But the doctors insisted she give it up: "It is the worst thing for your back; it accentuates the curvature. Indeed, it may have weakened those muscles," they told her.[21] Polio's effects on her body also left her cut off from the social body: "I had no companions; I could not do what the other children did; I shrank from companionship, except that of tiny children whom [I] sought."[22] Even several years after her diagnosis, she felt unrecognized and apart: "The world of physical activity was closed to my poor broken body. [Girls of her age] could swim and run and take long walks and play tennis and ride bicycles; I was cut off from that."[23] A portrait taken around that time shows an awkward Jessie, standing at an angle and wearing a dress that obscures the curvature in her back. She holds flowers in her hands, perhaps because she feels tentative about it, or perhaps because it is difficult for her.

Sociologists talk about a "loss of self" that happens to patients with chronic illness. You lose the self you thought you had. Not only do you lead a restricted life, but you feel social isolation, worry that you are burdening your family and friends, and experience stigmatization.[24] What happens when your self is lost?

But Jessie's days were also lit by introspection and insight. "I still daydreamed, I told myself stories, in which I was a beautiful, strong, useful and learned heroine, and I had imaginary companions, most frequently a fairy or cupid who came secretly to do my bidding. But withal I longed to understand life, real life. What was the meaning? The connection of things?"[25] Jessie's philosophical reflection came in, through, and with her disabled body. This is not to say, however, that Jessie thought these thoughts *because of* her disability, thereby reducing her insight to an effect of it.

Disability activists often explain that people with disabilities have experiences and subjectivities that are distinctive not just because of what they lack or the obstacles they face but also because they represent distinctively valuable ways of seeing the world.[26] I see so many of these in Jessie Sampter, beginning with her religious philosophies of body and mind.

———

One of the ways that Sampter discussed her understanding of the world was through her contemplation of God and theology. Though Sampter contemplated theodicy—the question of how a good God could let bad things happen—she never claimed to have it figured out. Often when Sampter wrote about polio and its physical effects, she reflected on the social world and its relationship to God. Adult memoir-writing Sampter recalled how teenage Jessie and her friend Nora talked. One conversation began with a playful, almost flirtatious, affirmation of friendship and devotion:

> I said: "I like you so very much.""I don't like anyone," she answered.
> "Yes you do, you know you like me."
> She couldn't deny it.[27]

Then the two, each of whom was physically disabled—Nora was blind in her left eye and missing the eyelid—talked about the difficulty of navigating society. "Of course, I'm extreme," she admitted, "but it's those social qualms. It's being afraid people won't like you, or that they only pity you. You know—We'll never get over it, so we might as well grin and bear it." They had deep conversations, exploring their feelings about being embodied creatures among others, in a social world. Jessie shared her own feelings of depression. Together they grappled with theodicy, how suffering could exist if God were good. And Jessie sketched her own theological view of the world, using her own experience to shape her ideas:

> "I hate society," I said. "I wish, so long as I have to go on living, that I could go into a convent."
>
> "Not me. To be shut in! I love society, I want society. But I don't want to be myself. Oh, I hate life!" And then she added: "A nice place for an atheist, in a convent!"
>
> "Nora, do you know, I don't think I'm an atheist. I can't be. I need God so much that somehow I feel there is something. I don't mean only wishing."
>
> "I've never called myself an atheist," she said, "but I don't think a God could be so cruel."
>
> "It isn't what I think or don't think," I answered, "I don't think anything, I can't know anything. I just feel something. I can't explain it. I don't know what life is for, I don't know what death is. But when I stand on the earth, I know the earth is supporting me. I stand on something. And so I feel that life rests on SOMETHING. I cannot pray. I don't know God or understand him or justify him, but though he makes me suffer, yet I trust him."
>
> Although he would not slay me, yet did I trust in him.[28]

Sampter had written, "I can't explain it," and then crossed it out. Explaining it was, in a way, exactly what she sought to do in this part of her memoir. Sampter-the-adult-memoirist used her embodied experiences as Jessie-the-teen to think through the question of the existence of God. She sought to explain, as best she could, her understanding of the world, which she had arrived at through her bodily experiences as well as her reason. This vignette, as well as the genre of autobiographical writing, suggests how time loops back on itself in the story of a life. The adult Sampter returned to her younger and newly disabled self to explain a cosmology. In one way, we might say that this brief story tells us more about the way the adult Sampter would construct her religious world than it does about the young Jessie. But in another way, it shows us how the two times existed together; it was through this simultaneity that Sampter could best create and explain her worldview.

Sampter concluded her recollection of her conversation with Nora by citing a twist on Job 13:15, part of the Hebrew Bible in which the eponymous character suffers repeated loss and pain at the hands of God. In it, Job declares, "Although he slay me, yet I trust him." Here the adult Sampter remembers a dramatic young Jessie who sometimes wished for death while trusting in a God who would not allow her death, even though she desired it. Unlike Job, who found himself seemingly unjustly slayed, the teen Jessie had sometimes thought she *wanted* God to take her life, sometimes considering suicide "romantic," even as she had resolved not to do it. The reflective adult Sampter added the textual layer of biblical citation (and adaptation) in the past tense to what she presented as already complex adolescent theology. Like Job, Sampter never claimed to fully comprehend the reason for suffering.

But even if we today, like Sampter and Job, cannot understand how or why a good God would allow suffering—or perhaps even more so *because* that question seems unanswerable—we often try to make sense of disability. There is a strong temptation to suggest that there is something noble, valiant, or edifying about suffering. When Bertha Badt-Strauss wrote a 1956 biography of Sampter, she did just this: "Jessie's fateful illness may have turned out to be a blessing in disguise," she wrote. "It did not vanquish her will-power; on the contrary, it strengthened her power to resist and enabled her to go her own way. 'What does not defeat you strengthens you!'—Only a girl who knew suffering as Jessie did was fit to become the frail woman but great educator and humanitarian whom we admire."[29] Yes, this is one way of narrating Sampter's life so that it is a redemptive story. And it solves the problem of theodicy by saying that God hands out suffering because it makes people better.

But to me, writing this story, it rings hollow. It would also have rung hollow to Sampter, who never believed in a God who guided the daily affairs of the world and never discussed her own disability as an experience of edification. Disability studies scholars and activists now revile the idea of victorious narratives of disabled people as extra-virtuous (*supercrips*, to use a term that began in activist circles) and their lives as narratives of triumph and overcoming—a genre activists like Stella Young have called "inspiration porn."[30] Disabled people are people: some persevere, some love a challenge, and some are upbeat regardless of circumstances, but some are grumpy, others are impatient, and some are cranky. Although disability theorists have not put it in these terms, to assume that people with disabilities are kinder, more perseverant, or closer to God, as many people do, is one way to answer the question of theodicy. But it's not convincing to many disabled people, including Sampter.

I want, then, to write Sampter's life in a way that does not instrumentalize her life for the edification of others, or reduce her story to a tale of overcoming, a narrative of virtue in suffering, or a lesson about perseverance. But, equally, I do not want to overlook her bodily experience or deem it irrelevant. To declare someone with a disability "just a regular person," or to say that she was smart or successful *despite* her disability, as if a disability is something that can be cast aside or ignored, comes from a place of good intentions. But this denies the importance of disability and the body in its particulars. Like declaring that you don't "see" race, refusing to see disability makes you miss important aspects of how the person sees herself, how others treat her, and how social structures affect her. To think well about Sampter and her experiences, her story must include pain and illness.

Sampter rejected theological accounts that explained suffering as a tool of punishment or a tool of ennoblement, and she also rejected the idea that her pain and disability made the rest of her life pitiful. Near the end of her memoir chapter, she wrote, "The child Job had something still to lose—O much still to lose. How lovely are the blossoming fruit trees in our garden, how the young grass starred with dandelions! There is that—and God." Though financial troubles soon forced the family to move out of the Harlem house where she grew up, she still had her mother and sister, nature was still a source of beauty and joy, and she had not given up on God.[31]

Jessie's pain recurred throughout her rehabilitation: "Every touch was like a stab. I screamed."[32] But her treatment also brought her conversation partners who fed her growing theological curiosity. The adult Sampter narrated the exchanges through the perspective of a know-it-all teenager:

> Even my massage treatments afforded intellectual stimulus. They were given me by a mul[l]ato girl of about nineteen, a devout Baptist, with whom I soon entered into profound religious discussions. I became keenly conscious of the superiority of my Jewish monotheism, but my interest and affect for my dark and pretty Pearl made me a delighted listener to her tales of divine purification through walking out into a lake and allowing oneself to be sprinkled. A Mrs. Kennedy, a devout

and plain looking Presbyterian with missionary tendencies picked me as a good subject, and presented me with a New Testament, in which she had marked ~~all~~ the passages dealing with hell-fire and brimstone. To her I listened in amused silence. She seemed not worth enlightening.[33]

Jessie, motivated by her fascination with deep religious discussion and perhaps also by her massage therapist's beauty, found her interactions with Pearl deeply moving. Pearl's baptism in a lake appealed to Jessie's strong sense of the connection between religion and nature, even if she did not sign on to its Christian theological implications. Perhaps having imbibed American cultural stereotypes about African Americans as inherently more authentically religious, or perhaps feeling safe because of the gap between their racial and social positions, Jessie talked with Pearl and deepened her sense of her own religion. And Jessie participated in these formative theological conversations while in terribly bodily pain.

Her account of Mrs. Kennedy is quite the opposite. While Jessie was at the sanitarium in western New York where she went with her family and received physical therapy, the proselytizing Mrs. Kennedy was no dialogue partner. The embodied aspect of their encounters emphasized distance more than connection: the woman is plain looking, and so there is no eros; she is set in her ways and dour; and she marks biblical passages instead of telling her own story. She is, in Jessie's estimation, unworthy of enlightenment, but she is also not generative of Jessie's own theological development.

Through this time in her twelfth and thirteenth years, Jessie became a "cripple." I don't mean this in the sense that she never walked again but in the sense that disability became integrated into her life. And I use the word *cripple* here intentionally. There are two major reasons for this. First, Sampter herself used it. At first, as when she recalled using a wheelchair, she used it as a word of horror: "A cripple!" But far more often, when she wrote about her life as an adult, she used it to call attention to something she saw as a matter-of-fact mode of existence—and not a mode of existence that was necessarily worse than any other embodied state.

Second, disability activists have reclaimed the term, often shortening it to *crip* (though *cripple* is generally still rejected). Like lesbians and gay men embracing and recoding the word *queer*, many people with disabilities have taken up the idea that disability is a distinctive and valuable way of being in the world, not just a life of impoverishment and obstacles or a medical problem to be treated. Like the "crip time" discussed in the introduction, attention to embodied failures and limitations can make us see the world differently, whether we are disabled or not. After all, everyone has bodily failures and limitations, and to recite a truism, if we live long enough, we all become disabled.

Crip talk has not been uniformly embraced by people with disabilities. Some choose not to use the term because of its racialized associations with the US gang called the Crips, or for the more theoretical reason that it draws so heavily from queer theory as to position people with disabilities exclusively as "a subset of the queer narrative" or is just too academic and therefore insufficiently in touch with disabled people's lives.[34] Others use it affectionately with one another or find it politically powerful.

Long before disability activists reclaimed the term, Sampter at times saw being crippled as her subject position in addition to being an obstacle in the world. Today disability activists sometimes talk about cripping an idea or a social space. By that, they mean revaluing it and changing its norms, a process akin to the queering of queer activists. Though she never used this language, and certainly went along with many norms of embodiment, there are moments in Sampter's life and thought that resonate with crip theory. They also suggest that its insights about time and the foibles of embodiment apply to all humans, not just those we might identify as disabled.

Life "after" Polio

What did it mean to Sampter that she was "a cripple"? Many things. She told herself these stories: that it was somehow her fault, that it was an obstacle in the world, that it wasn't inherently bad, that it was in itself a valuable mode of being in the world. These modes were not sequential in her life; they coexisted, moving in and out of the background.

Even on her best days, the curvature of her spine meant that walking long distances would never be possible for Sampter, and the muscle damage and thumb deformity precluded most physical labor. And even though she survived the initial infection—some did not—it would haunt her later in life too. Today doctors call what Jessie experienced *post-polio syndrome*. New muscle weaknesses appear, muscles fatigue more quickly, and endurance decreases. In essence, because some nerves function overtime to make up for lost nerves, they lose function faster. "When a muscle does not have a full supply of 'motor units' it may still be able to function for a limited number of repetitions but it 'wears out' sooner," explains a pamphlet for patients with post-polio syndrome.[35] Most centrally, past muscle weakness and pain haunt the body, taking it back in time. One polio survivor wrote, "My demon has a name. It is polio—and it has come to take me back to hell."[36]

"If only the——headaches would stop," Sampter wrote to her sister, Elvie Wachenheim, in 1927.[37] The outburst of almost-swearing was uncharacteristic of her, but the headaches were not. Headaches are common in those with post-polio syndrome. Scoliosis and imbalanced bodies often cause unusual head positions and neck strain.

"Pain is always new to the sufferer, but loses its originality for those around him," observed Alphonse Daudet in his account of living with syphilis. "Everyone will get used to it except me."[38] In some ways, Sampter agreed. Pain demands the bearer's attention. "Suffering always insists on attracting attention. A toothache, for example," she explained from intimate experience with the phenomenon, "will distract the attention even of the ruler of a state."[39] But thinking of it another way, disabling pain like Daudet's and Sampter's has an element of being thrown back in time. Pain wasn't always new to Sampter; in fact, it confounded the idea of time as evenly incremental forward progress. If we are not bound by linear and one-directional temporal thinking, however, we might say it brought her back in time. It was recurring, referential, and even sometimes retrospective. Or might we even say it projected her forward in time, making her like a "normal" elderly woman even when she was in her thirties. Pain and disability moved Jessie around in time.

In my own life, as well as the lives of many in industrialized countries, time is structured by work more than anything else. In the job I have now, I have to teach certain classes on certain days at certain times. My past jobs have been even more structured: as a lifeguard, I had to punch in and punch out on a time card. When I worked in a pediatrician's office and when I worked for Habitat for Humanity, I kept a time sheet. As a tutor, I worked with one student for an hour at a time, beginning and ending precisely on the hour. Lateness, even by a few minutes, was a serious problem. Work, productivity, pay: these are fundamental ways that time has been structured for me.

Sampter never held a job with regular hours. She never had to report to work at a set time each day. She never did manual labor for hourly pay (or any other kind of pay). In her first year in Palestine, the Zionist Organization of America paid her a modest salary, which she received as a lump sum. After that, she often received pay for her articles, but she also received regular checks from her brother-in-law, Edgar Wachenheim, who was the financial custodian of her family's money. Had her family not sold its New York property and placed the money in an account for Jessie and Elvie, she would have struggled to make ends meet in Palestine. Would the timing of her body—its regular and irregular pains and its slowness—have conflicted with an economy and a political culture in which production was crucial?

Sampter's insights about time and the body weren't just about herself; she also noticed the way other disabled people had distinctive and valuable experiences of the world. Upon the death of her dear friend Helen, who also had a disability, Jessie reflected, "Those of us who have had physical handicaps to contend with all of our lives—our relationship with death is different. It gives one a broader survey—one lives outside of life as well as in it, as it were."[40] She also observed the way one experiences the time of a life when she wrote of Helen's death as "her end which has been so near her all her life."[41] Crip time, in this way, could bring the end near to all the other moments in a life.

After she moved to Kibbutz Givat Brenner, she wrote to her sister about her "sweetheart"—a word that might have surprised Elvie when she first read the letter. Romance was wholly uncharacteristic for Jessie's letters. It turned out that her sweetheart was a neighborhood boy who had had polio as a child. The boy was the only person she ever referred to with this kind of affection; even her daughter, Tamar, never got a cute nickname in her letters. Jessie clearly felt a close affinity for the boy: "He likes flowers, but automobiles are his favorites. He is three years old, and at five months he had infantile, which has left him lame. His mother is a Canadian. He comes often to visit me and now brings me the red anemones which are just beginning to bloom."[42] The next month she gave her sister another update: "My little lame boy received the book of paper dolls—he is just four years old—I cut out a few things for him, and I wish you could have seen his delight. Being so much confined, he is more developed than other children in his appreciation and care of toys."[43] His disability had emotionally moved him forward with respect to normal developmental time, and he experienced appreciation but also joy at the small details and the tactility of paper-doll play.

Pain and disability also functioned as a way of keeping time for Sampter. In June 1921 she wrote to her sister with more evidence of marking time by illness: "Some day I'll take a carriage. I have not been in town in months, not since my illness. I simply don't walk here in the summer."[44] She experienced even the seasons of the year through her disabled body: summer was the season of rarely walking beyond her own garden. One of her final unpublished short essays, "Eternal Values," made the case for peace through the one true center of universal brotherhood, seeing the neighbor not as *like* oneself but *as* oneself.[45] In Jessie's handwriting at the top, where I expected to see a date, it says, "Written for the *Palestine Review* the day before my illness." The human body, unlike the eternal value of neighbor love, is very much at the mercy of time.

In the weeks after this illness, which turned out to be malaria, she wrote to Elvie, "Sister, dear, again I have to write you a very short letter telling of illness. I am now getting well, the illness past, but so weak I cannot sit myself up in bed—malaria! Which happens everywhere in Palestine sometimes, and, in Givat Brenner, occasionally one or two cases a year." She had had a burning fever and ached all over but asked her sister not to tell her daughter, Tamar.[46] The following week, she sent a longer description of her malaria: both she and Leah Berlin, who lived together, got it; they were sleeping in bed together. But Jessie seemed far worse than Leah and wondered if she might die. "I was very eager to have Tamar find me sound and well, so I decided not to die." Beginning her recovery was no easy task either, and it made her feel like her toddler grand-nephew. "I thought of Edgar III when I had to learn to stand alone all over again."[47] The illness, combined with her disability, moved her in time to feel like a small child. She also compared her feeling to the way she felt when she had "infantile" (polio).[48]

This time movement makes me think about how disability works with regard to the life cycle: children who cannot care for themselves are not considered disabled; old people experience disability, but we tend to see it as "normal" aging rather than disability; but when middle-aged adults cannot stand on their own, we read it very differently. Susan Wendell, critiquing the United Nations definition of disability, explains that what counts as normal depends on the society. She takes herself as an example: she "can walk about half a mile several times a week but not more," and so as a woman living in North America, she is not "significantly disabled" when it comes to walking. US and Canadian cultures and built environments often do not require walking longer distances. But if she lived in rural eastern Africa, "where women normally walk several miles twice a day to obtain water for the household," she writes, she would be much more severely disabled—not because her body would be any different but because what counts as normal in that society is different. This difference is not merely one of perception: Wendell would be more disabled because she would need help performing an essential daily task for livelihood: transporting water.[49] Rather than depending on absolute criteria, then, disability is always about cultural expectations about an individual body (influenced by age and sex, for example) as well as the expected ways of interacting with the physical environment. So disability itself is always about the body in culture and in time.

The Many Meanings of Disability

For all the help that disability studies brings to understanding Sampter, however, it has largely ignored a central part of her story: religion. Though many, perhaps even most, memoirs about disability reflect on religion, crip theory rarely mentions it, and scholars have yet to theorize the relationship of disability and religion. The few disability studies scholars who do address religion tend to dismiss it as oppressive or tell a narrative of secularization in which interpreting disability used to be the realm of the theological and now is the realm of the medical.[50] Lennard Davis, for example, writes in his discussion of disability and diagnosis, "Without making too much of this point, could we not see the physician as displacing the divine for the source of certain knowledge?"[51] But he never pursues the question at all, never asks of what knowledge "the divine" might now be the source. He assumes a process of secularism in which God and theology disappear. How could a field that is so attentive to other sorts of differences, such as race, gender, and sexuality, pay so little attention to religion?

I think there are two answers: first, disability theory, especially the version that goes under the heading "crip theory," has modeled itself on queer theory. For instance, each theory reclaims a slur. Each challenges the collapse of the normal with the normative, where *normal* means "good." Queer theory has also largely (though not completely) neglected religion and at worst has been overtly hostile to religion. In the case of queer theory, this makes some historical sense. As religious studies scholar Anthony Petro writes, "White feminist and queer activists often targeted religious institutions as sites of oppression. Historians of the women's rights and LGBT movements have regularly slotted religion on the side of conservatism, overlooking moderate and progressive movements within religious groups."[52] Religious communities have been sites of pain and rejection for many queer people. Religious texts have been mobilized to withhold rights and recognition.

But this isn't true in the same way for people with disabilities and religious spaces or texts. The dynamics are different. Many Christians have declared that gays are going to hell or even that "God hates gays." They did not direct these kinds of overt, even loudly public, denunciations toward people with disabilities. When Christians have denigrated disabled people, they have often done so through pity or charity. They have sometimes seen disability and assumed that people needed healing even when they did not. Interpretations of scripture have both valued *and* belittled people with disabilities. Some religious communities in some moments have marginalized or diminished the lives of disabled people, while others have been a major source of support, both materially and politically.[53] Some have even done both at the same time.[54] When Rosemarie Garland Thomson and Lennard Davis each call disability activists and evangelical Christians "strange bedfellows," they demonstrate the misunderstandings that some disability activists have about religion and theology.[55] These bedfellows are strange only if you see an evangelical church as a fundamentally right-wing political entity; they are not necessarily strange if you see it as having a theological way of seeing the world (otherworldly oriented, primarily invested in the saving of individual souls) that can lead to right-wing politics. This is not to let religious communities off the hook but to note that queer theory's model of understanding (or overlooking) religion isn't the right fit for analyzing disability. Yet much of crip theory still relies uncritically on that model.

Second, disability studies very often engages with the scholarly idea of intersectionality. Intersectionality calls attention to the ways that various aspects of a person's embodied life—race, gender, sex, ability, and/or class, most often intersect to produce particular forms of marginalization or oppression. To understand Black womanhood, for example, we cannot simply add up what we know about Black experiences and women's experiences. Despite their close attention to the particulars of social life, scholars of intersectionality rarely consider religion as a critical part of identity, and many disability scholars have followed suit.

This disconnect is unfortunate because disability theory relies very heavily on personal narratives, and when we look at many of these narratives, most of them talk about God or theology in one way or another. Sampter's contemporary Helen Keller based her own poignant plea for the equality and worthiness of blind and Deaf people on theology: "We are capable of willing to be good, of loving and being loved, of thinking to the end that we may be wiser. We possess these spirit-born forces equally with all God's children. Therefore we, too, see the lightnings and hear the thunders of Sinai. . . . We, too, go in unto the Promised Land to possess the treasures of the spirit, the unseen permanence of life and nature."[56]

Today's memoirists, too, have theological understandings of their bodies, and they speak and even argue with God. A man who is paralyzed from the chest down becomes a yoga teacher through his newfound Hindu theologies (blessed by his mother's Protestant pastor, who heard in a dream that the man would take an "alternative path"), a woman orients her own story of disability and that of her unborn child through the Jewish liturgical calendar, and a woman with schizoaffective disorder, bipolar type, and panic disorder needed to "redefine how I understood God, myself, my disorders, and the world in general" to articulate her own experiences.[57] Sampter herself reflected on the prominence of theological conversation: "Jews and Christians can easily speak together of the same God, especially when one is ill," she wrote.[58]

Moreover, theological language shapes common cultural narratives about disability. Darla Schumm has observed how narratives of sinners and saints work in American church life today.[59] If only you had sufficient faith and prayed more fervently, then God would heal your affliction. Or, that person over there with the intellectual disability is so sweet, she must be closer to God—or maybe God sent her here with a purpose. These are the kinds of narratives Schumm heard over and over again.

The centrality of religion in so many stories should come as no surprise: the majority of Americans are religious, and there's nothing like suffering (whether physical, social, or both) to make a person ask big questions and contemplate theodicy.[60] Even nonreligious people confront religion and disability. A mother of a child with Down syndrome wrote, "Lots of books told us that our child was an angel, or that God had chosen us to be his parents," which made her feel all the more alienated.[61] In response to others' frequent invocation of God, a woman who uses a wheelchair declared, "God as idea wasn't going to make one bit of difference in my life now. . . . God wasn't going to help me deal with my weak bladder or help me deal with the old-lady swollen feet I get on a hot day."[62] Cultural responses to disability are so entwined with religion that even these people who were not inclined to think theologically about disability found themselves having to talk about God, even if it was in the negative. If many people with disabilities take religious ideas very seriously—or even see them as central to their lives , as some do—then to neglect religion in our own understanding of disability fails to do justice to many of the people we seek to understand or advocate for.

Disability as Sin

Within her crip time, there were moments when Sampter teetered on the edge of imagining her disability as her own fault. In her autobiography Jessie included a letter to herself:

> Physically you are clumsier than anyone else I ever saw. You are ill-built, and a little deformed. (I don't care what I say, for you already hate me.) . . . It is funny, that thing the palmist told you. She said you were morally weak, because of the depression in your thumb due to paralysis. Perhaps it is so. If you had the courage to exercise your thumbs until they became strong, perhaps you would have the courage to live properly. You have a good many things to do. Among them is that exercising, you hate it. You almost always hate to move. It is laziness, I think; but sometimes, and usually when you are despondent, you find it almost impossible to make an effort. You almost think you will fall where you stand, but that is imagination.[63]

Sampter told herself a story to answer the question of theodicy: she was morally weak and cowardly, and so she suffered. Her interpretation does not precisely pose disability as sin, not least because sin played almost no role in her theological categories. But she did hold herself accountable and blame herself for not undertaking physical improvements.[64]

Doctors sometimes played into this narrative from a medical perspective. After receiving a "lecture" from two different physicians, Sampter wrote, "I have resolved to take wonderful care of myself for a while." The doctors insisted that Jessie's vegetarianism was contributing to her pain and illness, and so they prescribed a new diet, which included eating five meals a day, including a quart of milk, four eggs, meat, and "plenty of butter." Also, she reported, "I am taking some sort of good-tasting medicine, and I am getting inoculations of strychnine."[65] (Oh, good!) Both Sampter and the physicians agreed that she was at least partly at fault for her own disabilities and that if she was a good girl and did as they prescribed, she would be healed.

In both these instances Sampter, like many cultural and religious systems, connected moral deficiencies with physical ones. Christianity, Judaism, Hinduism, and other religions Sampter knew well all have traditions that connect disability to moral corruption. Of course, they all also have traditions that claim quite the opposite. But, interestingly, despite her knowledge of the Bible, Sampter did not cite biblical texts in which disease, blindness, or other disabilities appear as divine judgment. In Leviticus 26:14–16, for example, God says to Israel, "But if you will not listen to me and carry out all these commands, and if you reject my decrees and abhor my laws and fail to carry out all my commands and so violate my covenant, then I will do this to you: I will bring on you sudden terror, wasting diseases and fever that will destroy your sight and sap your strength." In 1 Kings 14, God makes King Jereboam's hand shrivel up in paralysis when he tries to have a "man of God" from Judah arrested.

Popular early twentieth-century culture in the United States and Europe made similar associations. For example, the 1919 issue of *Photoplay*, the most prominent US film magazine, had ads for both Hermotone hormone tablets and Kondon's Catarrhal Jelly—both medical products Jessie used regularly and mentioned by name in her letters. In the same issue, there were also two ads that announced "Deafness is Misery" (an ad for a hearing aid) and, even more telling, "Don't Be a Sickly Failure!"—an ad for a book telling you how to overcome all sorts of weakness and sickness, no matter how long you have been "mired in the slough of despondency or struggling under the handicap of physical irregularities." "You can't make yourself count among your fellow men if you are sickly, weak, anemic; tied hand and foot to chronic ailments that weigh you down and hold you back. You can't be anything that's worth while."[66] The latter marketed one man's plan for making anyone into a healthy and well-adjusted person and placed the blame for any physical ailments squarely on the person. "Make yourself fit!" it demanded. "You can overcome the physical disorders that are sapping your health and strength, unfitting you for work that gets anywhere and making a miserable failure of your life." The inflated rhetoric sounds almost humorous now, but the ad demonstrated cultural assumptions about physical disability. As Rosemarie Garland Thomson has observed, in language that avoids religion but nevertheless evokes it, "Western tradition posits the visible world as the index of a coherent and just invisible world, encouraging us to read the material body as a sign invested with transcendent meaning."[67]

Disability studies has often been quick to condemn religions, especially Judaism and Christianity, because of the theological interpretation of disability as sin or an advertisement for divine power. For example, according to researchers on social work and disability, "Judeo-Christian Beliefs" have caused people with disabilities to be "ostracized and stereotyped" and considered sinners or possessed by demons.[68] A 2017 article about disability and Shakespeare sets up the New Testament and "sacred society" as the oppressors of disabled persons: "As in many societies, it is the 'normals' who define, control, and manipulate what counts as disability; as in the New Testament of the Bible, disability is simply the platform for a display of God's power. . . . [T]he disabled person meets both ridicule and violence; and, in the end, the disabled man is run off the stage and out of the sacred society of the normals."[69] There is no doubt that some religious texts denigrate people with disabilities, but this is a vast oversimplification of both the New Testament and "many societies" if the sacred is always on the side of oppression. Others generalize further: "Religion—over time and across societies—has been a particularly potent force in separating people as 'abnormal,'" the *Handbook of Disability Studies* explains.[70] If you listen to this scholarship, religion and the Bible seem to be replete with texts and beliefs about the negative meanings of disabled bodies.

But instead of drawing on biblical religion, or later Jewish or Christian tradition, or even appeals to popular cultural assumptions, Jessie found evidence for this story of her disability as moral weakness in her visit to a palm reader. Jessie saw her visit to the palm reader and her encounter with the Ouija board not as occult practices but as ways of connecting to parts of the world she could not normally access with her own senses. And yet her senses, the Judaism she embraced, and her broader philosophy all denied the validity of this story of disability as a manifestation of sin.

Disability as an Obstacle in the World

Sampter did not always blame herself for the state of her body; in fact, it was only in rare moments that she did. At other times she saw her disability in perhaps the most common way most of us imagine disability: as an obstacle in the world. It prevented her from doing things she wanted to. In 1921, during her third year in Palestine, she wrote her regrets to her sister, Elvie, that she had "no strength for walking" so she couldn't buy stamps for young Edgar to add to his collection.[71] Near the end of her life, she told Elvie, "If you are learning book binding—how I envy you! It is something I have always wished to do, but am told it is too difficult for my hands."[72] But not only pleasurable activities were hard for Jessie—it was also sometimes basic needs.

Some disability theorists rail against any understanding of disability that uses the "medical model." This model conceives of disability as a problem of an individual body, sees disability as a problem to be solved, and focuses on cures and treatment. For instance, your need of a wheelchair is the problem, not the building's lack of a ramp; your hearing impairment is the problem, not our failure to provide a microphone; your post-traumatic stress is the problem, not our unwillingness to provide flex time at work. These scholars and activists note that the medical model provides excuses for not addressing larger social problems and structural environments, and so they advocate for a "social model" of disability instead. The social model presents disability as a social construction, created by societies' ideas of what is normal and what is abnormal. In this view, environments are disabling, societies deem a physical body abnormal, and people and institutions marginalize. Instead of being an empirical biological fact, disability is a label and a situation created by human culture and the built environment.

I am convinced that the social model works far better for inclusion and advocacy. However, in writing about a woman who lived a century ago, I found that I could not do justice to her and her own understanding of her life without also thinking about the medical model. Making a strict division between the medical model and social model, as well as using the social model to the complete exclusion of the medical model, doesn't quite work for understanding Sampter. First, like many people with disabilities, she saw herself through the medical model. To understand her own self-image and relationship to her body, I needed to understand her diagnoses, her interactions with doctors, and her attempts at self-treatment. This is not to endorse the medical model as the "right" way to understand disabilities but to try to understand a disabled person's embodied or mental differences as she herself saw these differences. Second, the medical model deeply informs the social model. Societies have created the social model in large part through conversations about medical research—however good or bad—and its production of expectations of how life should be.

Third, a purely social model works less well to explain the experience of people with certain disabilities. Chronic pain is one of them. No amount of change in Sampter's culture and environment could have created a situation where she felt normal and good in her body. Even if there were a bed in every room and she had her own solar-powered hover car, she still would have felt pain and exhaustion. She might have felt it less often, and so I certainly don't mean to say that we should dismiss accommodations in the case of people with chronic pain. But when the social model seems to imply that changing our social expectations and built environments sufficiently would cause all disability to go away, this is a mistaken view. The vast majority of people with chronic pain want a cure for their pain; they want treatment. They would like to have no chronic pain, and this is not because they have internalized the medical model or social pressures to be normal. As Tobin Siebers writes, "Pain is not a friend to humanity. It is not a secret resource for political change. It is not a well of delight in the individual. Theories that encourage these interpretations are not only unrealistic about pain; they contribute to an ideology of ability that marginalizes people with disabilities."[73]

Disability theorists such as Alison Kafer offer models that acknowledge that a single lens is unlikely to give us a whole picture. She uses a "political/relational model," which frames disability through the particulars: interpersonal relationships, social norms, everyday effects of architecture and the built environment, what counts as "common sense" about bodies in that society, pain, and the way people's bodies feel—all while refusing a set definition of disability.[74] Sampter's life and thought are impossible to understand without her relationships: her relationship to the political ideals of Zionism, to the land in Palestine, to the ideals of womanhood, and most of all, to people. Henrietta Szold wrote to Horace Kallen in 1918: "I saw her yesterday, and as I held her hand, I felt she might vanish from my side."[75] That line made me feel Szold's love for Sampter. I know that Sampter felt it too. Several years earlier, during a particularly difficult time for her health, Sampter was tempted to attend her friend Henry Hurwitz's lecture but warnings from "my doctor and Miss Szold" helped her check the impulse, she told him.[76]

Kafer finds disability in people's encounters and experiences, rather than as a fixed identity. Of all the approaches, mine comes closest to Kafer's. However, Kafer neither analyzes nor theorizes religion in any of its aspects My hope here is that my own quiet theorization of religion and disability is a step in that direction: it posits that encounters and relationships can include the divine, that interpretations of bodily experiences can include the theological, and that religious ideas about natural and built environments can be powerful.

One year, Sampter spent several weeks as an inpatient at the Hadassah hospital, diagnosed only with colitis. Even though she wrote, "I am much better and hope soon to be able to walk a respectable distance. Five minutes is still enough for me" in January 1927, that would not mark a wholly upward swing in her health.[77] Walking half a mile to the dentist was far beyond her capability that August, and so she had to arrange for a car to take her.[78] During the second half of 1936, she was feeling weak and in significant pain more often than not. That year, she wrote to her sister a fairly typical account of her health: "I don't feel bad, only very weak, and everything is a strain, so I won't write very much."[79] The next week she wrote, "My ear has almost stopped running, and I feel well except when I try to do anything more strenuous than resting."[80]

Perhaps even worse, doctors did not always know what was wrong, and that did no favors for her mental health. In the spring of 1932, she wrote that she thought she was finally getting over the year-and-a-half-long "indefinite thing" that made her weak and in pain.[81] One doctor told her that her recurring pain and weakness were because the curvature of her spine had caused the displacement of her heart: "Through my curvature the heart became displaced so that there is pressure upon it, and the nerves of the heart have been affected. Hence the periodic difficulties and even the 'murmur.'"[82] But that did not explain her other symptoms. From our historical vantage point, we can say that it was likely post-polio syndrome, but at the time she experienced the mental anguish that people experience when they are ill but can't find answers about exactly what is happening. She saw a psychoanalyst for several years after a "breakdown" in 1918, first in New York and then in Palestine. (In fact, her friend Edith Eder suggested she become a patient of Sigmund Freud, but timing and travel limitations prevented this.[83]) And, as Sampter would have told us, bodily experiences and mental ones are not separate. Physical pain and mental pain are connected. One could even exacerbate the other, as when she reported that she was too physically ill to make it to her psychoanalysis appointments.

She tried to avoid wallowing in weakness and pain, and though most of the time she accepted it as her way of life, she also sometimes expressed a desire to be otherwise. She reassured her sister after her difficult start in Palestine: "Really, I have had less illness than usual, and as you know, I always have spells when I have to rest."[84] During an especially good time in 1921, she wrote, "It is wonderful how much I can walk now!" Fellow American Zionist Henrietta Szold's house was about a mile away from where she and Leah were living in Jerusalem, and she could walk there.[85] In late 1936, in the midst of a long stretch of weeks in which she rarely left the house and spent much of her time in bed, she wrote, "I am awfly [sic] weak. . . . I can walk and work—outside of writing—very little. I am determined to change this situation. See if I don't!"[86] More typically, after two months of serious illness and pain, she wrote, "I am feeling much better but cannot walk much."[87]

Life in Palestine meant that Jessie experienced more disability than in New York because the cultural norms around work, walking, and physical ability were different. Zionist ideals meant the valorization of physical work, even for those who were highly educated, for example. Before the two moved to Givat Brenner together, Jessie would often stay with Leah in Jerusalem. During one visit, Jessie went to see a doctor about her pain. "I met a doctor in Jerusalem who had exactly the same sort of heart trouble as I, after pneumonia. It's a sort of collapse or muscle-strain, and he says one [cannot] overexert."[88] That meant not too much walking, limited gardening, little physical labor, and even limited participation in youth scouting, which she was invested in.

One spring she wrote to Elvie, "I myself have quite suddenly taken a great stride forward in health. I have practically reached my normal and usual capacity, and I am still so excited and delighted over the event that I have to boast of it. I can walk as usual without losing breath or being exhausted."[89] Her joy—and this was the closest to exuberant I ever saw her in many thousands of pages—is not that she is normal but that she is normal for her. And, like "normal" bodies by social standards, her normal is actually her highest level of function. Her joy also reminds us that disability is contextual. In Palestine one needed to walk. Cars were few, and much infrastructure was still in the process of being built. Whether she or her doctors thought the root cause was her own body or the infrastructure around her, disability could function as an obstacle preventing Sampter from doing what she wanted to do. But her disability had other meanings too.

Disability as a Complication for and of Zionism

In addition to her pain and illness being more disabling in Palestine than in New York, Sampter's disability presented an obvious complication for her Zionism. Not long after she arrived in Palestine, she wrote: "'A healthy soul in a healthy body.' That is the motto of our youthful Maccabees."[90] She offered no critique of this sentiment. This was her Zionism too—but it wasn't the whole story. (As chapter 4 shows, her Zionism also had much more complex and inclusive ideas about what kinds of bodies should be valued.) She would hardly have described her own experiences as "a healthy soul in a healthy body." Soul, usually; body, only intermittently. As soon as she arrived in Palestine, she needed to be admitted to the hospital. Her life there continued to be characterized by pain, weakness, and episodes of acute illness.

When she and Leah Berlin decided to move in together, the move to the new place was difficult for her, and Leah spent much of her time caring for Jessie. Frankly, Jessie's memoir makes Jessie sound rather insufferable:

"Two days later, limp from the fever, I dressed and went to the new house, and watchman's duty in the business of moving. I had to go to bed, in the sunny room—the sunniest and quietest in the house—that was to be mine. A day or two later my passion for making order overruled reason, and I was not only up and in every room giving Leah the benefit of my judgment in revising hangings for our sitting and dining rooms."[91] Not long after, Jessie went into town, got caught in a rainstorm, and then needed to be admitted to the hospital. "No one here needs me, not even Leah; perhaps my death would relieve her," she complained.[92]

Although she wrote about herself (in letters to her family and friends) and frequently wrote about Zionist ideals (for a vast array of publications), she often remained silent about how her own embodied life fit with the Zionist project. When she thought about finances, she wrote to her sister, "I can't depend on my earning capacity, which would indeed be a worry in my present state of health."[93] At times she recognized the disconnect between her labor socialism and her own embodied reality. "I wonder how a person like me on the one hand a socialist and closely allied with labor forces, on the other physically unable to depend on myself for an adequate livelihood," would fare when left without an income.[94] She also got snippy with Elvie when she opined that Jessie was dependent: "You mustn't have opinions about other people's doing if you want to hear them. I mean generalized opinions before you know everything. Such as about 'dependent women'. What does that mean? I'm sure I am about as independent a woman as ever lived—except for the weather. I am frightfully dependent on that."[95] Occasionally she would use the active verbs of Zionism even when she could not participate. For instance, she said that she "built a house" when she had workers build the house for her and her daughter, Tamar.

In addition to her writing, she performed her Zionism in the garden. She grew, among other things, roses, portulaca, nasturtiums, pansies, and dozens of other flowers. She looked forward to the Burpee seed catalog each year, even occasionally sending them extra money because she knew she'd soon want to order something additional. Leah remembered her in the garden at Givat Brenner: "Jessie loved going out to the garden in the morning, wearing a big hat, picking flowers for the house, as if she were engaged in holy work."[96] But her body also often limited how much of the gardening she could do: "I am able to work in my garden one to two hours a day, and I love it. I carry a stool about with me, and sit down much of the time. I can't dig, but I can water, cut, and prune. As a consequence, I don't go out at all, as I can't do any more walking than that requires."[97]

Gardening can be exhausting work. Even watering means carrying a heavy can or hose. Cutting and pruning means getting down on your knees, reaching, and using grip strength. Tending to plants involves bending over, standing up, bending over, standing up . . . It's enough to give the fittest person an achy back. I often come inside with sore hands, dirt crusted under my nails, and sweat running down my face. Sometimes I'm sore the next day, especially if I've spent a lot of time weeding or digging. When Sampter decided to garden, she often knew she was spending her small amount of physical energy all in one place. But she loved it.

In the winter of 1933–34, she and Leah went to live on Kibbutz Givat Brenner, but joining a kibbutz with communal finances would present another problem: How could she do her share in the community when she was unable to perform most of the tasks of the workers? The kibbutz members debated whether they should allow "aged" women, one of whom was "crippled," as they called her. Should they be allowed to join, especially given Jessie's physical condition?[98] Although Jessie wholeheartedly loved the idea of the kibbutz, she could not do what others there could. She could not work the land, nor care for a large group of young children, nor plant orchards, nor build buildings.

Jessie's Zionism, then, did not match her embodied experience, but her disability didn't preclude her from being a Zionist either. Disability studies often critiques political theories of nationalism for their ableist assumptions. For example, Carol Breckenridge and Candace Vogler write that "an assumed able body is crucial to the smooth operation of traditional theories of democracy, citizenship, subjectivity, beauty, and capital."[99] Political theories tend to assume people have able bodies that can work productively, be self-sufficient, and thus contribute to the nation. Given Breckenridge and Vogler's critique of this system, it may be surprising to learn that even disabled bodies can work to create a nationalism. Sampter's story suggests the ways that a disabled person might still work to support these explicitly ableist nationalist structures but also ways that she might form alternatives within a nationalist vision.

Although Sampter was firmly committed to a Zionism that celebrated healthy, strong, reproductive bodies, she still saw disability—and, more generally, the particulars of different embodied experiences—as a reason for making its ideology more inclusive. She gave all her money (save a small sum for Tamar's schooling) to Kibbutz Givat Brenner, where she and Leah moved, so that they could build a convalescent home for workers whose bodies no longer worked as well as they once did. At one point, a woman

Sampter in the flower garden, 1930s. Courtesy of Givat Brenner
Archives, Yesha Sampter papers.

named Devorah moved to the kibbutz but seemed not to make any progress learning Hebrew. It turned out that she had little time to practice her new language because she had a baby with a disability: "He is a beautiful baby. But he will never speak Hebrew." He would never speak any language at all, she explained. "Besides being blind, he is also deaf, idiotic, and epileptic." Sampter railed against some of her fellow kibbutzniks who would not budge from their language standards in Devorah's case. "If you have a baby," one man insisted, "you must learn Hebrew. If you do not learn Hebrew, you will never be able to speak with your child."[100] Sampter wrote, "Some people are so principled that they can see nothing but principles in life. Whenever they meet a particular case, they apply their general principles to it. They are forever cutting off other people's feet in order to fit them into their own beds."[101]

She was also instrumental in bringing education for deaf people to Palestine. In the early 1930s, she wrote a lengthy essay called "They Have Ears but They Hear Not," a reference to both Psalm 115 and Jeremiah 5:21:

> I went with my friend the violinist to hear her make music at the school for deaf children. As I saw the miracle in their faces, my thoughts wandered back over the long and steep and rocky path that had led up to this miracle.
>
> 1916–18: Two children born deaf two years apart to a Jewish mother in Palestine who has had three normal ones. ~~Their defect is a memorial to~~ They were born and conceived during war, terror, and starvation.
>
> 1929–1931: A rich Jew dies in Shanghai and his will leaves a sum of money to the Alliance Israelite in Paris for a school for deaf and dumb children anywhere in the Near East.
>
> Meanwhile Amos and Ruth, in their desire for speech, had been the means of creating a school in Tel Aviv for the deaf children of Palestine. Their mother, arousing in them, had stirred up a sore problem. Yet for them it was almost too late. When, after a couple of years of search for ways and means, the school was opened in 1930, Amos was already fourteen years old and Ruth twelve, and they could be given in private tutoring only a small key to a little part of the vast world that is locked away from them. Nevertheless they did find the way to the word through eye and hand; and their need has saved many others.[102]

The essay framed the history through the stories of two children, and in addition to its intended pathos, it revealed some of Sampter's shifting ideas about what it meant to be disabled. She typed, "Their defect is a memorial to war, terror and starvation," but then edited in her own handwriting to say, "They were born and conceived during war, terror and starvation." Like the theology of Ezekiel, she rejected the initial narrative in which "the parents eat sour grapes and the children's teeth are set on edge."[103] No, it was neither the children's fault nor their parents' position amid suffering that caused their deafness. And she also moved away from the language of "defect," though she would return to appeals to sympathy from her audience of potential philanthropists later in the essay.

Although Sampter did not have the language of Kafer's political/relational model to describe disability, her writing shows resonance with seeing disability in this way: "If these children can attend school until the age of fourteen, with its preliminary vocational training," she explained of the deaf school's pupils, "they will then be equipped to enter the world of man as equals and as workers."[104] To Sampter, children who could lip-read and speak could participate fully in economic and social life. They could work like other workers—an essential for the Zionist cause. The only thing holding them back was the way society marginalized them and failed to educate them. In this way, she almost presaged today's Deaf movements, many of which see Deafness as a minority language and culture and not a disability. Yet she also presented their deafness through a medical model: each individual body had a problem that required intervention.

The essay didn't say how intimately Sampter herself was involved in founding the school, Palestine's first educational institution for the deaf. Not only did she help raise money in 1929, 1930, and 1931, but she was also an animating personality of the seven-person committee in charge of its creation.[105] Her commitment to organizing and fundraising always included doctors and hospital space, so the medical model also structured how she thought about deafness. Although some histories say that the Jerusalem school was the very first organized effort at deaf education, it began with Sampter's committee in Tel Aviv. In 1929 she wrote to her sister:

> Deaf-mute affairs are progressing famously. An excellent teacher, who is also a fine gentleman and a Hebrew scholar, suddenly turned up right here in Palestine, in Tel Aviv. The two Zevilo children are going to board and study privately with him, on the money I got for them from America. Dr. Salzberger came down from Jerusalem to meet me, the teacher, and another ear specialist at Dr. Zlociosti's on Saturday, and we had a very fruitful meeting. We have the promise of rooms in the Straus Health Center in Tel Aviv. We have everything ready for the school ex-

cept the $3000 budget we need for the first two years. I returned home to find a letter here saying that the deaf-mute committee of the National Council of Jewish Women is interested and will probably finance the work for us![106]

Louise Waterman Wise, the wife of the prominent American rabbi and Zionist Stephen Wise, sent $1,000, "so we can begin," Sampter reported. The committee continued to meet, and its members raised funds and later visited the new school, which operated out of the Straus Health Center in Tel Aviv.[107] The school, as the Deaf interest monthly *Volta Review* reported, had "two large, sunny rooms," a kitchen, and a garden "patterned with the bright bloom of flowerbeds," and "a space [was] set aside for their vegetable garden which the deaf and dumb children work with their teachers and which helps to supply their table with fresh greens."[108] Sampter's influence was clear.

After the school's first year, Sampter also recruited her younger friend Zilla to be the new kindergarten assistant at the school. When Jessie, Zilla, and Tamar visited, "the school made an excellent impression. I'm most satisfied. I shall write it up for our committee in New York and send you a copy. Only, we are not satisfied with the kindergarten assistant, and Zilla may take her place next year."[109] She did. Zilla enjoyed the job and was disappointed when the arrival of specially trained deaf educators meant she would no longer continue.

The arrival of new educators also prefaced another move: the center of deaf education would soon go from Tel Aviv to Jerusalem. The school had struggled in Tel Aviv, especially for funding. November 1932 marked the Jerusalem opening of the school for the deaf—what is now the Hallie Friedland School for the Hearing Impaired. It was (and is) connected to the Alliance Israelite Universelle, an international education-focused Jewish organization. The school hired Marcus Reich, a German Jewish teacher who had established a school for deaf children in Germany in 1873, to serve as its central figure in its early years.

Sampter was still involved, although far less actively, until the end of her life. In 1935, when Stephen Wise and Louise Waterman Wise visited Palestine again, Mrs. Wise gave Jessie a twenty-pound check for the "little deaf and dumb boy in Rehoboth [Rehovot] so now he can be sent to the school in Jerusalem!"[110] The exclamation point was unusual for Sampter, but the abiding interest in deaf education was not.

Jessie's involvement with the school for the deaf, and her relationship with her "sweetheart," suggests that the Jewish land she wanted not only made space for but actively included those with disabilities, those whose bodies might not align with a muscular Zionism. Sometimes Sampter's political and intellectual activities helped her pass as able-bodied, even though that was not the case. And sometimes she joined others in thinking that disabled persons should be pitied. But she worked toward a nationalism that made more space for people with disabilities and created fewer disabling spaces.

Disability as a Metaphor

In 1915 Hadassah published Sampter's *A Course in Zionism*. There she framed the Jewish problem in terms of chronic illness, which reflected her own disability from childhood polio: "We are a sick people. Our national will has been atrophied by age-long inertia. But here and there certain organs are coming back to life and action. We must exercise and strengthen them with work, and through their force and activity the whole body shall be revived."[111] Sampter imagined all Jews shared a collective body. Even beyond a body politic (though Jews might become that too), Jews shared experiences and connections at an almost physical level.

But what are we to make of her insistence on thinking about a social situation as illness and disability? Disability activists often object to the use of disabilities as metaphors: saying someone is "blind" when we mean they're missing something obvious, "schizophrenic" when we mean inconsistent, or the familiarly offensive "retarded" for "stupid" or "ill thought out."

Of course, these people are right when they point out the problems with disability as a metaphor. But must disability metaphors always be insensitive? Could bodily metaphors of disability ever help us understand political situations, for example? And what does it mean that Sampter, who so intimately experienced illness and atrophy, identified her people's plight as illness and atrophy? When Sampter evoked these, it was not merely a shaming of disabled bodies; it was a close identification with disability as an embodied way of understanding the political situation around her. When Sampter refers to atrophied limbs, she knows of what she speaks. She knows about "exercis[ing] and strengthen[ing] muscles" in the hope that a body will be able to do things.

The ethics of Sampter's metaphor are complex. When Sampter writes about a Jewish collective body that is disabled, she hopes for its healing. Yet her metaphor also takes the perspective of a disabled person and shows us how that experience leads to political insight.

Disability can also be a kind of metaphor—a metonym, even—for the whole person. In this mode, people who interact with the disabled person see the disability as the central and relevant part of the human in front of them. In one of the few moments in disability studies when a scholar thinks seriously about theological categories, Rosemarie Garland Thomson discusses when a disabled person serves as the occasion for others to exercise the virtues of compassion or even pity. Those Christians, for example, who believe that salvation depends on good works rather than predestination need an object for their good works. Thomson writes of this move in the nineteenth-century context of *Uncle Tom's Cabin*: "The perfect beneficiary is this innocent, suffering disabled figure; the more repugnant the sufferer, the more noble the Christian who loves him."[112]

Robert Orsi has a moving reflection on how the priests and sisters in the Catholic parish he grew up in saw his uncle, who had cerebral palsy, as innocent and special. "Cripples are holy people" was their message. By imagining the group of Catholics with cerebral palsy as holy, the volunteers and priests could imagine their closeness to a suffering Christ. But imposing holiness also meant distancing them: "Being 'holy' meant that they were not like the rest of us, that they did not have the same needs and desires we did, and so they did not have to be treated in the way we expect to be treated ourselves."[113] Here the effect is more mixed than the denigrating slurs of "schizo" or "OCD," but it nevertheless sets disabled people apart, distancing and instrumentalizing them. Darla Schumm's work shows how people with disabilities experience this "saint" paradigm—a set of stereotypes little better than its twin "sinner" paradigm.[114]

But might disability metonyms, too, be used for political good? In 1914 the Zionist monthly *Maccabaean*, where Sampter often published, printed on its front page an allegory that sought to illustrate the "Zionist contention that the Jew is the Man without a Country." The allegory for the Jewish people as a whole was a man with a mental illness. The man was born in Russia and then immigrated to Brazil and then to New York, where "after a few months [he] became insane." The United States ordered him deported to Brazil, but Brazil refused him admittance "on the ground that, being an alien who had once left Brazil, he could not be allowed to return." His former town in Brazil also refused to take him back, and when the ship's captain tried to leave him in Rio de Janeiro, the officials refused. No steamship company would take him back to Russia. "What is to be done with this human being? He has a civic status nowhere. He belongs in the twilight zone where no law applies. In truth, he has no rights, for rights belong only to a person who has a legal status."[115]

The editor was most concerned to show this man as a metonym for all Jewish people in terms of his statelessness, but the man's disability is also instructive. Seen as a dependent, pushed from institution to institution because each sees him only as a liability, and recognizable because of his difference, this man and his story highlight the plight of the Jewish people (at least in Zionist eyes). Rather than framing his disability as sin, an object of pity, something to be overcome, or an occasion to count our blessings, the article identifies its readers with him. His humanity and status as a person deserving rights are central, and the article blames the nations that fail him rather than faulting him for a failure to make himself desirable to those countries.

To say that this disability metonym might be used for political good is not to say that it is entirely unproblematic. It is to say that these metaphors and metonyms do not have to denigrate people with disabilities. They may even have the effect of bringing disability and the normal closer together.

Disability as a Way of Engaging the World

Among Jessie's unpublished papers, I came across a one-page reflection on disability, normalcy, and what counts as a real life. I read it, paused, and then read it again. It was poignant and astute, the words of an introspective woman looking back on life in her body. And then I realized that she wrote it just months before she died.

> For forty-three years—since I was twelve years old—I have been an invalid, or, rather, what is called a semi-invalid, half an invalid. For all that time, the valid part of me has been striving desperately to be normal, to think, feel and experience the ordinary human thing. The other half, the damaged half, has been striving desperately to suck out of its wound all the salt and sweetness of the extraordinary, the exotic and the parasitic. It has formed beautiful galls, as beautiful as leaves and flowers and much more fantastic.
>
> I have stopped striving. I have stopped to look and examine and make my account with life. The pain has been very sweet; it may have been hard to bear; death would at any time have been easier; but, having been borne, it is good to look back upon. The happiness, the ordinary human thing, has been cracked through and through by inadequacy; it was always only half: a child that was not born to me, love without do-

mesticity, walks from which one had to drive home, and independence with strings to it.

And yet, as I figure up the account, it seems to have been all valid. Every kind of life is life if one lives it.[116]

This candid reflection, on walks cut short by pain and disability, on feelings of inadequacy, on the struggle to make sense of seemingly incongruent parts of a self, showed a woman who reflected deeply about how her own embodied experiences shaped her life.

I have quoted it at length because I think it shows, in Sampter's own voice, the richness of her own understanding of her life. It shows how she might have moments of seeing disability as sin, as an obstacle, as an issue for Zionism, or as a metaphor, but it was also a profound and valuable way of seeing the world. It was *her* profound and valuable way of seeing the world. "Validity" prefigures many of the movements in current disability studies. Memoir and first-person reflections have become standard-bearers in disability studies, and here Sampter anticipates many of the philosophical and theoretical foci of that literature. Her essay speaks of pain and sadness, and yet in the end the speaker does not disavow these or reject a faulty body but rather claims all parts of her life as a real life. A valid life.

Sampter saw her own pain and disability as inseparable from her experience of the world. "I don't look upon suffering as a problem," she wrote to her sister in 1936. "The only problem is how to meet it."[117] This wasn't a glass-half-full attitude; it was a deep-seated sense that pain and suffering were an integral part of what it means to be human.

In a more philosophical vein, she wrote, "He that understands it does not suffer it. He does not suffer. Life is joy."[118] This unpublished essay worked through the ideas of pleasure and pain and their relationships to a good human life. "Pleasure is good, no matter how insufficient and unsatisfactory. Pain is bad, no matter how instructive and interesting. Which does not mean that we are to go seeking pleasure and avoiding pain.—Nor the opposite. To do either is stupid." So if pain is bad, why isn't it simply to be avoided? Sampter explained, "Pain is an indicator, pain is direction. Pain is a mold, pain is that un-desire which gives desire shape. It is the lever of action, the springboard of desire." She saw her pain as the thing that would help her direct her choices wisely and well. In letters to her sister, she discussed "enjoying" troubles, by which she meant gaining perspective and being motivated by things "we don't like."[119] So Sampter described her pain and disability as ways of experiencing and learning from experience in the world. Unlike

Elaine Scarry's account of pain, in which "even though [pain] occurs within oneself, it is at once identified as 'not oneself,' 'not me,' as something so alien that it must right now be gotten rid of," Sampter sought to make sense of her body and her life *with* her pain.[120] To riff on Scarry's terms, pain was also part of the making of Sampter's world, not just its unmaking.

In her discussion of pain, Sampter also claimed that the problem of theodicy was, as a problem, entirely a human invention. "Pain is not—to say the least—pleasant, but that is its virtue. The nature of pain is to be unpleasant, and our business is to dislike it, to cast it out. But we thought it was God's business, and so we created the silly problem of evil and solved it with a thousand superstitions."[121] Taking religion seriously—that is, not dismissing it as false consciousness or merely incidental—is crucial for understanding Sampter's relationship to disability. If disability studies and activism follow suit, I think we will find that is true for many others too.

Conclusion

In February 1938, she wrote, "The less I can do other things, the more I write."[122] It wasn't strictly true; in fact, she sometimes had trouble writing. "I have let Tamar send off a letter to you without writing at all because I felt so ill weak," she wrote the following month, and the next week she explained that the gap between letters was because she had been hospitalized in Petah Tikvah for pneumonia.[123] She had been quite ill, and Leah had cared for her at home and then accompanied her to the hospital when it became more than she could handle. The following week she reported, "Today I got dressed for the first time."[124] She was feeling better a week later, but, she wrote, "I tried, foolishly, to do a little walk in the garden, and I had a little setback."[125] Her days became short: she was up at 10 in the morning, back in bed from 1:30 to 4, and back in bed for the night at 8:30. In mid-September she was still writing little. "Writing is hard," her letter to Elvie and Edgar said.[126] She would be dead before the end of November.

Until the end, Sampter championed Zionism, a political and religious project that valorized the strong, productive body. Although she never explicitly criticized that ideal, she also held that her own experiences were valid, not in spite of her own disabled body but in recognition that it afforded her a distinctive view of the world.

She never claimed a simple answer to the question of theodicy. Only in fleeting moments did she wonder if she "deserved" disability. And perhaps most surprisingly for a woman who prized the life of the mind, she never suggested a philosophical separation of the body and the mind so as to say that her "real self" was her mind, which she could have described as healthy and productive. She never wavered from her insistence on the unity of body and soul. "The body is the soul," she wrote. "Physicians argue whether worry causes indigestion or indigestion causes worry, whether to heal colitis with psycho-analysis or hysteria with diet. And suddenly, in the midst of modern medicine, they make the absurd statement that mind influences body or that body influences mind. But the mind is the body." This was as true in the embodied experience of illness as it was in the philosophical realm. "One cannot treat the body or treat the mind; one can treat only the body which is the mind, the mind which is the body. Every act is a change in thought; every thought is a bodily act."[127] Sampter's story is a story about disability and embodiment. It's a story about the particular: as a "cripple," Sampter saw the world differently; she experienced the world differently; and these differences matter. It's also a story about the universal: it does not allow its audience to avert their eyes from Sampter's embodied experiences, which should remind us that we all have bodies and that they structure all our experiences.

CHAPTER THREE

A Queer Life

When Jessie Sampter applied for a US passport in April 1919, the first line read, "I, *Jessie Sampter (single)* a Native and Loyal Citizen of the United States, hereby apply to the Department of State, at Washington, for a passport, ~~accompanied by my wife~~." No, she did not have a wife, so she crossed out that part of the form. Nor was she married to a man, which was quite unusual for women passport seekers. Perhaps an official told her she should write it there, or perhaps she decided on it herself, but either way, there it was in the name blank: right next to "Jessie Sampter" was the word *single*, a sign of the way she never fit the expectations of gender and sexuality of her time.

In this chapter I tell Sampter's story as a queer story. At its heart, this means telling her story through her relationships. Janet Jakobsen once asked, "What would happen if we thought of queer . . . as a verb?"[1] *Queer* can be a noun (when it is used to refer to a gay or lesbian person), an adjective (when it is used to describe either a person or a thing associated with nonheterosexuality), or a verb (when it is used to indicate the action of resisting dominant ideals and ideas about what is normal). Jakobsen's point pushes us to think about queerness not merely as an identity—as we see in one of its most common uses as a synonym for *gay* or *lesbian*—but as ways of doing things in the world. Identity can seem essential, individual, static, and fixed, whereas verbs allow for doing, relating, and changing. And using *queer* can homogenize very real differences if it is used to imply a unified experience of gay men, lesbians, bisexuals, and other people with nonnormative sexualities. Here I am using *queer* as a relational term, a term about the ways a person makes her social world. It is most often an adjective having

The original and each copy of an application for a passport must have attached to it a copy of the applicant's photograph.
A loose signed photograph of the applicant must accompany the application.
The photographs must be on thin paper, should have a light background and be not over three inches in size.

Fee for passport, one dollar.
Fee for executing application, one dollar.

A woman's application must state
whether she is married or not, and a
married woman must prove that her
husband is a native citizen.

[EDITION OF 1917.]

FORM FOR NATIVE CITIZEN.

APR ~~ 1919

UNITED STATES OF AMERICA,
STATE OF NEW YORK,
COUNTY OF NEW YORK.   *ss:*

I, _Jessie Ethel Sampter (Single)_ a NATIVE AND LOYAL CITIZEN OF THE
UNITED STATES, hereby apply to the Department of State, at Washington, for a passport, ~~accompanied~~
~~by my wife.~~
(Name and place of birth.)

I solemnly swear that I was born at _2138 Fifth Avenue_, _New York City_, in the State of
New York, on or about the _22_ day of _March_, _1883_;* that
my {father} _Rudolf Sampter_, was born in _Posen (Grandfather was citizen)_
and ~~is now residing at~~ _died in 1895 in New York city_
[that he emigrated to the United States from the port of _Came to U.S. at age of nine years_
on or about the _____, 1___; that he resided _64_ years uninterruptedly, in
the United States, from 1 _859_ to 1 _895_, at _New York_; that he was
naturalized as a citizen of the United States before the _Grandfather was citizen_ Court
of _____, at _____
on _____, 1___, as shown by the Certificate of Naturalization presented herewith];
that I have resided outside the United States at the following places for the following periods:

never, from _____ to _____
_____, from _____ to _____.

that I am domiciled in the United States, my permanent residence being at _N.Y._
in the State of _____, where I follow the occupation of _Zionist Educational work_; that
I am about to go abroad temporarily; that I intend to return to the United States within _1_ {months}{year}
with the purpose of residing and performing the duties of citizenship therein; and that I desire a passport
for use in visiting the countries hereinafter named for the following purpose:

Palestine _Educational work in Palestine_
(Name of country.)   (Object of visit.)
England _en route_
(Name of country.)   (Object of visit.)
France Italy _en route_
(Name of country.)   (Object of visit.)

I intend to leave the United States from the port of _N.Y._
sailing on board the _____ on _Feb 22_, 191 _9_
(Name of vessel.)   (Date of departure.)

My last passport was obtained from _never_ on _____
and was _____
(Disposition of passport.)

OATH OF ALLEGIANCE.

Further, I do solemnly swear that I will support and defend the Constitution of the United States
against all enemies, foreign and domestic; that I will bear true faith and allegiance to the same; and
that I take this obligation freely, without any mental reservation or purpose of evasion: So help me God.

Jessie E. Sampter
(Signature of applicant.)

Sworn to before me this _FEB 17 1919_ day
of _____, 19___.

[SEAL OF
PASSPORT AGENCY.]

Fee Received
APR 1919
Forenoon

_____
Passport Agent, Department of State.

* A person born in the United States should submit a birth certificate with his application, or if the birth was not officially
recorded, affidavits from the attending physician, parents, or other persons having actual knowledge of the birth.

[OVER.]

Sampter's 1919 passport application. Courtesy of Givat Brenner
Archives, Yesha Sampter papers.

to do with relationships and occasionally also a verb showing how those relationships buck the dominant social norms. It sometimes has to do with sexuality, but it does not fixate on sexual acts or declarations of sexual self-identification as *coming out* does. Rather than focusing on labeling Sampter herself as an essentially queer person, I think about two parts of her life in terms of queerness: she expressed *queer desire* in her writing, and her life was characterized by *queer kinship.*

Centering queerness does not wholly eclipse religion or disability in her life. In fact, it illuminates them from different angles, especially through her relationships. Relationships are at the core of how we experience the world; they "provoke love and hate, peace and violence, and activity and passivity," and so we cannot understand the religious person without understanding her relationships with other people.[2] In spite of how disability studies often focuses on the disabled person and her relationship with society, all we need to do is read memoirs to see the absolutely central role that intimate relationships play in the way disabled people tell their stories. Christina Crosby writes her life before and after her bicycle accident as a story about her relationship with her partner and her brother, and it is often through those relationships that we learn about even seemingly personal things, like her body and how she relates to it.[3] No polio survivor's story I have read would be the same without a mother, a friend, a brother, a lover.

Sampter "never had a family of her own," as the expression goes for remaining unmarried and not having her "own" "biological" children. But she always surrounded herself with people she saw as family. Her "supplementary mother," Josephine Lazarus; her partner, Leah Berlin; her Yemenite daughter, Tamar; and her fellow kibbutzniks were each, in their own way, Jessie's family. Some historians have used the idea of marriage as a model for historical same-sex relationships.[4] Instead, this chapter explores the category of queerness and considers how it can help us understand both Sampter's life and the broader social norms that structured it. Was she a lesbian? What does it mean that she also expressed romantic feelings for a male friend? Was she bisexual, then? What are the right words to describe her relationship with Leah? Should I call it a partnership? A marriage? A friendship? More than one of these, or something else entirely?

I have decided that *queer* is the best analytic fit for Sampter. It might at first seem an odd choice. Few people used the term when she was alive, and those who did used it pejoratively, and so Sampter certainly wouldn't have called herself queer. During her lifetime, doctors and psychoanalysts were in the process of describing—and thereby creating—homosexuality as a perversion linked with neurosis and sexual deviance.[5] The category of homosexuality emerged in law, medicine, and the new sciences of psychology and sexology, and in none of these places was it considered good.

And yet the contemporary theoretical concept of queerness has shed its pejorative past—or, more accurately, it has transformed a past in which sexual or gendered difference was disparaged and pathologized into a present in which sexual or gendered difference has a distinctive value. Homosexuality and other "deviant" sexual practices no longer appear in diagnostic manuals not because same-sex acts have changed but because cultural and medical interpretations of those acts have changed. The historian Carolyn Dinshaw, for example, uses medieval England to show how sexualities have historically specific meanings that are entangled with religion, law, and location. Yet she also shows that these differences do not preclude the idea of queer communities across time or today's readers feeling affinity for queer people of the past.[6] Because queer studies has theorized gender and sexuality as changing concepts, including their relationships to one another, and especially because scholars have often done so with close attention to historical and social context, the idea of queerness helps to interpret Sampter's embodied experience even though its meaning today differs from its historical meanings.

Queer also draws attention to the multiple possible modes of relation to other people, whereas *lesbian* or *bisexual* focuses more on the identity of one's preferred sex partners. Women's intimate relationships in past eras often confound today's ideas about love. As Carroll Smith-Rosenberg wrote in a classic essay about women's letters, our contemporary tendency to see love and sexuality in a "dichotomized universe of deviance and normality, genitality and platonic love, is alien to the emotions and attitudes" of the nineteenth-century women she studied.[7] Love and sexuality mean different things in different times, and importing either-or ideas like homosexuality versus heterosexuality, or romance versus friendship, would be alien to many women of the past, to use Smith-Rosenberg's language. In the late nineteenth and early twentieth century, personal propriety dictated that women not write about explicitly sexual matters, even if they were part of, say, a recognized heterosexual courtship or marriage. Silence also characterizes many historical intimacies between people of the same sex. In keeping with the genteel norms of her own time, Sampter never wrote about her sex acts in letters to her sister, autobiographies, or poetry. There are hints but never declarations.

The time period makes matters even muddier for describing her sexuality: in the late nineteenth and early twentieth century, it was common for women to write letters that were romantic and sensual, but these letters did not always correspond to physical acts. It was also common for women to touch, kiss, and caress one another, but they interpreted these connections as nonsexual. Sexuality, we might say, is contextual. What counts as sexual, and what counts as sexy, differs considerably from historical moment to historical moment. In Sampter's case, however, we know both her writings and many of her intimate social arrangements. She wrote frankly about gender relationships in Palestine, and sexual desire for both men and women is evident in many of her unpublished works.

This is not a problem unique to Sampter. For example, her contemporary Jane Addams—an upper-middle-class urban Protestant woman who was a pioneer in the settlement house movement—also shared her life with women and rejected many of the gender norms of her day. After she and Ellen Gates Starr visited a settlement house in London, the two women decided to found their own. They leased a large home in Chicago, moved in, and began to serve the community—sometimes more than two thousand men, women, and children a day—through educational, social, athletic, and arts programming. Soon thereafter, Mary Rozet Smith became a major donor to Hull House, and she and Addams spent the next thirty years doing things that couples do: they owned a house together in Maine, they traveled together, and they expressed their love in letters. They also worked closely together professionally on a variety of philanthropic projects. But many biographies of Addams make little mention of her sexuality or personal relationships. Some lament that she never married. One biographer wrote, "Life . . . forever eluded her"—a very strange thing to say for a woman who won the Nobel Peace Prize in 1935.[8] A few speculate about whether she was a lesbian, though she, like Sampter, would never have used the term to describe herself.[9] Writing a historical life requires wrestling with conceptual issues to make the past intelligible to us in the present. Telling Sampter's story as a queer story offers a chance to theorize how to translate an embodied past into something legible and relevant in the present.

Yet rather than concluding that figures like Sampter and Addams do not matter to a history of sexuality, I think the opposite. Sampter and Addams matter to the history of sexuality precisely because they do not fit easily within our contemporary categories of heterosexual, homosexual, and bisexual. They make us think about human sexuality and intimate relationships in ways that are more expansive than just what goes on in the bedroom.

To take one specific example, they remind us of the importance of money to sexuality: their class status allowed them to have nontraditional family arrangements that would have been nearly impossible for working-class women, who often needed to marry to have financial support. Put more generally, Sampter can show us a different configuration—one that is not primarily focused on the specifics of sex acts but instead on more diffuse desires, intimate relationships, and family arrangements.

The way I read Sampter's writing, as well as her social relationships, her life was characterized by queer desire and queer kinship. By *queer desire*, I mean both that she sometimes expressed sexual desire for women and that she occasionally expressed a desire to be male.

Queer kinship, then, describes the intimate social ties created beyond and in contrast to heteronormative family norms. Although originally anthropologists used the concept of kinship to think about descent and marriage, it has become a useful model for understanding social structures and deep personal bonds beyond those familiar ties. Intimate social networks of gays and lesbians have made explicit the idea of a "chosen family," which does not rely on traditional blood relationships but nevertheless has the through-thick-and-thin quality that takes it beyond the realm of friendship. Queer kinship need not always be kinship for queer people, but it often is, and it should be clear why people who are not heterosexual would create different kinds of family arrangements. This model of queer kinship fits Sampter: she lived much of her adult life with a woman partner and an adopted daughter and later had an extended "family" of fellow kibbutzniks. Though she also maintained a strong relationship to her sister, her everyday life had a queer model of kinship, that is, one that bucked the social norms around her.

———

"Religion and sex. I acknowledged their close relationship, and saw each exalted thereby," Sampter wrote in the mid-1920s.[10] Most people in the United States today don't often think of religion as sexual—or their primary association between religion and sex is sexual abuse. Many think that sex is bad, according to "religion," and that religion is the enemy of sex. While it is certainly true that some religious doctrines proscribe certain sex acts and partnerships and some religious communities have oppressed queer people, it is equally true that religion and sexuality have a long and intertwined history. Just to take some examples: medieval Christian mystics had sexual visions and embodied experiences of Jesus; one aspect of religious life for many Sufis is an ecstatic love mysticism; some Hindu devotional poetry depicts amorous relationships between Krishna (in a male role) and the poet/reader (in a female role).[11] Religion is no stranger to sex.

The reasons we rarely see disability and sex together are different, but, as with religion and sex, the cultural power of that denial is still strong. Popular images of disabled people rarely suggest they have sexualities. Sometimes they seem helpless; sometimes they seem angelic; sometimes they even seem heroic. But imperfect bodies are often desexualized bodies.[12] We rarely see disabled bodies in *Playboy* or even on covers in the supermarket magazine rack, and when we do, they rarely seem sexual—like on the cover of *Parents*, where they appear as children who need caring for (or even pity), or like on the cover of *Runner's World*, where they are inspirational.[13] Though more mainstream media now include people with disabilities, disability is still not part of the dominant image of sex.[14] Despite these widespread assumptions about how religion and sex, or disability and sex, don't really belong together, telling Sampter's life as a queer story shows that they do.

If Jessie's childhood seems an unlikely start for a Zionist because of her disability and her family's religious identification and social class, it also contained the seeds of her experience in later life when it came to gender, sexuality, and the family. For instance, queer desire echoed in many of her early recollections. Though she would not have used this language, even from a young age, Sampter had begun to negotiate between her own desire and gendered sense of self, on one hand, and what the society around her declared proper gendered ways of being, on the other. In her unpublished autobiography from the early 1920s, Sampter recalled a time when she had a boy playmate:

> Vague recollections of a small boy chum, Lewis Long, my "twin" in time of birth, who lived next door for more than a year when I was about six years old. We played together daily. . . . If we really were twins, I thought, I should have been a boy too. At seven I had a passionate desire to be a boy, and I then believed that my all-powerful father could effect the change by buying me a suit of boys' clothing and cutting my hair. For months I kept teasing him to do so. I used to pose before the mirror, which was always a mystifying and beloved friend, hold up my curls, as if they were short, and consider what a pretty boy I should make. Still, being a girl, I set great store by my curls.[15]

We might at first be tempted to think of this recollection as little more than another version of childhood make-believe or an indication of the ways that gender norms can seem more flexible for children. Even today most Americans think differently about little boys who put on their mothers' high heels and jewelry than they do about adult men who wear heels and jewelry designed for women. So, at first glance, perhaps Jessie's longing to be a boy seems merely a childhood flight of fancy. And yet Sampter included this "passionate desire" for her father to change her into a boy in an autobiography she wrote as an adult. That she thought to recount this in her narrative is in itself significant: even if her memories of her boy chum were only "vague recollections," her queer desire remained clear, and she thought of it as an important part of both her past and her present. Like the youthful discovery of her Jewishness, these play moments continued to resonate with how she saw herself as an adult.

Although her autobiographical writings include only a small number of scenes of childhood play, several of the others also demonstrate Jessie's gendered desires. Some are quite recognizable for any girl who identifies as a tomboy. Why can boys do things girls can't? "When we were still in Europe," she recalled of her preteen years, "we used to play 'doctor' with a little boy whose consulting room was in a cave in a hillside. There he examined our dolls. We were deeply concerned about their physiology. He could play only doctor because he was a boy, and boys did not play with dolls. Why?"[16]

At other times, young Jessie went beyond curiosity, or even indignation, about gender roles into an explicit desire to cross them. She recalled role-playing with her friend Belle: "One day Belle and I dressed as boys, in bathing trousers and blouses, and at my suggestion, we became lion hunters."[17] Other times she played games with heterosexual plotlines, where she played the man. Jessie recalled a time with her cousin Anita: "We play house. I am a soldier, and she is my wife and all our dolls are our children. Usually I ride to battle on her little brother's rocking horse."[18] Jessie's youth was marked with moments of queer desire—desire for her own body to be sexed differently, desire to do things associated with men, and desire to act out intimacy with a woman character. As childhood play gave way to the deep conversations of adolescence, Jessie developed new relationships and new desires.

"One of the Great Things of Life"

As Sampter wrote and rewrote her life, she recalled the bonds of her adolescence. Not long after her father died and Jessie was diagnosed with polio, she met Nora. She recalled the event as "one of the great things in life." In "The Speaking Heart," her recollections of Nora are wrapped up with discussions of beauty, the body, desire, and the nature of the world. Jessie and Nora were young teens when they met, and the adult Sampter wrote in a way that conjured up the intensity of her feelings:

> I loved beautiful persons. Physical beauty seemed a virtue to me, a service, that made it possible to forgive its owners even stupidity and graver failings. Yet ~~compassion~~ suffering drew me ~~even~~ more than beauty. At Christmastime—or rather Hanukkah—one of the great things of life happened to me: I met my friend, Nora. She, though a year younger than I, was taller and beautifully built, and the first thing I noticed was that her skirts were too short. Perhaps because I did not wish to look at her face. Already she had the ample build that later developed into the Venus de Milo or Winged Victory type; her golden brown hair fell in heavy braids almost to her knees. The right side of her face was beautiful, fair, a gracious profile; on the left side she was blind, an eyelid missing from birth; and the side of the nose was scarred by operations, the mouth drawn awry. I took her hand; it was muscular, vibrant, electric.[19]

As we saw in the previous chapter, the two had a deep and affectionate relationship, one that sometimes bordered on flirtation. And here Sampter reflected on Nora's physicality: she was "taller and beautifully built" and seemingly unaware that her skirts evoked sexuality. Her body recalled a classical feminine beauty of curves and long hair. Even Sampter's description of holding her hand arouses a sexual charge.

Later on, Jessie described her desire for Nora in terms that were more explicitly sexual:

> Incomprehensible yearnings! I used to wish Nora were a man, then— who knows?—we might marry. She drew me with a physical attraction that also repelled or frightened or troubled me. The touch of her electric hand on my heart would send a thrill through me, would heal or soothe the pain that still so often centered there. She was big and strong. Sometimes she would draw me down to sit on her lap, sometimes in a wild, desperate mood she would grab my throat and pretend she was going to strangle me. I liked it. I found consolation in our mutual sorrows, and to her alone I could speak without shame of the longing for death but I did not understand what was the force that drew us together, the deep, dark connection that sometimes made me suspect I had known her in some prenatal world, in a cavern of the pregnant earth.[20]

As this passage suggests, Jessie's reflections sometimes connected queerness and disability. In the case of her desire for Nora, the combination of suffering and beauty, encapsulated in Nora's beautiful and disfigured face, drew Jessie. She felt closeness and sameness ("know[ing] her in some prenatal world") as well as difference (feeling repelled or frightened), so often characteristic of romantic relationships. When Nora married years later, Jessie wrote, "I was happy for her, and I felt deserted."[21] Even though, by that time, the two had moved apart and could see each other only occasionally, Nora's marriage still stung, perhaps for romantic reasons, perhaps as a further loss of friendship, and perhaps for reasons that were not entirely clear even to Jessie herself.

Queerness and disability also entwined in Sampter's own self-conception. She wrote, of a time in her mid-teens, "My exceeding modesty was in part due to the defects of my body which I shrank from exposing even to women. I hid my heavy steel brace when I was not wearing it."[22] Jessie associated her disabled body with unattractiveness and tried to hide it. But she also thought of her disability in sexual terms that were not entirely negative. "When I began to surmise what marriage meant," she continued, "I marveled, though without fear, how anyone could endure it. Biological abnormalities of some sorts, of which I read in scientific books, thrilled me with horror. Especially the conception of the Hermaphrodite, man and woman at once. Suppose I were that? Would I know? Did I perhaps secretly and horribly long for it, as an escape from dependence on the love of others?"[23] Maybe if she embodied both sexes, she wouldn't have to conform to social ideals of heterosexual coupling. Here a fantasy of queer desire also entailed a fantasy of queer kinship: maybe if she had a differently sexed body, she could have a different kind of family.

As Sampter continued to write, and as I continued to read, I saw that her worldview subtly refused many of the social norms of family, sexuality, and reproduction. Her own life never included a husband or childbirth. Perhaps more interesting, she also found ways to push against these norms in her writing, though she did not uniformly reject them. As I thought about how to describe someone who made her own family from the people around her, sometimes without regard to blood ties, I realized that this model has been popular in contemporary queer cultures. It may include sexual practices, but it need not necessarily. Though she was never a member of such a subculture, Sampter's life was marked by queer kinship, and her writing was too.

Several years after she contracted polio, when Jessie was in her late teens, came her "second great event," as she called it. The first great event had been meeting Nora. The second great event would be the beginning of a lifelong friendship with Mary Antin. Antin is well known to historians as a memoirist of American Jewish life in an era of immigration, but she played a much more intimate role in Sampter's personal and intellectual life.[24] The two women became fast friends. Mary was two years older than Jessie and had been born into an observant Jewish family in Polotsk in the Russian Pale of Settlement. Both Mary and Jessie had begun writing at a young age, and each had already published poetry.[25] Though the two women came from different backgrounds, they bonded over big questions about religion, philosophy, nations, and war.

After twenty-year-old Mary married a Columbia University geologist, Jessie, too, began dabbling in geology and paleontology. The two women would remain friends and correspondents throughout their lives, through Mary's divorce, Jessie's move to Palestine, and mental and physical illnesses for both women.

Mary Antin also changed Jessie's life in another way: shortly after Jessie's eighteenth birthday, Antin introduced her to the writer Josephine Lazarus. Josephine and her older sister, the poet Emma Lazarus, had grown up in an established and culturally elite New York Sephardi family. Both women published work with Jewish and American themes, though Emma was the more famous sister. An Emma Lazarus poem is engraved on the Statue of Liberty's pedestal, after all. The people in their family's social circles mostly shunned Zionism, and so both Emma and Josephine came to it as adults, but each offered forceful articulations.[26]

Josephine was a generation older than Jessie and Mary, but she would often host the two young women at her home and discuss philosophy and writing. She encouraged both to write more, to edit their writing carefully, and to publish it. In fact, Josephine's encouragement was a major force behind Antin writing her best-selling memoir, *The Promised Land.*[27] She had a similarly inspirational effect on Sampter.

Beyond being a role model and inspiration, Lazarus also helped Jessie question the family structures and gender roles in the world around her. "Mother was almost jealous, for Miss Lazarus became a kind of intellectual mother to me, nursing me in things of the spirit; but we need more than one mother," Sampter reflected.[28] And if we need more than one mother, and biology needn't determine mothering, then perhaps other social expectations are not as set in stone as they seem. Josephine remained single and cared for an "invalid" sister in her own home.[29] "Why had Miss Lazarus not married?" Sampter thought. "She must have loved; there was in her such a fullness of experience."[30] Fullness of experience, then, could exist outside the bounds of nuclear families and heterosexuality. Sampter's relationship with Lazarus not only demonstrated to her intellectually that alternative kinship models were possible but also showed her experientially that they could be fulfilling.

Jessie dedicated her first published book, *The Great Adventurer*, to Josephine Lazarus. Part poetry, part essay, the book made the case that each person was an adventurer. From its very first words, the book questioned the value of ingrained social norms. Its first stanzas considered the utility of heterosexual sex for new life but suggested that neither heterosexual coupling nor heterosexual sex was in and of itself good:

> A man and a woman went forth by moonlight; they knew the planetary forces; they loved, they lived a rapturous moment of life; and, lo, there glimmered the face of a new man.
>
> A troop of soldiers rushed through a town, and stole its fairest daughter, and stupefied her and misused her; and, lo, there glimmered the face of a new man.
>
> A thoughtless couple was thoughtlessly united, for convenience and through the babbling force of many tongues; and, lo, there glimmered the face of a new man.
>
> Like bubbles upon water, like clouds shaped by the wind, so shadow-like and accidental is a human face.[31]

Heterosexual sex could lead to children regardless of its value—it might be loving, it might be cruel, or it might be thoughtless. But in Sampter's writing it was not privileged.

Nor was marriage or blood relations necessarily privileged above other human connections. Jessie's own mother died just a decade after her father, leaving the twenty-three-year-old without biological parents. But even before her mother's death, Jessie began to think of Josephine Lazarus as more than an intellectual mentor and even more than a friend. Josephine "was, to me, a second, complementary mother," she wrote.[32] Even from this early stage of her life, Jessie created her own family, not adhering to cultural norms regarding the kinship of marriage and blood. A poetic interpretation of her nonstandard—even queer—sense of family and mothering as divorced from procreation appeared in *The Great Adventurer*. The voice who spends her time wanting a child, or a husband, misses out on the true modes of creation and of human connection:

> I live upon a promise. In winter I live upon the promise of spring, and in spring I live upon the promise of autumn. Forever am I like a mother

expecting the birth of her first child; forever like a bride awaiting the bridegroom. But I may die before night.

Is it all promise? Is nothing to be fulfilled? . . .

Woe to me, I have missed the fulfillment! I did not see it.

While I was awaiting spring my window was brilliant with roses of frost and lilies of ice. While I was awaiting autumn the cherries were already ripe upon the trees. Behold, she who was awaiting her first child had him already in the stillness, closer than ever again. Behold, the bride awaiting her bridegroom hears his voice singing into her ears.

Though the mother and bride die before night, yet are they no less mother and bride. . . .

The true fulfillment is the promise. . . .

Mine only is this endless present, with its vision of the past and future.

Most delightful of all present things, most living and nearest to my soul, is just its promise of the future.[33]

Queer theorists have offered the idea of "queer time"; that is, human time need not be oriented toward a future that takes heterosexual coupling, reproduction, and the figure of the child as its emblem.[34] This future-oriented time becomes most obvious when Americans talk about "leaving a better world for our children" or cleaning up the water or funding social security "for our children." What if we asked, What other ways might there be to imagine time? Must time be oriented toward the future? And if it is, must it focus on reproduction and children?

Sampter's longing and emotional pain suggest both the power of such critiques and also their inadequacy for understanding the lives of gays and lesbians who do want to become parents. Her writing critiques the idea that the real meaning of life is to be found in a heterosexual marriage with children, yet she still looks to the future as part of her present and still sometimes longs for a child. Sampter uses common reproductive, family-oriented images—bride, mother, child—but suggests that taking them at face value limits the possibility of fulfillment. She presents the idea of marrying and bearing children but then insists that if that is all we can see, we will miss out: "Mine only is this endless present."

Perhaps Jessie looked around her and saw the social expectations for women, but then she also saw Josephine Lazarus, and wondered how to make sense of it all. How could a "spinster" find her life fulfilling? The poem rails against this question, insisting that human bonding and creation could be just as meaningful in the absence of a husband and children. But in this way it also shows how Jessie assumed the value of these norms of bonding and creation: she wanted to show that they were available to unmarried and nonchildbearing people too.

As I read more of Jessie Sampter's writings, I wondered about my own historical distance from her. Her sexuality and her embodied experience are available to me only in writing and through the occasional photograph. I do not know how she moved in the world, nor can I know what her voice sounded like, nor precisely what kind of pain or pleasure she experienced and when. Did she have sex with women? I do not know this either.

How, then, should I write about a woman who recorded her erotic desires toward women and would later share decades of her life with another woman? I might, like Sampter's 1956 biographer, pointedly ignore all the homoerotic moments in her writings, downplay the homosocial character of her social and personal life, and lament that Sampter never married a man.[35] But to do this would be to assume that heterosexuality is the default sexuality and to regard a person as straight unless they explicitly detail having sex with a person of the same sex. This approach is not faithful to Sampter, a woman whose desires were never defined by normative sexuality or gender, a woman who had a "passionate desire to be a boy" and "incomprehensible yearnings" and physical attraction toward Nora, and a woman who shared many of her years with Leah Berlin. Perhaps, then, I should declare Sampter a lesbian. But this will not do either: Sampter's queer kinship is not reducible to contemporary ideas about women who desire women.

Jack Halberstam writes that queerness is "more about a way of life than a way of having sex."[36] In this sense, Sampter's life was a queer one. Sampter defied social norms at many turns: she never married; she moved across the ocean alone; she had a flourishing career; despite not having a husband, she adopted a child from another culture; and she had a rest home built where she and Leah would live on the kibbutz. In spite of losing both her parents at a young age, Jessie Sampter made a family that was characterized by emotional and intellectual ties. While these may seem more pedestrian than the punk rockers and club kids Halberstam discusses in his research, Sampter refused dominant ways of doing family, religion, and economics. As I read through Sampter's papers and could put together her story of growing into an adult and embracing Zionism, I saw these refusals even more prominently.

Queer Kinship and Sampter's Relationships

In addition to nurturing her through friendship and even kinship, Mary Antin and Josephine Lazarus also both fostered Sampter's eventual turn to Judaism and Zionism. And, like her kinship arrangements, neither Sampter's Judaism nor her Zionism quite adhered to traditional norms. Zionist life, as she would explain, should mean far less gender differentiation, far more personal freedom in terms of sexuality and religion, and a new structure of kinship once the nuclear model of man-woman-children would no longer be dominant. Most strains of Zionism sought to change gendered expectations. Sampter went beyond them. Nevertheless, her Zionism was never fully queer (if indeed such a thing is possible) insofar as she retained some traditional ideas about gender and sexuality. In short, Sampter's Zionism, both in her journalistic writings and in her more philosophical ones, would queer notions of gender, sexuality, and kinship.

Even as a child, Sampter recognized that although marriage might be "normal," it was hardly inevitable. In her teen years, a beautiful young woman came to live in the apartment above Jessie, Elvie, and their mother. Mrs. Ritter was "delicate, very pretty, with eyes like black cherries and short brown curls. She played the piano not well but with feeling. I loved her; I formed a passionate friendship. . . . At last I was understood. We had long, dreamy talks in her bedroom." Until one day Sampter said to her earnestly, "There is only one thing in life that can be perfectly sure, and that is death." "No," answered Mrs. Ritter, "marriage too." Sampter balked. "This remark seemed to me so stupid that though I continued to appreciate her sweetness, my idol was shattered, my worship at an end."[37] Marriage was not perfectly sure. As a young, disabled woman who watched young men court her sister but offer only friendship to her, Sampter knew well that a lifetime without marriage was quite possible. Sampter objected to Mrs. Ritter's pronouncement not just because she saw it as factually and experientially untrue but also because she found it ideologically objectionable. To insist on marriage was to hem women in, to insist that the "normal" course of getting married was the only legitimate course for a life. Although she wouldn't have known it at the time, as it turned out, many of the most influential women in Sampter's life—Josephine Lazarus, Henrietta Szold, and Leah Berlin—never married.

The idea of marriage nevertheless appealed to young Jessie, though its appeal was more about the children it might produce than the idea of romance with a man. After her father's death, when she learned that her mother had remained in bed for six months of her pregnancy with Jessie, she decided that she could honor her parents' sacrifice only by making something significant and lasting from her life. "The ambition grew to serve, to become great, to be remembered; thus I would repay Father for his love for me. I would be a poet. . . . I would write my name in the annals of mankind." And related to this desire for immortality through intellect was also an immortality through genetics: "I would marry and have children. Now I understood why Mother could no longer have a little brother for me, since Father was dead; so I must have my own children very soon."[38] Throughout her reflection on this phase, the adult Jessie gently chided the young Jessie for her ideas about the potentials of childbearing. She developed a crush on an older cousin but remembered this puppy love as more disheartening than charming. Soon after, Sampter insisted that marriage was not for her at all. "I should never marry. Had I been a Catholic, I should have gone into a convent," she declared.[39]

Marriage was not inevitable, then, and soon she would also decide that neither was giving birth to children. When she reflected on her work at the settlement house, she wrote, "More children! My mother instinct seemed satisfied, and I no longer consciously had the passionate desire to bring forth my own."[40] Sampter held tight to her youthful idea that she needed a legacy—but that legacy need not take the form of biological creation. It could be intellectual or spiritual. In her experimental 1909 book *The Great Adventurer*, she wrote, "For the power that is in a man must go forward and ripen in season; and if it cannot bear physical fruit, it shall bear spiritual fruit."[41] Her youthful desperation to have children as her way to shape the future had opened into a wider vision: each person had a legacy, and intellectual and spiritual legacies were at least as important as the physical legacy of biologically related children. "Every man is a spring of the waters of life. The force that is in him must pass onward, like the water that is pouring from the mountains. Through the calm, broad river or the seething narrow chasm, in clouds or spray or cataract or subterranean stream, it must pour down to the sea. So the force of man, through body or spirit, through good or evil, pours down through the ages. Where there is room and passageway his children shall pass. One is the father of heroes and another is the father of prophecies."[42] In her early twenties, as she began to write more seriously—poems and essays, mainly—she began to think of her writing in these terms. She kept her unpublished manuscripts by her bed. "I treated them as my children; they seemed very precious to me, irreplaceable; and Mother, who shared the feeling, called them my babies."[43] When Sampter used *man* as her word for the generic human, she shared in the convention of her time. *Man* was universal. But she was always quite careful with her words, and so her use of *man* for the default human also demonstrates how she unconsciously replicated some of the gendered assumptions of her time.

Simultaneously, however, she took stances against social expectations for women. When the journal *Menorah* published her poetry in 1914, its editor wrote to Sampter to ask for a photograph and a "little vita." But don't worry, he wrote, "We don't ask for birth years in the case of the masterful sex!"[44] She wrote back, demurring on the photograph and life details. As for a "feminine aversion to recalling the year of one's birth, I fear I don't share it," she declared. "That being the least personal of all the events of my life—I don't even remember it—would also be the least private. I'm neither ashamed of my age nor displeased with it."[45]

The second half of the 1910s was a turning point for Jessie. She wrote feverishly, deepened her commitment to Zionism, and struggled with worsening health. When the cousin on whom Jessie had a crush was dying of tuberculosis, Nora "had only to lay her hand on the aching spot and the pain would be drawn out, melt away in a kind of yearning, and sleep would come to heal." Nora had "the art of love," Jessie discovered. "Her vibrant, magnetic hands!" she exclaimed. Yet Nora's physical comforts left Jessie feeling a little unsure: "Why did I doubt whether these ministrations had yet something unholy in them?"[46] Sampter associated sexuality with unholiness but couldn't quite place her feelings and what they meant.

During this time she also wrote of her attraction to her friend Louis, who enjoyed her company but was not interested in a romantic relationship. In that, he, too, associated sexuality with unholiness and lack of sexuality with holiness: "He does not love you in that way. He says you are holy, pure; he had not thought of you as one who would want to marry," Sampter recalled her friend saying after she had talked with him.[47] His demurral was more than a cop-out; his reaction echoed social attitudes toward both disability and queerness. Disabled people can be seen as holier than others—think of disabled children who are called "angels" or people with physical disabilities who are regarded as "spiritual heroes"—and their sexuality is often ignored or denied.[48] And his surprise that Sampter might want to marry suggests both queerness (whether because of an attraction to women or a commitment to staying single) and disability. Although Jessie described the development as deeply disappointing, her words lacked the intimate and almost urgent language she used to describe her "great events." Even before they met, she recalled, "I longed for male attention, for a lover."[49]

And yet, immediately following this confession in her writing, she noted how a "beautiful" man, whom she thought she could love, turned out to be "a rather silly flirt." Love sounded romantic in the abstract, but she did not find the particular men around to be real candidates.

Does the hope of a relationship with a man at this point in her life make her not queer? (I think not.) Should we acknowledge that changing sexuality is a part of every person's life, and this might also include the gender of the people to whom one is attracted? (I think so.) I also think we should see her as part of a long tradition of queer people who seek out male-female relationships for a variety of social reasons, only some of which have to do with sexuality. Sampter frequently asked herself, "Can an unmarried woman remain normal?" and wondered if her "temptations to acts of sexual perversion" might be a consequence of not marrying.[50] Even if she sought a romantic relationship with a man, she surely also had other kinds of sexual desire that resisted social norms. But in the end, I think, the details of her sexual acts are far from the most interesting part of the way she defied norms of gender, desire, and kinship.

For much of the time I was researching this book, I lived together with a friend. But we were more than friends; we affectionately referred to ourselves as husband and wife; we anticipated each other's needs; we supported each other emotionally; we shared jokes about the crummy people we knew and the strange malfunctioning appliances in the Tel Aviv apartment we had rented for a summer; we ate together, whether it was late-night pizza or her fabulous home-cooked meals; we divided up the housework. (I will never outlive my gratitude to her for always being the one to clean the bathroom.) We went on vacation together. We drove places together. It's not carpooling if it's family, right? We were family. We no longer live together, but we still are.

I suppose this is a case where my life turned out to feed my research method. I didn't plan my living arrangements so that I could experience what it's like to have two smart, strong-willed, professional women running a household together. I didn't set out to learn what it means to have a chosen family. And yet I did learn those things.

I also learned how people reacted: sometimes assuming that two adult women under the same roof must experience conflict and jealousy, sometimes assuming that we must have the handyman on speed dial because what would we do when something broke? Those gender stereotypes have changed, some, from the ones Leah and Jessie faced. But I met plenty of people who thought a household without a man—a family without a man—must be missing something. I met those people in my own life, and I recognized them in Sampter's archive. I never quite figured out how to say, "This works for us" in ways that convinced the ones I met, and I can't imagine I would have had more luck with the historical ones. Maybe they would never be convinced. People's ideas about gender are pretty hard to change. But I think it's worth it to try. I am sure Sampter thought so too.

Married to Palestine

Some Zionist art seems to be homoerotic. Early twentieth-century artists like E. M. Lilien featured images of sculpted male bodies. Lilien drew naked, well-muscled male bodies carrying grapes, a naked angel wrestling Joseph, and naked male angels playing instruments while flowers grow, just to name a few. Despite what these images suggest, however, Zionist ideologies assumed heterosexuality. When Sampter became a Zionist, she began with a fairly standard view of gender in Palestine and the Zionist cause: "The cooperative colonies had been begun in Galilee and groups of young Hebrew speaking pioneers were laying the foundation of social justice, the plow in one hand, the pistol in the other. There was danger, on this frontier land, from attacks by thieving Bedouins, and these young men and women took their lives in their hands, and sometimes laid them down for their people."[51] As she became more involved with the political movement, her views became more complex, with respect to both gender and the political situation. She began teaching courses on Zionism, Henrietta Szold encouraged her to speak publicly, and she published essays on Zionism in the American press. In many ways, this is the story of the next chapter: Sampter's story as a story of Zionism, nationalism, and transnationalism.

But Zionism is also important to Sampter's story as a queer story. In both her intimate relationships and her philosophical ideas about the Zionist movement, Sampter's queer kinship and queer desire arise again and again. Soon after she entered the Zionist fold, she and a Zionist friend went on a summer retreat. The friend took her niece, and Jessie took a young woman mentee from the settlement house, "so we were a small family."[52] "We took long walks, she towering dark and tall and slim above me, we went collecting new flowers, watching for rare birdsongs, losing our way among fields and thickets. We walked hand in hand like two children and dreamed. Our children were running ahead."[53] This was queer kinship—and a little bit of queer desire too. The walking and dreaming were not overtly sexual, though eros saturates her description. As she continued her recollection, religious desire also weaves into the mix: "Peace and joy filled me. I thanked God for friendship, I thanked him for life, for work, for my people, for God. I lifted my heart to him at night on my bed, and it throbbed as if it would break, it seemed fluttering to escape, to snap the bonds of life and be free. A radiance was shining just around the corner of my mind, just beyond my vision; a little door was open. . . . Was it death I wanted or God? A great yearning filled me, the yearning that is peace."[54]

People with disabilities are often seen as childlike or helpless and are rarely portrayed as sexual, let alone sexy. Yet sometimes these negative assumptions can grant them some respite from the pressures of gender norms. Eli Clare writes, "I think about my disabled body, how as a teenager I escaped the endless pressure to have a boyfriend, to shave my legs, to wear make-up. The same lies that cast me as genderless, asexual, and undesirable also framed a space in which I was left alone to be my quiet, bookish, tomboy self, neither girl nor boy."[55] Sampter wore dresses and stockings and always considered herself a woman but nevertheless chafed at many social expectations for women.

Soon after Sampter became a Zionist, she also cut her hair short. She wanted to in part because her arms were weak and styling hair meant holding them aloft for longer than was comfortable but also because the style would look less feminine. At first, her sister, Elvie, pleaded with Jessie to keep it long. Jessie didn't want to cause trouble over something seemingly so trivial. But after Jessie's pneumonia, Elvie relented, and so Jessie cut her hair short. "Oh, what freedom and comfort! I have never since let it grow," she wrote many years later.[56]

Instead of becoming an aspiration, as it would for many single women, the idea of marriage served a different purpose for Sampter. Sampter used marriage as a metaphor for closeness and commitment, and also for desire, but less so about a relationship with a man. When she made the decision to move to Palestine and the Zionist Organization of America approved, she wrote, "It was as if I should be married. I took my savings from the bank and went shopping with Sister, for my trousseau; I indulged my taste for gay colors, which I had always a trifle suppressed. . . . My friends gave me presents, whatever I wanted, and when I wanted nothing, money to use for Palestine."[57] She also joked about marriage: "I'm awful about personal anniversaries. I don't 'keep' my own birthday at all, generally mention it the day after if I think of it. As for my wedding day----," she jested in a letter to her sister many years later.[58]

In 1919 Jessie packed a trousseau and drolly declared herself "married to Palestine." Palestine—as well as many homelands—was frequently gendered feminine for those who imagined it to be their homeland. But what did Jessie mean when she thought of marrying Palestine? Had she gendered it male, thinking of it as a husband, or had she thought of it as feminine, with its soil passively waiting and yearning for the active farmers and builders? Her desire for the ambiguously gendered homeland was also subtly linked to her disability. She wrote to Elvie just before she left, "I write in the full consciousness that my not returning to America is among likelihoods, either because I may not outlive the year of probation, or because at the end of that year I shall have found in Palestine that spiritual fulfillment, that 'at-homeness.'"[59] Jessie thought she might very well stay in Palestine, either because the land was the spouse she awaited or because her body would not let her leave. Though she would make several visits back to the United States, each of her predictions had an element of truth.

When she arrived in Palestine, ill and physically exhausted from the long voyage, Jessie went to the Hadassah hospital in Jerusalem. After her release, she stayed briefly at Hotel de France, the headquarters of Hadassah's physicians and nurses, where visitors arrived for Rosh Hashanah. "One stands out now," Sampter recalled, "a large, broad, stately woman of my own age, with straight dark brown hair and gray eyes, impressive and yet simple." They spoke in Hebrew.[60] The woman was Leah Berlin, a Russian Zionist. Her father and grandfather were Lubavitcher Hasidim, and she was a committed socialist. She had grown up in Riga, where she joined the revolution first as a participant and then as an organizer. She remembered a pivotal moment: a railroad engineers' strike in which she participated. She was thrown in jail with forty other (mostly Jewish) women by the Cossacks, and after they were released, she made her first public speech against the czar and his "proclamations."[61] After several more years as a revolutionary in Russia, Leah moved to Palestine and worked for the Zionist Commission. When she and Jessie met, she had been coordinating a war relief effort that focused on teaching women and girls to make a living by sewing.[62]

Shortly after meeting, Jessie and Leah moved in together. For the rest of Jessie's life, Leah would be a significant presence, both physically and intellectually, and their close relationship was clear to others who knew them. "She is a large woman, large physically and spiritually, built on large lines in every way, and her admiration of Jessie is whole-souled," Henrietta Szold wrote to Sampter's sister in 1920. "She can bring Jessie down to earth, when it is well for her not to soar. As you know, they share a room."[63]

Jessie Sampter and Leah Berlin, probably late 1930s. Courtesy of Givat Brenner Archives, Yesha Sampter papers.

Jessie, too, referred to their space as "our home" and wrote to her sister of how "we" spend the days.[64] After a few years, Leah's mother, who had just moved to Palestine, joined them. One writer called Leah "Jessie's devoted companion."[65] What were these two women to one another?

I have decided to call Leah Jessie's *partner*. The term is now common for long-term gay and lesbian relationships, and it is also increasingly common in long-term heterosexual relationships. But I've chosen it because it is far more expansive than this. You can be a partner in a law firm. But you can also be a partner in crime or a partner in crime fighting. You can have a short-term partner, like in social dancing where your partnership might last only the length of the song. *Partner* also has a long history in gay and lesbian communities; before gay marriage was legalized, the term often signaled long-term intimate commitment. In all of these cases, partnership is a bond, and Jessie's relationship with Leah was most certainly a bond.

It wasn't love at first sight. In fact, even when they became friends, Jessie first saw Leah as spiritually inferior: "She seemed to me a younger sister, a child, in things of the spirit, though she was as old as I and a powerful person with capacity for leadership. She wanted to find me perfect. That is the weakness of woman's love for woman in so impulsive a nature as hers . . . but I felt in her, too, a deeper bond, the strength of her direct nature."[66] It is easy, from Jessie's letters, to forget that Leah was a formidable revolutionary. But you cannot miss Jessie's admiration for her. "A quick decision moved me: 'Shall we not live together?'" So they decided. "But it was another half year before we were able to find suitable rooms, or, as it happened, one room."[67] They saw each other daily.

Jessie and Leah had decided to move in together, but they still had to decide on a place. "I have not yet decided about moving, or rather, Miss Berlin is not quite decided. We have seen two very desirable rooms, one of them quite enormous, for . . . less than $15, and I may decide to room with her and use the other for a sitting room. . . . Miss Berlin is very strong and practical, and she wants to take care of me. She has promised to do all the moving for us. I like her very, very much. . . . If we wanted to pay $5 more, we could get a third room, but I doubt whether we shall care to do it."[68] As if it were obviously related, she followed her joyful recounting of her life with Leah with an immediate reference to her friend Louis, with whom she had earlier wanted a romantic relationship. He had instead married a mutual friend. "I am delighted that Louis has his heart's desire."[69] When the rooms fell through later that month, she updated her sister: "It is not pleasant for me to receive visitors here. And Leah and I could have a pleasant little household, as everyone who knows us agrees."[70]

The longer they continued to live apart, the more Leah appeared in Jessie's letters to her sister. "I am sorry not to be with Leah Berlin, as I like her more and more," she wrote in the second week of December.[71] "How I wish you could know Leah Berlin," she wrote in the third.[72]

Finally, in March 1920, they moved in together, and the next months' letters were glowing. When they packed up and moved, she wrote to Elvie, "This is *my* busy week, for I am moving! I meant to send you a long type-written letter today, but Leah Berlin came in to help me with my packing—or rather, to do it for me—and I am snatching a moment to scribble, in between directing her."[73] "Those who know me think I have never before looked so well."[74] "Leah sends greetings."[75] As soon as they were settled, Jessie wrote that she finally had "truly a home of my own." She sketched the whole floor plan, including "our room," for her sister. "Leah and I are going to make two rooms of ours, by stringing a yellow oriental curtain across the middle." They would use one side of the curtain as a bedroom, including two beds. "We are keeping house together, sharing half and half. . . . I love it!" Jessie wrote, displaying an uncharacteristic level of excitement.[76] Elvie wondered if the room arrangement was, perhaps, cramped or "narrow," but Jessie assured her the close quarters were just right.[77] In June they added a puppy to "our family."[78]

But in July they had their first real fight: "Our living experiment in this little house has not worked well," she wrote to Elvie one evening. "I have been deeply disappointed and hurt. . . . So Leah and I are going to try what we originally planned, separate housekeeping."[79] This was Jessie's first mention of a plan for "separate housekeeping"—presumably separate cleaning and shopping because they still planned to dine together. But logistics were not what really bothered Jessie. It was the emotional turmoil of the fight. She later reflected, "It was our first difficulty and left me sore and puzzled. I accumulated anger because I could not answer; I was submissive and resentful. I became uneasy and found in [Leah], the big, strong, masterful, secure, a use of strength that I could only interpret as hidden cruelty, it no doubt added to her attraction for me; it also repelled me."[80] That moment "I could not bear that my love should go unappreciated. So we passed from love to hate and from hate back to love, [Leah] more expressive, I more intense. And because of this greater intensity of mine, I began to fear she no longer loved me at all."[81] Kinship means conflict as well as support.[82]

And yet, the next week, Jessie's letters went back to singing Leah's praises and speaking of their lives, and even tastes, in the plural: "We—Leah and I—like them very much"; "Leah and I are going to Hebron" to "spend four days during the holidays"; and, in a paragraph otherwise entirely about what Jessie eats and how much food costs, "Leah and I have similar tastes" in food.[83] And the house regained its glow in her letters: "We are so comfortable and cos[y], and I think our sitting room is really beautiful."[84] The two of them shared intellectual passions. They discussed Zionism. They read countless books together, including some writings of Sigmund Freud. Jessie's mentor approved too: "Miss Szold," as everyone referred to the Zionist organizer Henrietta Szold, "loves Leah," she told Elvie.[85]

When I arrived at this point in reading Sampter's letters, I paused for a moment. I thought about some of the cultural narratives about being gay I heard when I was growing up: if you come out, your family will disown you;

you'll have to choose between being a child to your parents and being who you really are; when it comes to your family of origin and the queer community, you can only have one or the other. Even then, for most people these were false choices, but they were powerful stories. Sampter, like many gays and lesbians in the decades after her, never faced exile from her blood relatives. Queer kinship for her meant making a life with Leah, but it did not mean forsaking her family of origin. She missed her parents, she loved her sister, and she adored her niece and nephew. In fact, the whole reason that I could know so much about her relationship with Leah was because of Jessie's closeness to her sister, Elvie. Without that, there might have been merely perfunctory letters, or perhaps no letters at all.

Their friends and colleagues remarked on their relationship. Some of them even romanticized it. Tamar de Sola Pool, an American Zionist, wrote about Sampter, "It was not long [after arriving] that she found a companion with whom to share her home, a vigorous active young woman in charge of the war relief workshops for girls. It was Leah Berlin. Miss Berlin spent her days creating and directing young girls and women whom the war had ravaged." De Sola Pool painted Leah as strong and dynamic and Jessie as frail but brilliant. The two were complementary, and together they helped the women and children of Palestine: "While Leah directed the machine shop, Jessie, lying flat on her back with her hands in the air, helped to create the first toys the children of Jerusalem had after the war. The little orphans would stuff old stockings and sew them up and Jessie, with fingers only partially under control, would paint charming little features that turned stuffed old stockings into beloved dolls."[86] De Sola Pool was convinced that the relationship with the strong and dynamic Leah had changed Jessie: "How the miracle happened, I know not, but the next time I see Miss Sampter sharing fully the throbbing life of Jerusalem as an active member of the community."[87]

Leah traveled for her Zionist work, and Jessie missed her when she was gone: "Leah went to Egypt for two weeks on business, and of course I missed her very much. Not that I was lonely, for I don't object to being alone and I had more than enough company, but I missed her. We are very happy in our cos[y] little home, and Leah was glad to get back too."[88] Jessie explained that she wasn't lonely—it wasn't that she just needed someone around—it was that she missed Leah in particular and their domestic life together.

Yet she was also proud of Leah's work. In a 1936 article, she recounted Leah's work before the two knew each other:

When all the Jews of Palestine who were subjects of allied countries—that meant, chiefly Russians—were banished from Palestine by the Turks, an American battleship carried hundreds to Egypt, where they spent two years in concentration camps, until they could return under the protection of the British flag. On that battleship, a woman, one of the exiles, was seen organizing the people, feeding and caring for their children. When they arrived in Alexandria, the British officers there turned to this woman to ask her to continue her activity. She was Leah Berlin, trained in public work through long years of activity as a Russian revolutionist.[89]

After returning to Palestine, Leah continued her work running factories to train girls and women, which also included trips back to Egypt to order materials. British barracks and hospitals became steady customers. Jessie described her: "Leah looked business-like, in her simple straight dress, a black braid folded like an epaulette over each ear. She had the carriage and the manner of an officer."[90] Jessie also admired the difference that Leah made: many of these young women had been homeless and ashamed, and Leah taught them skills and the dignity of work.

Jessie's partnership with Leah even made her disability seem less disabling. Of course, for many reasons, living with a friend would certainly be less disabling for a person with post-polio syndrome, fatigue, and spine and hand issues. But Leah's presence went beyond that: it also made Jessie's disability less emotionally disabling. Sampter's writings from the previous decade had described feelings that today we would characterize as depression, physical and emotional feelings for which she sought medical help. In her unpublished autobiography, she wrestled with describing her disability and its implications for her professional and philanthropic work. She edited the tenses, never quite sure how to represent her disabled body in time. And yet as soon as she transitioned to discussing her life with Leah, verbs became present tense, and the editing stopped: "I cannot could not work. Life was never ^before so empty of service, personal or communal, for I am was weak and often still ill. But is it not enough to live pleasantly? To have a friendly, simple and pretty home in our own land? To make a home for [Leah], harassed by the uncertainty of existence in her own workshop from day to day?"[91] Partnership, supporting Leah and being supported by her and having a home together in "our own land," gave her meaning. This may have been a queer kind of homemaking, but Jessie and Leah certainly made a home.

In addition to their queer kinship, Leah and Jessie's more conventional kin also mattered in their lives, sometimes as support networks and sometimes as complications. When Leah's father died, her mother and twin brother and sister, who still lived in Russia, decided to move to Palestine. Jessie wrote to Elvie, "She used to be jealous of my letters, but now I will be the jealous one."[92] Later she reflected, "Since our life together, I had often refrained from speaking to [Leah] of my letters from Sister, because I noticed that my pleasure in them made her sad, but now I said to her, I could be the envious one. My family would never come."[93]

Leah sensed Jessie's sadness and reassured her that she *would* have a family in Palestine: "You are going to stay with us," Jessie recalled Leah saying. "You will love my good old mother, and I know she will love you. You will be in my family."[94] Leah's mother, brother, and sister planned to make the trip via Egypt, and so when Leah left to buy goods in Egypt for work, she also planned to meet her brother and sister there. "When she kissed me goodbye," Jessie recalled, "she said: 'I hope to come back to you in two weeks with a brother and sister.'" Other friends, recognizing what a change this would be for Jessie, supported her while Leah was gone: "My friends, knowing [Leah] to be away, came to visit."[95] But Leah's brother and sister made the journey more quickly than they had expected, and they wound up arriving in Palestine the day before Leah returned. Jessie welcomed them into their home and wrote to Leah: "'I love your sister already more than I do you,' I say to Leah. She is not jealous. She laughs."[96]

But Leah's homecoming the following day was dampened by Jessie's illness: "The afternoon Leah returned, I fell ill with fever, to her annoyance and my own, as we wished to move in two days. . . . [S]o happy was Leah in her new-found children [her brother and sister], who told her long sagas in Russian, that I hardly noted how my head was throbbing in the midst of the confusion and Babel. I relished her joy and was unaware of my pain."[97] Although Jessie had a fever, aches, and weakness, Leah's presence made Jessie physically feel better. At least, she wrote, she did not feel the pain.

While Leah tended to her sister's recovery in the spring of 1923, Jessie took care of all of Leah's affairs.[98] And in many of her letters, life after Leah's mother and siblings arrived sounded very much like life before. "The rest of our cooking [apart from the dinners they had sent in] we—chiefly Leah—do ourselves," Jessie wrote.[99] Leah brought her new handkerchiefs from Egypt, and Jessie wrote to her sister requesting underwear for them both: "I'll write to you about my winter underwear which I cannot get here.

Leah wants some too, and I want to measure her."[100] She put in an order, complete with measurements, in the next letter to her sister.

The arrival of Leah's siblings and later her mother made Jessie more aware of her illness and disability, but it did not stop Leah from caring for her. At Passover, Leah hosted a seder, much to Jessie's joy: "A seder in my own home, for the first time in my life. Leah has taken this trouble chiefly because she knew it would be impossible for me to go out."[101] Jessie did sometimes feel left out. Life wasn't always easy. "Fact is, I should never live with Leah's mother except for Leah's sake," Jessie wrote to Elvie on one of her crankier days.[102]

Even on the toughest days for their relationship, Jessie continued to reject more traditional alternatives. She wrote, "Suppose I could find the friend—man to marry me—an absurd hope—would it be worthwhile?" She vehemently dismissed the idea: "I should rather die, as a solution."[103] Though Jessie did not want to give up on their domestic arrangement, she was still ill and was suffering from serious depression. In 1924 she wrote about a dream she had about a rose begonia plant. She saw the plant as a metaphor for her shared life with Leah, and in the dream Jessie's half was dying. As she contemplated leaving Palestine for medical treatment in the United States, she worried about her relationship with Leah: "Our rose begonia is dying, and I do not know what ails it."[104] She soon made the trip to the United States, in the hopes that psychiatric care would help her depression.

Jessie returned to Palestine the following year, and soon after, her family changed again: she adopted a Yemenite orphan, whom she named Tamar. Since her arrival in Jerusalem, Jessie had been engaged with Jewish Yemenite communities in Palestine: she had advocated for more educational opportunities, often helped out at the orphanage, and, along with Sophie Berger, had created a group of girl scouts "with a nucleus of 11 girls from the orphanage."[105] During a 1922 illness, the children came to visit her and brought her flowers. Later that year, after her return from the United States, Jessie began to consider adopting a girl from the orphanage. "The other day, I saw a little girl, in whom I am going to interest myself—(with a view to adoption?). She is a darling, with dark curls and big appealing black eyes."[106] Sampter's kinship crossed not only ethnic bounds but also lines of privilege when she adopted Tamar. In fact, many Jews imagined that Yemenites were a less civilized people in need of uplift. A generation later, the new Israeli government would take this to an extreme by taking newly arrived Yemenite children who were ill to the hospital, away from their families, and sometimes not returning them. They explained that the children had died. And often they had. But there was also more to the story: doctors had performed medical experiments on some children, and other children may have even been adopted out to Jewish families in the United States or Holocaust survivors in Israel.[107] Even today, many Yemenite Jews wonder if children they thought had died were actually either subjected to medical experiments or adopted out to other families. Sampter adopted Tamar decades before this, but it shows how many Zionists (and later Israelis) saw the differences between Ashkenazi Jews (those including Germans and eastern Europeans) and Yemenite Jews.

Tamar moved in with Jessie and quickly became part of the family. In 1924 Jessie decided that the two of them should live in Rehovot, a small settlement with a population of about two thousand about twelve miles south of Tel Aviv. Jessie wrote to a friend about laying the cornerstone for their house: "When I say 'we' I mean Tamar and I."[108] Educating Tamar and seeing her grow up in Palestine brought Jessie happiness. In 1931 Jessie took Tamar on a trip to the United States, where she met Elvie, along with a host of Jessie's friends and associates. When her cousin Rex had fallen ill with tuberculosis in the 1910s, she wrote that she would happily care for his favorite little brother, Ronald. Then she wrote elliptically, with three enigmatic dashes, "Ronald should be as my child; he should grow up--- differently."[109] She knew that Tamar was not getting a "normal" upbringing, but Sampter felt that she could educate and raise her better than just normal.

Even once Jessie adopted Tamar, and Jessie and Leah lived apart, it was a rare month that the two women didn't see each other. For example, in May 1927 Leah threw a party in Jessie's honor and gave a loving speech about her.[110] The next month Jessie wrote of the "beautiful Turkish vase that Leah gave me."[111] When she went to meet her friend and fellow Zionist Irma Levy Lindheim in Jerusalem at the end of that summer, she stayed with Leah, who still lived in the city.[112] She wrote letters to her sister from Leah's room, stayed with Leah while Tamar had an elbow operation ("I sleep in Leah's room with her," she explained), and planned visits to Jerusalem around Leah's schedule ("Leah Berlin's going on a vacation later, and I like to go to Jerusalem while she is there").[113] When Leah was working in Tel Aviv, Jessie wrote, "I am staying in her room with her, where there is a large couch besides the bed."[114] Leah also visited Jessie frequently, sometimes spending her two-week vacation at Jessie's home.[115] In 1931, after Leah went to the Zionist congress hosted in Basel, she stayed with Jessie for a while. "She has not decided on her future work. It may keep her near here," Jessie wrote to her sister hopefully.[116]

During these years, Leah also cared for Tamar on occasion and visited her when Tamar began to attend school in Tel Aviv. In September 1931 Tamar stayed with Leah, and then Jessie and Tamar spent all of the fall holiday of Sukkot there.[117] Leah especially cared for Tamar when Jessie was unable. "When Tamar wrote to me of this [the school would not allow children to leave overnight because of an outbreak of whooping cough, scarlet fever, or measles at the school], Leah went at once to see what was what," Jessie explained to her sister.[118] (It turned out to be diphtheria, and Tamar did not have it.)

Perhaps predictably, Jessie and Leah did not live apart forever. In January 1933 Jessie reported to her sister that she and Leah had made a big decision.[119] "Leah and I like being together again," she reported in her next letter.[120] They would live together from that moment until Jessie's death, though it would be several more years until their plans came to fruition.

Jessie did not share her plans with her sister initially, but she wrote to her about the money that Elvie's husband managed for Jessie. "I may want to invest the money very soon, in a few months, in the work that Leah and I want to do together. I almost wrote 'to live together,'" she told her sister. She declined to discuss her "plans—shall I say dreams?—that may be revised several times before they are carried out," but if Elvie knew her sister at all, she would know that it was a plan to make a Zionist contribution to Palestine.[121]

The plans, though they certainly did undergo revisions, were to create a Zionist rest home for workers located at Kibbutz Givat Brenner. But designing and building it took what seemed like forever. "Leah and I are both sleeping outdoors now," she wrote one week.[122] They stayed with Leah's family in Tel Aviv for the next month.[123] When they moved onto the kibbutz, she wrote that she and Leah were sharing a room. "In the Rest Home I shall have my own room. I don't like sharing a room permanently. I have a deep conviction that every human being—married or single—should have a room of his own, and on the whole this very deep conviction is very deeply shared by most of our comrades, and, with three in a tent, our dream is, a single room for each member."[124] Her conviction about having her own room, then, was about individuality rather than about a fizzling partnership with Leah. Evidently her brother-in-law thought she was protesting too much and predicted that the two would continue to share a room. In response to his prediction and his reminders of the perks of sharing with Leah, she wrote, "I'm still rooming with Leah but expect a change soon, despite your prognostication, Edgar, Sr. And you're right about the compensations."[125] The two women still shared both intellectual and intimate aspects of their lives; when Jessie traveled, for example, she asked her sister to send her letters to Leah.[126] If Elvie's package for the two didn't arrive in time, Jessie would share her stockings with Leah. They provided aesthetic advice for each other too: "Leah advises me not to send the 'solo' picture, which she says is very bad, but to have another made."[127] Jessie also felt something was lacking while Leah was gone. She explained of their rest home project during one of Leah's trips, "It goes perfectly well without Leah, but it needs Leah!"[128]

When I spent time at the Givat Brenner archives, I asked one of the members of the kibbutz what she thought about Jessie's relationship with Leah. "Ah!" she said. "Let me find this for you." And she set to looking through old documents. She couldn't know anything for sure, she explained, but a few years earlier, when they did a retrospective for the kibbutz's seventieth anniversary, they looked at all the plans for kibbutz buildings. As she showed me the architectural drawings, she pointed out two small bedrooms: "And the original plans for the rest house had Jessie's room at one end . . . and Leah's room at the farthest opposite corner!" she told me. She and other kibbutz members suspected this was because there was gossip about their relationship, and so Jessie and Leah made sure that they would have two rooms and that they were as far away from each other as possible. I wouldn't have arrived at this conclusion on my own from just looking at the architectural plans, but the way she explained it helped me see that on the kibbutz, both then and now, Jessie and Leah were partners. They weren't the only women on the kibbutz who never married, another kibbutz member explained to me, but they enjoyed a special relationship with one another.

As the kibbutz members of their time told it, Jessie and Leah were opposites—one a frail and spoiled woman from New York, the other a big, practical woman from Russia.[129] And like many relationships of opposites, they seemed to do very well together. Jessie's writing shows this too. Jessie was quite serious and, to be frank, often rather humorless. And yet when she lived with Leah, she was more lighthearted and even occasionally funny. "Sister, dear, many, many thanks again for all your gifts packed into the magician's hat—I mean suitcase," she wrote when her sister sent gifts for her and Leah.[130] Both Jessie and Leah needed teeth pulled, "so we went on the spree together," she wrote to her sister about their visit to the dentist.[131] A guest who spent an awfully long time arranging a salad became "the salad artist," in a nearly unheard-of moment of Sampter's snark.[132] "Leah is very well, too, and we are as happy as this crazy world and its newspapers will permit us to be," she wrote amid the growing international political turmoil in 1936.[133]

When Jessie died, Leah wrote to Elvie. She apologized for her letter, written only "as good as I can" because "my English secretary, my dearest, dearest friend left me forever and so suddenly." She recounted their last days together and also remembered their entwined lives for Elvie: "I don't know if you know what Jessie was to me. For the last seven years we have been all the time together. I did nothing without consulting her and so did she. I have three sisters in Tel Aviv but she was more to me than my sisters, she was a dear friend, such a friend you have only once in life. We are of the same age and I did not expect that she will leave me so soon."[134]

Queer Kinship and Zionist Ideals

Sampter's queer kinship and queer desire extended beyond her personal life, beyond Leah, and beyond Tamar. They also shaped her Zionism. Although the next chapter covers her Zionism more fully, queer kinship plays a role in the contours of that Zionism, so it is also a part of her queer story. As her months and then years in Palestine ticked by, her Zionist poetry, correspondence, and journalism began to focus more on physical labor and collective work. The main character of her short story "Plow Deep," published in the Menorah journal, found her true love in collective farming, after being jilted by a lover and contemplating suicide. "I love my land. That is why I came. I shall love it, I shall work for it always. O my land, my land! You are myself, my body."[135]

Though this was Sampter's Zionist ideal, it was not a Zionism in which Sampter could participate fully. "I did not come to Palestine to build houses," she wrote in 1923, "but to see and to tell the truth, that those who know how to do may know what to do."[136] She would have to continue her role as a literary pioneer rather than a physical nation-building pioneer. Sometimes, though, she wrote as if she had forgotten the particulars of her own body in favor of offering a (seemingly) more universal model. She wrote to Elvie, "The question Zionism poses is simply this: Do you want to live a healthy, normal, free life in Palestine? Or, if you do not, do you want a section of the Jewish people to have a chance to do it?"[137] Sampter accurately described much Zionist ideology: the settlement of Palestine would help create healthy, "normal," and free Jewish bodies. Sampter herself, however, was never healthy in the way this ideology imagined, nor did her life fit within the bounds of the normal, in which marriage and reproduction figure as main life events. But still she wrote as though it were self-evident that every Jew should want these things, if not for herself, at least for others.

In 1925 Sampter took a prolonged tour of the Emek (the Hebrew term for the Jezreel Valley) sponsored by the Jewish National Fund. Inspired by that trip, she published *The Emek*, a book of poems that painted intimate portraits of the men and women workers and their relationship with the land. The images that accompanied the poem, woodcuts by the American Zionist Maxim Gottlieb, showed muscular men plowing, robust women working, and fertile lands. And yet despite these typical Zionist images, the poems in *The Emek* queered not only abstract or ideal notions of what family and gender might look like but also intimate portraits of what gendered social life did look like, at least through Sampter's eyes. "Regeneration" celebrates "the lone woman farmer of Nahalal," whom Sampter describes as "roughing and tramping it, fearless yet careful." And though Regeneration is alone and without children, "she is creating, she is bringing forth."[138] Regeneration became a creator not through reproduction but through the Zionist ideal of bringing forth sustenance from the land. Other poems celebrated the disruption of gender norms in less explicitly Zionist ways.

'I think that boys,' she says, 'should be given dolls
That they may get the parent-instinct too, As well as girls,

one kibbutznik says in a prose poem.[139] In Sampter's description of an idyllic kibbutz nursery, a girl hammers while a boy washes.[140] Her writing echoed these ideas before and after her trip, but it was in these poems that it became tied so closely to a location and a socialist Zionist way of life.

The valley, through Sampter's eyes, was also a place where sexuality was not so tightly confined by the social norms she assumed her readers had.

Where there is hard working and hard living
There is hard loving. And love is not fenced with the thorns
that make it forbidden fruit.[141]

Fittingly, when her poems were published as *The Emek*, it was Leah who lovingly did the legwork of sending it to stores, shipping copies to people, and promoting it to others. On her tour of the Jezreel Valley, Sampter seemed to imagine that kibbutz life could be a space for realizing the possibilities of queer kinship—true Zionist social groups should not be governed, she thought, by the same norms of gender, sexuality, or kinship that she saw elsewhere.

Throughout her life, Sampter thought that men and women could be friends. On her relationship with her longtime Zionist friend Ben Shlomo, she wrote to her sister, "We have not the slightest intention or inclination to fall in love with each other. We have a strong common interest."[142] For a year, he lived in the "hut" on her property, and the two spent long hours reading and talking politics and philosophy. Jessie and Ben Shlomo clearly had a close and special relationship. As I read her descriptions of him in her letters, I wondered if their intellectual intimacy was not also physical. Yet when he decided not to take a faraway job in part to remain near her, she insisted there was nothing romantic between them.[143] She refused to help others gossip, she explained matter-of-factly.

Traditional family arrangements might be customary, she thought, but that didn't mean that they were best for either the adults or the children. "I questioned monogamy as an institution," she wrote in the early 1920s.[144] She continued to think this way until the end of her life. "The important thing for children is that their parents should love each other and be happy together, not that they should have a marriage certificate. . . . The word 'bastard' sounds to me as obsolete as 'dastard,' and the idea is going out of date too," she wrote to Elvie in 1929.[145]

Similar critiques had come from socialist feminists, like the nineteenth-century suffragist Victoria Woodhull, who championed "free love"—not quite in the 1960s sense but in the sense of being allowed to marry, divorce, and bear children, or not, all without government involvement. In an 1871 speech, Woodhull declared, "Yes, I am a Free Lover. I have an inalienable, constitutional and natural right to love whom I may, to love as long or as short a period as I can; to change that love every day if I please, and with that right neither you nor any law you can frame have any right to interfere."[146] Sampter's public writing was less polemical than Woodhull's, but the two shared a sense that the institution of marriage was far too rigid and held too much power in the societies around them.

Collective living, with its different expectations of family and sexuality, appealed to Sampter. And so it made sense when Leah proposed that they move together to a kibbutz.

As was typical of kibbutzim, at Givat Brenner Sampter was asked to work according to her capabilities. Some kibbutz members felt that these limited work demands allowed Sampter to keep a more rose-colored vision of Zionism. Jessie did not experience kibbutz life primarily through the grind of physical labor or as a practical collective that made others feel like "cogs in the machine," as one of her friends wrote.[147] She would sometimes help make clothing, but she spent most of her time writing poems and essays. She was the organizing personality behind the daily kibbutz newsletter and quickly garnered a reputation as an intellectual.[148]

She published an article titled "Married Women in Kevutzot," which was translated and republished in English, Hebrew, and even Hungarian.[149] It described gender roles in collective living arrangements, such as kibbutzim and kvutzot, where the members had rejected the familiar model of one household for each nuclear family. "Individualistic homing," she explained, was an "old habit"—that is, a cultural rather than a natural way of living—"and the Palestinian working woman who has the strength to overcome it lives a freer, richer life, does more work and has more time than the farmer's wife" in a traditional arrangement.[150] In kvutzot, she explained, women and men work equal hours and spend equal time tending to children, who are reared more communally, usually in "children's houses" rather than with their parents. "We are pioneering not only on the land but in the kitchen and the nursery, on the frontier of new ways of living together, as men and women."[151]

In her 1937 article in the *Reconstructionist*, Sampter described the way sexual coupling at kibbutzim worked: "In sex as in religion, personal freedom is complete, except as it threatens the freedom of another, and the only coercion is that of public opinion, which is strong but takes no measures except gossip. Official marriage is not required or considered necessary, but most couples eventually marry. A couple asks for a room or a tent together, and the moving in is celebrated with flowers, goodies and a reception. Couples do not ask for a room until their relation presages permanence, for changes have unpleasant consequences in the form of gossip."[152] It was not just her kibbutz, or even the kibbutzim in the Jezreel Valley, that would reconfigure sexual and social life: Sampter saw in Zionism the necessity to revise the idea of family. Zionism required the queering of kinship ideals well beyond her own life. Sampter claimed that nuclear families were conventional but neither natural nor the most ethical form of relationship. In a *Reconstructionist* article, Sampter challenged Mordecai Kaplan's Zionism on similar grounds: "Is Dr. Kaplan's idea of civilization as fluid as all that? Accepting Socialism as the only type of organization compatible with our Jewish social values, is he ready to face a new setting of the family which will inevitably follow when couples are no longer economically dependent upon each other, when the family is no longer a cooperative economic unit?"[153] Although she admired Kaplan and was even publishing in his movement's journal, she suggested that his Zionism did not reach the true ideal of Zionism, in which a rearrangement of economics would also mean a rearrangement of kinship that no longer privileged the heterosexual couple. Three years earlier, as a response to his discussion of the American family in *Judaism as a Civilization: Toward a Reconstruction of American Jewish Life*, Sampter had written to Kaplan, "The family, as understood today, is doomed. It is nothing but an ingrown cluster of selfishness." It was inefficient (why must every apartment have its own separate kitchen and laundry?), unethical (it teaches selfishness and insularity), and organized around sexist principles ("The patriarchal unit has long lost its cogency, and rightly so"). "The unit today ought to be a revolutionary group," she wrote, perhaps echoing Leah's revolutionary politics.[154]

She saw gender as closely related to politics both in Palestine and abroad. As the 1930s wore on and the situation for Jews in Europe became worse, Sampter wished she could do more to help. She wrote to her sister, "If men could be legalized by marrying citizens, I should marry at once, and even make an attempt to practice polyandry. You surely never suspected you had such a wicked sister."[155]

Kibbutz life, however, was not always an idyllic place of gender flexibility. She had expressed her displeasure when women had to cook instead of work the fields:

It's a pity
The girls who cook had learnt no skill abroad
Hard to cook in huge cauldrons for a hundred
With nothing good to choose from, and a longing
To plow and plant the earth.[156]

During the Arab Revolt in 1936, she wrote, "Shall half the community protect the other half? Shall half lie on the floor while the other half is facing shots? What will our children say? What will our daughters say when they grow up and are differentiated from the little boys with whom they now share everything?"[157] "Married Women in Kevutzot" lamented that fewer women than men entered leadership positions and that women often voted for men rather than other women during these elections. Yet she was hopeful for the future: "The younger the group, the more active the women are in public affairs," and so the next generation would do better.[158] A kibbutz was a place where traditional gender roles should not be followed, Sampter insisted, but it would often be a struggle to live up to those ideals.

This struggle also raises the question of what it would mean to queer or crip a political movement like Zionism. Does it count only if there are no traces left of what is normative? What makes it a success or a failure? It seems to me that no political project can ever fully buck normativity—or, put another way, nothing is ever 100 percent queered or cripped. And if every queer or crip project is an incompletely queered or cripped one, then Sampter's work exists on that spectrum, but there is always more work to do.

Conclusion

There's something queer about religious desire. "Religion often appears 'queer' when looked at sideways," Elizabeth Dolfi, a scholar of religion and sexuality, writes.[159] Many of today's evangelical Christian men ask Jesus to "come into me"; they sing songs like "He Touched Me" and "Your Love Is Extravagant," the latter of which includes the lyrics:

> Your love is extravagant
> Your friendship, it is intimate
> I feel like moving to the rhythm of Your grace
> Your fragrance is intoxicating in our secret place.[160]

Medieval mystics see themselves sucking on Jesus's wounds—wounds that are often vagina-like in their imagery. Kabbalists fill themselves with divine seed, in Jewish mystical imagery, and scholars see Kabbalah as "a total language of feminine erotics," a place of homoerotic relationship of the male student to God and a place of gender-bending sexual fluidity.[161]

Perhaps there can also be something religious about queer desire. Sampter's visions of a Jewish society based on queer kinships, like what she hoped the kibbutz would be, resonated with her religious worldview in which all beings were profoundly connected. Her desire to have kinship and family beyond the bounds of one man, one woman, and their biological children reflected her theological sense of the oneness of humanity and the divine: if everyone is fundamentally connected, an insistence on nuclear families is merely conventional. It is also limiting. Having social, even familial, intimacies that were not tied to biology reflected the greater theological truth of oneness.

On a more theoretical level, queer theory and scholars in religious studies offer overlapping ideas about what it means to be a person, a self. Neither claims that a person is an autonomous self, a pure agent going through the world making whatever decisions he deems best. Instead, they see selves as dependent, always in relationship with other selves, and shaped by forces beyond their control.

Sampter's queer story is not just about sex, then; it's also about both disability and religion. Though sex plays a role in the story, queer desire and queer kinship point toward a broader category of queerness, in which queerness is about defying gender and family norms. Heterosexual courtship, marriage, and reproduction did not mark the turning points of Sampter's life, but her life was still profoundly relational. Intellectual intimacy, engaged philanthropy, illness, caring and being cared for—these structured her days. Her relationships with Nora, Leah, Josephine Lazarus, and even Ben Shlomo defied the expectations of how family and intimacy worked. Sampter's queerness disturbed the "normal" timeline and replaced it with the different relationships of queer time.

In *The Seekers*, one of Sampter's students used the language of queerness to try to make sense of brilliance: "Geniuses are often queer," said Henry. Sampter replied, "What we usually call genius is but a larger power of understanding, a sense of duty, of the relations of things."[162] Sampter framed Henry's question of queerness not in terms of sexuality but in more general terms of defying the norms of perception. Queerness might be odd and abnormal, but it also meant being able to see things differently. "We all have that, in some degree," she said. "So we all have genius. It is not a matter of quality but of quantity." In Sampter's eyes, all people had seeds of genius—and queerness—and that was something to cultivate.

CHAPTER FOUR

A Theological-Political Life

"I preach labor, with limp hands," Jessie Sampter wrote from her home in Palestine.[1] How queer, for a disabled woman to champion an ideology that promoted manual production and sexual reproduction. But Sampter's Zionism never quite toed a party line. To do so would have been challenging in any case, given the variety of positions that different Zionists held: there were labor Zionists, political Zionists, cultural Zionists, and religious Zionists, and dozens of ideological disputes divided even these groups. Sampter brought her own queerness to Zionism—and she also subtly tried to bring Zionism to queerness, not in the sense that she actively promoted same-sex sexuality (she didn't) but in the sense that she challenged its gendered, religious, and political inclinations.

This chapter tells Sampter's life as a political-theological story—a narrative about how someone could simultaneously espouse nationalism and internationalism, pacifism and state building, Zionism and democracy, gender ideals and the reality of inequality, and about how she could make sense of the gaps between the ideal and the real. Just to take one example, when Sampter arrived in Palestine, Arab non-Jews outnumbered Jews there (somewhere between five to one and ten to one, depending on who was counting and where). So if Zionists were really in favor of democracy, as almost all Zionists claimed to be, how could they reconcile the demographic reality that any democratic movement would go against the creation of a Jewish state? How could Sampter be both for Zionism and for democracy?

These gaps between the ideal and the real are part of the human condition. When Sampter sought to understand and then deal with these gaps, she had the same set of options available to all of us: pretend there is no gap, claim that the gap is mere illusion, adjust your ideal to match the real, or work to change the real to match your ideal. She did a little bit of each. When she worked to change the real, she also worked to challenge the norms that made social ideals as she saw them. She queered Zionism when she praised nonnuclear families and living arrangements. Disability activists give the name *cripping* to the process of upending bodily norms; Sampter did this too, such as when she wrote the short story "Bed Number Six," which featured a weak, chronically ill Zionist stuck in a hospital. Although her Zionism never became fully queered or fully cripped—there is always more work to be done—she wrestled with the gaps between the real and the ideal until the end of her life.

To tell Sampter's life as the story of a Zionist thinker is to attend to her own voice. But it is also to attend to a road not taken. In spite of her prodigious writing and her famous associates, Sampter did not become a prominent Zionist icon. Israel has no major street named after her as it does for her fellow Americans Henrietta Szold and Judah Magnes. Today's Zionists rarely cite Sampter, and all of her books are out of print. But in the breadth and depth of her writing, she rivals many male Jewish thinkers of her time, and she was clearly in conversation with many now-canonical authors. Perhaps most important, to tell Sampter's life as a political life shows how embodiment can matter profoundly for political and religious writing.

Scholars who study modern Jewish philosophy have very little to say about thinkers' bodies. Jessie Sampter's hands were limp. But what about the Jewish philosopher Benedict de Spinoza? What were his hands like? His back? His face? Students in Jewish studies hear that the thinker Moses Mendelssohn had a hunchback—and at least one scholar has theorized why this matters to his thought about aesthetics.[2] But what about Hermann Cohen or Martin Buber? What were their bodies like? The assumption is that bodies matter only when they are disabled, or when they are different. I see a close parallel to the field's gendered assumptions, under which it matters for scholars trying to understand their philosophies that Hannah Arendt was a woman but not that Emmanuel Levinas was a man.

Our bodies are not just sacks of meat and bone designed to carry around our thoughts. Our brains need our bodies—and, in fact, they are *part of* our bodies. Our bodies are the way we experience the world, whether we are men or women, able-bodied or not. At times, Jewish philosophy has pushed against mind-body dualism, especially a dualism in which the mind takes priority over the body.[3] Theologies in which the body is inherently sinful while the mind or soul can be purified are more commonly Christian than

Sampter at Kibbutz Givat Brenner, 1930s. Courtesy of Givat Brenner Archives, Yesha Sampter papers.

Jewish. From either a scientific or a Jewish theological perspective, then, we should see the mind and the body as intimately related, dependent, and intertwined. Sampter's story shows us that to understand Jewish thought more fully, we must also pay attention to thinkers' bodies.

Paying attention to Sampter's body has been a key part of my quest to understand her. And part of that meant paying attention to my own body, even when I was doing the seemingly physically uninteresting work of writing itself. I'd ask myself, On which days can I write well or a lot? When does my back hurt? How is my writing different when I'm exhausted? And beyond that: which conversations, events, and relationships from my life affect my writing? Like other scholars, I was already attuned to how public, political affairs of the day might affect a person's philosophy. But I also learned so much more when I considered when Sampter or those around her were aging, full of energy, fatigued, or injured. Or feeling lonely, inspired, expectant, or frustrated. I asked myself what it *felt* like to be in Jerusalem,

Rehovot, and Givat Brenner—and what it meant that those places felt like home to Sampter. In a political sense, yes, but in an emotional and physical sense too. Those were never separable for her. For me, either.

Path to Zionism: Universalism and Particularism

Writing about Zionism today is complicated, to say the least. What gets called Zionism before 1948 is very different from what gets called Zionism after that. (In fact, as a writer, I rarely use "Zionism" to describe movements after 1948; I prefer "support for the State of Israel" or "support for Israel as a Jewish state" because they are more specific and descriptive.) Sampter lived in a time when Zionism meant support for Jews as a "nation," but almost all the details were contested, not only from without, but also from within. Some insisted that the goal was a nation-state, while others did not. Some emphasized the need for territory (whether it was in Palestine or East Africa, as Theodor Herzl once advocated), some prioritized revitalizing the Hebrew language and Jewish culture, and some wanted to focus on building a Jewish civil and economic society. Some, like Sampter, wanted to make sure that both Jewish and non-Jewish Arab cultures flourished side by side. Others did not.

We now have the benefit, or the curse, of knowing how some of these things turned out. Yet Sampter and her story remind us that Zionism once encompassed many alternatives. The history we know was not inevitable. Nor is the future.

This isn't a book about whether Zionism is good or what Zionism should look like. But it is a book about the sort of Zionism that Jessie Sampter thought was best. And perhaps it can be a book that makes you think newly about today's Zionism and its relationship to the past.

Sampter never wrote her own life as a story about religion, queerness, or disability. But she did write her life as a Zionist story. The year before she died, she penned a two-part article in the *Reconstructionist*. Her friend and teacher Mordecai Kaplan had founded the journal as part of the new movement called Reconstructionist Judaism, which conceived of Judaism "as a civilization" and endorsed Zionism.[4] Though Sampter, then living in Palestine, did not identify herself as part of his movement, she and Kaplan shared many political and religious positions. He sent her his 1934 *Judaism as a Civilization* when it came out, and she found it "immensely stimulating," though she wrote, "I differ completely from you" about how to approach the question of the future of Jewishness.[5] She reminded him of "the importance of your teaching in shaping my thoughts in the early days of my return to my people," but she reflected on how much "live contact with the Jews of Palestine" and world events had changed her perspective. In response to an invitation from the *Reconstructionist*'s editor to write an article, she decided to write something different from the sorts of pieces she usually wrote for publication. Her writing so often described others, life in Palestine, and her Zionist and religious philosophies. But she rarely described her own life in publication. She probably sat at her typewriter in Kibbutz Givat Brenner, outside of Rehovot, from where she told a tale of her earliest years in the bustling metropolis of New York:

> I was born into a German-Jewish, third generation American upper middle class, well-to-do, completely assimilated, highly cultured bourgeois and individualistic family in New York City where *trefe* meat was eaten as often as three times a day, where Christmas trees and Easter eggs obliterated all traces of *Hanukkah* and *Passover*, whose prophet was not Moses but Darwin. My maternal grandfather on *Yom Kippur* and my paternal grandmother made fun of people who kept kosher. I am now a citizen of Palestine, a vegetarian. I am a member of a Socialist-Zionist commune of agricultural and industrial but highly cultured workers, the chief aim of whose rapidly growing and penurious settlement is to bring as many Jews as possible, as quickly as possible, to our ancient home land.[6]

When Sampter recounted the trajectory of her life in the *Reconstructionist*, she dramatized the events for effect. Though the details were truthful, her story sounded just like a conversion narrative: she once was lost but in Zionism was found.

This story of Jessie Sampter's life begins when she was seven, when, in her account, children on the street called her Jewish and her parents confirmed that it was true. As she explored Jewishness, Sampter grappled with an age-old question for Jews: Was Judaism about particularity—specialness and difference? Or was it about universality—a religion for all? If the essence of Judaism was specialness and difference, wasn't that chauvinism and even prejudice against non-Jews? In contrast, if Judaism were universal, why not proselytize and work for the whole human race to become Jewish? Although these questions remain perennial, Zionism helped Sampter make sense of her own answer: Jewish national character had something unique to contribute to the overall project of humanity. "We are a religious nation. It is our mission as a nation to teach, or show, righteousness and justice to the nations," she wrote. "Our religion is universal. But being human, it must have a dwelling place in the heart and hearth of a people."[7] Zionism was the promotion of this unique national character, including Jewish history, literature, morals, and customs—what we might call *culture*. Sampter's Zionism, then, did not proclaim Jewish superiority, but it did claim Jewish distinctiveness. Just like the Irish or the Chinese, she thought, Jews had something special that should be nurtured.

She credited her conversations with her Russian immigrant friend Hyman Segal with lighting the sparks of her Zionism; his work made her feel "as if a door had been opened to her."[8] His poetry in *The Book of Pain-Struggle, Called: The Prophecy of Fulfillment* tells of a hero who lives in spiritual and physical worlds marked by pain and struggle. "In the beginning there was pain, pain, pain," begins one poem.[9] The hero finds himself in the desert, a setting where "the Strugglers of olden, the Painmen of my people . . . grew to manhood, Saw their visions."[10] After finding an ancient parchment, he hears a voice that says,

> The land
> Languisheth without its own people
> And man without his ancient faith.[11]

Segal's description of the spiritual and physical worlds as sites of pain but also of belonging and unity resonated deeply with Sampter.

Part of this resonating may have been the way that *The Book of Pain-Struggle* cripped Zionism. Rather than offering Zionism as a balm for Jewish suffering, Segal's work posited that chronic pain and suffering were fundamental to Zionism—and they were fundamental to Zionism because they are fundamental to the human condition. Its hero declared,

> I am of a Chosen People. . . . From the right hand of our Lord
> Runs a law of Pain and Struggle.[12]

And though he called this God "our Lord," it was the God of all:

> Pain is all, all is Pain. . . .
> All's alive with Pain. . . .
> Lo, the laws of the universe
> Show the ways that it always
> Responds to the pain of God, for Pain-Struggle is God![13]

Those who were "pain-lacking!" did not have truth or beauty, nor could they accomplish the divinely ordained quest of the pain-saturated hero.[14]

This Zionism took bodily (as well as spiritual) pain as its baseline, and only from that pain could the Zionist hero pursue his quest. Bodily wholeness and comfort could not give rise to the prophecy nor its fulfillment. Though religion was part of Sampter's path to Zionism, then, her chronic pain was another part.

Sampter could also have read Segal's poetry as that of a religious recombiner, given the possibility of reading Christological themes in it. The hero declared, "The Lord came to me in Pain-Struggle" and bellowed,

> I sought thee
> that thou bring that faith to mankind![15]

Completion of the hero's quest did not mean an end to the pain; it merely meant that the "pain-man" could help others see that pain was the source of all human thought and action. Sampter was not the only one to notice the way Segal had upended Zionism's traditional relationship to suffering. When the *New Catholic World* reviewed Segal's subsequent book, *The Law of Struggle*, the reviewer was appalled, perhaps because of the idea that a Jew other than Jesus could live a life of redemptive suffering on behalf of the human race.[16] (Although Segal's book could be read as engaged in cripping and religious recombination, it surely was not in the business of queering Zionism: throughout the hero's life, appealing girls and women appeared beside him, from the "little dark-eyed girl" companion of his boyhood to the "nobly-hipped and tall, and lithesome as a flame," host in the Land of Beauty.[17])

Segal helped bring Sampter into the world of American Zionism. He took her to Cooper Union to hear speeches in Yiddish and Hebrew, neither of which she understood very well. And yet the visit made a strong impression on her. The Hebrew lecturer was, she recalled, "a visiting Palestinian Jew. The speaker had a fine physique, a commanding brown beard that shadowed the coarseness of his features; but he was not a person; he was a symbol, as much a symbol as the white and blue Jewish flags that hung about the hall."[18] Sampter's description of the man leaves little doubt as to the gendered nature of Zionism: it exalted healthy male bodies that worked the land. Sampter, of course, did not have such a body, so she would have to engage with Zionism in other ways.

Her first experiences with Zionism kindled within her a feeling of profound kinship with other Jews. "The Jewish people: I realized the Jewish people," she wrote. "I have a people, a congregation. It is not in the church or the synagogue. It is in the streets, in the tenements, in the crowded pale of Russia and Poland, in the little agricultural settlements in Palestine. It is my people, a chosen people. God has called it, has chosen it for suffering and service. The God that is in me is also in my people."[19] Jewish people had spiritual and material needs, which she shared. Although she felt this sense of spiritual kinship, she also felt a social distance from most other Jews. After all, many of her friends, acquaintances, and neighbors were non-Jews. In the years following her adoption of Zionism, she moved into a settlement house in Harlem "in a congested Jewish quarter" and later into a YWHA (Young Women's Hebrew Association), where she was closer to immigrant Jews than to the acculturated life she had known.[20]

She also described her commitment to Zionism with language and theology that she knew—and that language and theology was not only Jewish but also reminiscent of Christianity and Hinduism:

> It meant social salvation, for the Jews and through the Jews for mankind. The Jewish people has a social religious ideal, the socialist foundation but with a watch tower facing the stars; the divinity, the holiness of man because God is holy, the equality, the oneness of man because God is one. . . . For the scattered Jewish people they are only dreams, but in our own land, lived by a community, they will become a beacon to mankind, a Messiah to the world. The Jewish people is the Messianic people; it is crucified; by its sufferings the world shall be saved, and its resurrection in its own land shall give life to mankind.[21]

Jewish national culture should create an example of justice and morality on the earth, and Zionism was the path to allowing this Jewish national culture to flourish. That part was typical of other Zionist thinkers. But the language of the "oneness of man" because of the oneness of God—as well as her belief in the oneness of God with nature, which included humans—was not. In fact, it recalled a Hindu-like theology. With this understanding, Sampter wrote, "So Zionism became my religion, the Jewish people my congregation."[22]

Perhaps even more striking, the crucifixion of the Jews as the savior of all peoples used the themes of crucifixion and redemption in ways far more familiar to Christianity than Judaism. Similar to Segal's work, Sampter's Zionism cripped the norms of the Zionism she saw around her: in her view, Jews would suffer for the redemption of all humans. Sampter's writing made the Christological theme of pain and suffering for the sake of humanity's redemption even more prominent than in Segal's work. Like a crucified and resurrected Jesus, Jews would suffer physically to bring spiritual and ultimately political redemption to all peoples.

As Sampter immersed herself in Zionist networks, she also turned to Judaism. Segal introduced her to Henrietta Szold, who served as a guide to both Zionism and Judaism—Sampter sometimes attended a Conservative synagogue with Szold and her mother, Sophie. Sampter began meeting with the rabbi and philosopher Mordecai Kaplan, who, she said, taught her to read the Bible—to read the Bible in a new way, she must have meant, since she had read it many times before. His philosophy fascinated her, though she did not always agree. He "sought a revaluation of Jewish values in terms of social science not of metaphysical disputations" and convinced her that Jewish history should take its rightful place alongside theology in her Zionism. "His interpretation of religious history as a place with political and social history first gave me that unified outlook which makes of history the proper study for mankind. In one sense, all history is prophecy; history lives only by the use we make of its interpretation in meeting the future," she wrote.[23] Although Kaplan's Zionism was not always orthodox, it did center on the image of the "viril[e], self-perpetuating Jew" in Palestine.[24] Despite Kaplan's influence, Sampter's never did.

Kaplan hosted small intellectual salons in his home. There Sampter befriended fellow Zionists Lotta Levensohn and Alice Seligsberg, both of whom would remain conversation partners for many years.[25] She also came to know Horace Kallen, a philosopher who advocated for Zionist causes and promoted "cultural pluralism" as opposed to the "melting pot" as the ideal model for American society.[26] Through her relationships with these men and women, especially under the tutelage of "Miss Szold," as Sampter always referred to her, she came to espouse a Zionism that included a return to the land of Palestine. Rather than focusing exclusively on political nationalist ends, she saw Zionism as a spiritual means of cultivating the Jewish people that she now cherished so deeply.

Sampter's erudition and interest in pedagogy made her an asset to the young American Zionist movement, and Szold recognized her writing as a much-needed addition.[27] In 1913 Szold wrote to her new associate, "I am glad that you are going to write. You will serve Zionism best in that way. I believe it is what we need—good writers from whose work Zionism will radiate as a fine aroma."[28] The Zionist movement in the United States was still small; Sampter estimated it at twenty thousand people in 1914. Szold saw Sampter's work as a more serious contribution than the "brochures, the apologia, the party pamphlet, the disquisition" that had characterized the movement until then.[29] Nor was she just flattering Sampter: she wrote to Horace Kallen that the most important thing for American Zionists was "literature, literature, literature."[30] Sampter would provide a philosophically serious literature, which would be both literary in quality and convincing in its claims, Szold thought. And in this she proved right: although Sampter remained an active Zionist and prolific writer until her death, she never became an organizational advocate or a political figure.

In addition to her literary skills, Hadassah valued Sampter for her commitment to education. She founded the Hadassah School of Zionism, for which she created materials so that each Hadassah group could teach and learn Zionist ideas and basic facts about Palestine.[31] She herself taught courses in New York, along with others, such as the educator Alexander Dushkin.[32] Szold praised Sampter's work with the school: "I am more convinced than ever that yours is our most important work."[33] Sampter thought of the school not merely as education but as an act of political and religious creation. She told the Hadassah convention in 1915, "The class in Zionism, conducted by the director of the school [Sampter herself], had before it an exceptional task, a piece of pioneer work. . . . There are no textbooks of Zionism."[34] Sampter, who had already been at work on her own Zionist course book, saw herself as a pioneer—not the sort of pioneer who would till the soil but one who would lead others by her literary creation.

From early in her educational work, she thought Zionism allowed for deviation from popular gender ideals. For example, what she described as Zionism's "ennobling" potential was in part about gender relations: "The effect of Zionism on the Jewish character, its ennobling, invigorating power, I observed in my associations with settlement workers and settlement groups. As a character-builder, quite apart from its direct aim, it was appreciated even by those educators who were anti-Zionists." When they were discussing co-ed Zionist clubs, an anti-Zionist settlement worker said to her, "My own feeling is that no serious work can be done by mixed clubs, that they tend to flippancy. But in our house we have only one mixed club, a Zionist club and this is successful. As theirs is a serious aim, it is not fair to judge others by them."[35] In Sampter's eyes, something about Zionism allowed for different relations between men and women.

Though she often had to cancel speaking arrangements at the last minute because of her health, she still took on new roles, such as heading the education section of Hadassah's Central Committee and serving as a consultant to set up Zionist education in Baltimore. These moves toward more intellectual and behind-the-scenes roles suited Sampter well. There is little evidence that she was a popular speaker; her speeches were dense and heady, and I would be shocked if anyone ever referred to them as fiery. But writing educational materials and designing curricula pleased her and Hadassah. Yet through all of these new responsibilities, she wrote, "Always the specter of illness."[36] During her early years with Hadassah, Szold wrote to Kallen, who had expressed concerns about Sampter's health, "You are entirely right about Miss Sampter. It is most important that she should do nothing to strain her health. She seems to me to grow more fragile day by day. I saw her yesterday, and as I held her hand I felt as though she were going to vanish from my side. But all the time her spirit burns with a brighter lustre. She is untiring in originating plans and in executing them for the sake of Zionism, which now possesses her whole being almost to the exclusion of everything else."[37] Sampter would remain a Zionist for the rest of her life, but she would find ways to make her Zionism a crip Zionism, a queer Zionism, and a religiously recombined Zionism.

Nationalism and Internationalism

Today many people are wary of nationalism.[38] The memories of Germany's Nazi-era nationalism, the oppression of North Korean nationalism, and even the ways that American nationalism can have racist ends worry us. Those of us who have as our goal a world in which people across the globe come together in peace are unlikely to see nationalism as the primary route to achieving it.

But this perspective is a present one. In the early twentieth century, many people, including Sampter, saw a simultaneous commitment to nationalism and internationalism as not only possible but also the most pragmatic path toward peace. Yet this was not a position Sampter came to easily. How could one claim to be an internationalist while also being a Jewish nationalist? If internationalists saw the ideal society as one that crossed national boundaries, decried isolationism, and defied any nationalistic chauvinism, how could an internationalist also be a nationalist?

In the spring of 1914, Henrietta Szold asked Sampter to give a speech to a Hadassah gathering. Sampter decided to use the speech to tackle just this problem: how to square her newfound Zionism with her ongoing commitment to internationalism.[39] The speech was well received, and Hadassah later published it as a stand-alone pamphlet called *Nationalism and Universal Brotherhood*. She began by rhetorically asking what she could reply when people said, "We want universal brotherhood. We want to do away with nations. Then why try to establish another nation?" It was not an easy question for her: "The reason I find it hard to quarrel with them is that I agree with them in their main contention. I, too, want universal brotherhood. As a Jew I see that the idea of universal brotherhood is the crowning of Jewish prophecy. And yet the Jewish prophets were all nationalists. If I had to choose between universal brotherhood and the Jewish nation, I should of course choose universal brotherhood. But I do not believe that I have to make that choice."[40] How could she avoid such a choice? Sampter had an answer: internationalism was the larger philosophy, and it could encompass individual nationalisms. Internationalism does not mean the destruction of nations to make way for one vast, undifferentiated humanity but the cooperation of a society of nations. "Nations are the units in internationalism as individuals are the units of society," she told her audience. "Evolution is from the family to the tribe and free city, from the city to the nation to the international tribunal. Each one of these is a step towards peace."[41] But, she noted, as humanity makes these larger steps, it need not sacrifice families or cities. Likewise, nations could work in the service of the larger internationalist project.

Each person should have a nation and therefore a national culture and history. It was these things they brought to the internationalist table. "I hope for a confederacy of all nations, for a world-wide solution of economic problems, for universal free-trade, for internationalism, for the fulfillment of Jewish prophecy. Palestine, when it becomes a Jewish state, a sure legislative possession of the Jewish People, must be a neutral, international state, a citadel of peace."[42]

Sampter even told her (overwhelmingly Jewish) audience that the Bible was the source of both internationalism and Jewish nationalism: "What kind of universal brotherhood did the prophets teach? Was it not international righteousness, international morality? Universal brotherhood includes the brotherhood of nations."[43] In the years after her Hadassah speech, Sampter continued to ground her internationalism in the Bible, as she wrote in 1918: "I believe with the prophets that humanity is one as God is one. . . . But also with the prophets I believe that internationalism implies the existence of free, orderly, self-respecting nations, of which the normal Jewish nation is to be one."[44] She described the "mission" as expressed in the Bible: "As a nation, a people, that shall carry out the laws of God in its national life and so be a constant historical spectacle—a sort of morality play—for the nations of the world until they, too, shall walk in the way of the Lord."[45]

In Sampter's eyes, though the Bible was the source of these ideas, history and sociology also strongly supported the mutual embrace of nationalism and internationalism. In a pamphlet about Jewish history, she wrote, "In America we have begun to see that one can be loyal to more than one country. We can work for both America and for Zion. Indeed the truer Jews we are the truer Americans we can be, for America needs what religion and social ideals the Jew can give her through her love for Zion."[46] Her proclamation sounds a lot like the words of Louis Brandeis, who famously declared, "To be good Americans, we must be better Jews, and to be better Jews, we must become better Zionists."[47] Both declarations rested on the idea that the United States benefited from cultural pluralism, in which each cultural group has something special to contribute to the country. Sampter also took it a step further and insisted that each nation had something to contribute to humanity as a whole. Many years later, on then Supreme Court Justice Brandeis's eightieth birthday, Sampter remembered him saying something very similar about the broader value of a Jewish national culture: "Working with Jews in labor disputes, seeing their peculiar genius for democracy, I had the wish that this people should be given the chance to develop its own commonwealth, to let the world see this new thing it would create in democratic institutions."[48]

Both Sampter and Brandeis—as well as most Zionists—thought there was something distinctive about Jews. But was that distinctive thing cultural or hereditary? Learned or inborn? Sampter claimed it was both: "Besides a purity of race as great as that of any geographical nation, the Jewish people has also preserved at least four of the chief factors of national life, namely, laws, customs, history and language. A fifth nation factor, religion, has been the means of preserving by its sanction the other four. Religion has therefore been the chief national asset of the Jew."[49]

Sampter sometimes articulated her Zionism in racialist terms (that is, a kind of thinking that groups people into races and assumes these races share distinctive traits and tendencies but that is not necessarily racist), but she also resisted a purely racialist foundation for Zionism: "I say we are a people, a nation. This is a psychological fact in which race plays only a minor part."[50] Though race mattered, a group's self-definition mattered more, and that could be based on many different cultural aspects, of which race was only one: "Nationalism is based upon common history, traditions, sufferings, laws, language, race, land, religion, or any one or a few of these. Any section of humanity that feels itself to be a nation is a nation. And the Jews as a whole have never ceased to feel themselves a nation or to be so regarded by all the rest of humanity."[51] So while Sampter engaged in race thinking, as did so many of the American intellectuals of the early twentieth century, she refused any account of Jewishness that relied primarily on race. Instead, she saw religion as the real root of Jewish national distinctiveness: "Nationalism is the self-consciousness of a people. God-consciousness is the zenith of self-consciousness. It is this God-consciousness that has given to the Jew a nationalism capable of withstanding two thousand years of dispersion."[52] Perhaps unsurprisingly, after she moved to Palestine, she would write very little of race. The idea of race was central to intellectual and social life in the United States, whereas Palestine's social divisions were more often articulated in the language of class, religion, and culture.

In the late 1910s, she continued her Zionist work in the United States, but she began to wonder if she might be intellectually and politically happier in Palestine. In 1918 she had planned to work for Mordecai Kaplan two hours each day, but then Henrietta Szold asked if she might work for the Zionist Organization of America (formerly the Federation of American Zionists), even though the total for four hours a day was the same as what Kaplan had offered to pay her for two.[53] Nevertheless, she agreed: she was to write *A Guide to Zionism* because the first edition (her *A Course in Zionism*) was out of print. She had to write the Palestine chapters herself, but even reading dozens of contemporary accounts left her feeling unprepared to write a comprehensive guide. "But what could I do?" she asked herself. Her answer was clear: "Go to Palestine."[54]

After an initial no from the secretary of the Zionist Organization of America, the group granted its approval. Louis Brandeis, also initially reluctant for Sampter to leave, agreed in the end. The terms were straightforward and not terribly generous. She would go for part of the price of her passage and continue to receive her "present salary," which was about $2,000 a month in today's dollars.

Though living in Palestine would complicate her Zionism, she remained committed to both internationalism and Jewish nationalism throughout her life. In 1937 she entered an essay contest about how to combat anti-Semitism in the United States. The committee deemed her "Cure the Causes" a winner, and it was subsequently published alongside the five other winners. The collected volume, edited by Reform rabbi and prominent Zionist Stephen Wise, met with acclaim, including from the novelist and translator Ludwig Lewisohn, who gushed over Sampter's essay in his review of the book. He even gave the conclusion of his essay over to her voice: "And so Miss Jessie Sampter writes profoundly and eloquently at once words to which I am happy to give this additional currency," he wrote, and then finished his review quoting twelve lines from her prize-winning entry.[55] Those lines reiterated the necessity of Jewish nationalism for the sake of the Jews but also for the sake of a contribution to internationalism:

> As a living entity, a Jewish community conscious of its national heritage, rich in the culture of its own people yet discharging with a full heart all the duties and labors of love of American citizens, we challenge our foes, we call them out into the open to show cause why we should do otherwise. We shall not try to make ourselves liked by being agreeable according to the standards of our critics. We are what we are, an international people. Only internationalism—nations organized integrally—can overcome war. Only an international group with a national center can be strong enough to face the world in this new-old struggle for international and intra-national justice. A Jewish Palestine may not directly end anti-Semitism, as some of its protagonists hoped; but it makes a clear issue of it, a universal issue of the place of small nations in this distracted world.[56]

How would a Jewish Palestine—the "national center" of an international people—help combat anti-Semitism in America? Sampter saw two steps in this process: first, to "upbuild Palestine as a national center and develop Jewish values in America," which included organizing the Jewish community, learning Hebrew, studying Jewish history, and finding "your place among our people. The Jewish front is wide, somewhere you will fit in."[57] The next step was to "help to bring about democratic socialism in America, in the world."[58] Collectivist democracies were the best for Jews, as well as for all other peoples. She had refined this political conviction from her life in Palestine, and especially her life on the kibbutz. A Jewish national center in Palestine would support Jewish life in other countries, and it would also draw attention to the plight of "small nations"—or, as we might say, minorities—on the international stage. Jewish nationalism done well would both combat anti-Semitism and contribute to a more just internationalism.

In Palestine: The Real and the Ideal

Pacifism and State Building

In 1933 Albert Einstein gave an interview in which he said he was "against war." He had just written a foreword to Sampter's *Modern Palestine: A Symposium*, and so she had paid close attention.[59] Sampter wrote to her sister about the interview, "To be against war is about as sensible as being against scarlet fever or senile dementia. For both of these one seeks preventions or remedies."[60] For her, antiwar sentiment was sensible, even obvious. But she knew that no amount of wishing war away would make it so. Should every war always be avoided? Could one build a nation without self-defense? When non-Jewish Arabs already lived on some of the land and were willing to fight for it, how could one build a Jewish state in Palestine without engaging in violence? The costs of true pacifism could be high.

Throughout her adulthood Sampter remained opposed to war and violence, sometimes lonely positions. They were complicated positions too: she lost associates and political clout over her opposition to World War I and to armed conflict with Arabs. Being both a pacifist and a state builder was also complicated from a gendered perspective: while pacifism was often gendered feminine, state building was decidedly masculine. Sampter occupied both sides, even when it seemed contradictory.

Sampter became outspoken in her pacifism as a young woman: when war broke out in Europe in 1914, she rejected its wisdom on both the grounds that war itself was bad and that it was particularly bad for European Jews. She wrote in the *Maccabaean*, "There is one people, however, scattered among all these nations, which has to pay all of the tolls of battle, and yet to whom victory and defeat are alike a national calamity. These are the Jews."[61] She also wrote an unpublished essay, "The Ideal of Peace in Jewish Thought and Life," in 1915—"long suffering, non-resistance, and the healing peace of religious life" were both the ideal and the reality of Jewish life among "the oppressive nations," she wrote. "So abhorrent is physical contest to them that they have been accused of physical cowardice."[62] Yet because of their "obedience and loyalty," Jews fought in every war.

Sampter saved some of her strongest words, however, for the United States. When the United States entered World War I in April 1917, she joined the Women's Peace Party. Later that year she published *The Book of the Nations* (with the Hebrew subtitle *Sefer ha-Goyim*), which decried the evils of pitting nation against nation in a prophetic style. Using biblical verses and imagery, Sampter excoriated modern nations, especially Germany, England, and France, for imperialism and economic sins that had led the world into war. "I shall destroy the nations with their own weapons, saith the Lord," the book declared.[63] She later summarized its warning: "God would destroy the nations by their own weapons, as he destroyed in the flood, but Israel reminds him of his ancient promise to make of it a nation to save the nations. And he spares the nations for the sake of that hope, and he repeats the promise, in the face of despair, in the face of groveling, destroyed degenerate Jewry."[64]

Holding fast to a pacifist stance even after the United States entered the war proved very unpopular among both the Zionist elite and the general American populace, but throughout 1917 and 1918, Sampter continued to write her antiwar lamentations. Henrietta Szold encouraged her while she wrote, and she had great conversations with the reader for E. P. Dutton, *Book of the Nations* publishing house. She described him as "a Christian. A religionist. I could speak to him on matters of faith more easily than to most Jews, to any, I might say, except Miss Lazarus and Mary [Antin]." Although it never became a best seller (about five hundred copies were sold in the first six months), the book met with largely positive reactions. Even before *Book of the Nations* was published, Mary Antin praised it in a letter to Horace Kallen as "surely the best thing Jessie has done, and a master piece of work by any standards. . . . [It] resembles the Bible in more than form." Kallen had praised her earlier poems as "most novel," and Antin heartily agreed about the new manuscript.[65] After its publication, Israel Zangwill quoted it at length and wrote that she had "poured forth in the very idiom of the Old Testament her prophetic indignations against our modern Assyrias and Babylons."[66] Sampter must have been thrilled when a reviewer wrote, "The book might well have been written by a Hebrew prophet."[67] Sampter's friend Lotta Levensohn reviewed it glowingly in *The Menorah Journal*; Zangwill praised Sampter's writing and held her up as a paragon of Jewishness: "This book is still more remarkable, showing, as it does, the Jewish reaction to the doings of contemporary Christendom. The biblical form seems the natural expression of a Jewish soul saturated with the old prophetic literature of the race."[68] *The Mizrahi* magazine reviewed it positively, calling it "exquisitely conceived" and "vibrant with feeling," praising its "liberality of thought," and quoting its ecumenical query: "Is God a personal god, is He the God of Jew or Christian or Buddhist?"[69] Yet the *Lyric* complained that it reminded them of Segal's *The Book of Pain-Struggle*, which it called "the most badly written good book ever published."[70] Each had a distinctive style; neither, apparently, was to the taste of that particular reviewer.

On the heels of *The Book of the Nations* came *The Coming of Peace*, a collection of poetry that reaffirmed her pacifist stance. In the poem "What Is Man?" Sampter lamented both war in general and the Jewish nation's inability to stop it:

Once the Lord chose a nation to guide the nations,
Once he proclaimed the law, that God is one and Man is one,

And he said to this nation: All the nations are brothers,
And my house shall be called a house of prayer for all the peoples.
Where is that nation now?
Why does it not arise and cry? . . .
For this nation is outcast, tortured, and despised.[71]

"The Healing of Peace," published shortly after *The Coming of Peace*, offered a promise of a time after the wars of nation against nation:

But I will come quietly, as a woman to her sick child,
As the words of a friend, little by little.
And I will heal your wounds with the healing of peace.
And lead you up to my mountain to prophesy, said the Lord.[72]

These poems subtly drew attention to the gendered dynamics of war and nationalism: nations are "brothers" who fight and persecute other nations. The Lord, who will ultimately bring peace, is motherly, "as a woman to her sick child."

The rift between Sampter's convictions and her American sense of belonging pained her: "My pacifism threatened my Americanism, my Zionism, and yet not their intrinsic spirit, but the false ideal set up for a moment by a war-mad people."[73] She bought Liberty Bonds after Woodrow Wilson's Fourteen Points speech in January 1918, but then she was upset. The coupons had mottoes: "For every bond bought, a Hun is hunted" and "Bonds buy bullets." Sampter panicked: "I was murdering, I had gone to war, had blood on my hands." She was the sole "no" vote on whether the Zionist Organization of America should encourage enlistment.[74] Sampter, Henrietta Szold, and four other members of Hadassah's Central Committee, as well as several male leaders (such as Judah Magnes and Gotthard Deutsch), took outspoken pacifist stances, much to the dismay of most of the Zionist leadership.[75] Sampter and Szold each offered their resignations from official Zionist positions over their antiwar stances. Brandeis and others insisted they stay, telling them that pacifists could be good patriots too. After the war's end, she wrote, "I lost my country in the shame of victory."[76] Maybe her heart was already partway to Palestine.

Even before *The Coming of Peace* was published, Sampter, exhausted from writing and Zionist work, contracted pneumonia. It was during this time that she used a Ouija board to contact her deceased mother and ask what she thought of Sampter's embrace of Judaism and plans to move to Palestine. Sampter deemed the experiment successful, but it left her exhausted and on the brink of mental and physical collapse. Then, Sampter explained, she had religious visions. One writer calls these visions a "nervous breakdown," and Sampter's sister, Elvie Wachenheim, thought something similar, though Jessie insisted that, debilitating as the experiences were, she was able to talk to God. She even called herself a prophet. Elvie helped arrange for her to see a psychiatrist, which both sisters deemed helpful. He even encouraged her to continue with her plans to move to Palestine, though he suggested limiting the trip to one year. Then she went to a (vegetarian) sanitarium run by Seventh-Day Adventists for four weeks to rest. "'How much can I work?' 'Not at all,' [the doctor] answered." She reflected for a moment. "I resolved to begin work at once."[77]

Her work soon took her to Palestine, where her pacifism would be tested anew: How could Zionists build a Jewish state when there was conflict with the non-Jewish Arabs who already lived there? How could a Jewish pioneer be a pacifist when Jewish villages were violently attacked by Arabs? These conflicts ranged from small-scale raids to internationally visible, bloody riots, such as those of the early 1920s and 1929. Some Zionists, often called Revisionists, advocated not only self-defense but also strategic offense. Others insisted on armed and trained Jewish defense, like the Haganah (the Jewish defense force founded in 1920) and later the Irgun (an underground and more right-wing Jewish military organization founded in 1931).

Living in Palestine made the gendered layers of pacifism more apparent. In the most visible sense, fighting was done overwhelmingly by men. Women played only minor roles in the Haganah and Irgun and were less likely to be armed in any more local defense strategies. Even beyond women's marginalization from the front lines, Sampter's ideology of pacifism had gendered aspects. In a hybrid short story–essay called "The Mother," Sampter wrote:

> "But we women," said Sonya, "we do not think one can prove anything by killing. We know god hates killing. And so we make, make, make—we knit. It is all war. Half the world kills and the other half makes. And so, if I have to be in the war, I will be the half that makes." . . . "Sonya," I said, "it is the mothers who make the world for the future. Maybe when this war is over there will be justice at last, justice for the little nations and the big nations, justice for the Jews, justice for the mothers. And meanwhile, my little girl, we must have patience, we women. We must conserve, we must conserve the life of the world for after the war."[78]

Sonya summarized, "It is we mothers who have to make the world different."[79] Sampter remained hopeful that Jewish women could be a force for change and that the Jewish nation would provide an example of peace.

Sampter also chided masculine ideals of conquest for their roles in the misery of war. "To the Jewish Teacher," published in the *Maccabaean* shortly after she arrived in Palestine, hinted at these gendered aspects of war and peace:

> Who shall inherit the world? Shall force reign? . . .
> Shall the plutocrat reign
> and the factory conquer
> And all men be one
> In a tyranny of steel and oil?[80]

No, the will to own and dominate, whether through war or industrial production, was not the path to a better future:

> You shall inherit the world:
> A nation shall rise
> Whose banners for peace are unfurled[81]

Inheriting the world was not about imperialism; it was about setting a gentle and pacifist example of what a nation could be. Once the Jewish nation had a geographic home, it could rise to become this ideal.

Yet in the real Palestine, banners were not always unfurled for peace. Sampter was shaken by the violence between Arabs and Jews in the early 1920s, not long after she had arrived. "I am filled with rage and grief," she began an article about the riots during Passover in 1920.[82] She blamed the British: "Three times the British Administration had allowed Arab agitators—not our simple, kindly Arab peasant neighbors, but demagogues and tools of Western imperialism—to organize anti-Zionist demonstrations in the streets of Jerusalem."[83] An accompanying poem decried "the blackness of empire and the sin of the strident west."[84] The British rule of Palestine not only encouraged Arab violence, she thought, but also failed to protect Jews: "Threats of murder were printed and spoken unchecked. Riot had once broken out, and a Jew had been beaten. No wonder our young men organized for self-defense."[85] Perhaps Jewish self-defense was even necessary, she began to consider. To some of her fellow Zionists, Sampter's pacifism, or her radical critique of the British Empire, went too far: the *Maccabaean* printed her article with the editor's warning that "we cannot subscribe to all the conclusions drawn by her." [86]

These questions of empire, violence, and self-defense would not go away. During the 1920 riots, she had picked out an easily accessible weapon for self-defense: a kitchen knife. Three years after the 1929 riots, when Sampter was living in Rehovot, she bought two guns. (A pacifist who bought guns?!) In a letter she sent with a friend rather than through the oft-censored mail, she explained to her sister and brother-in-law:

> You probably know that in the riots of 1929, Rehoboth and others of the agricultural villages were not attacked chiefly because it was well known that we were inwardly strong and protected by arms; you may also know that the Government, except for a few permits, practically forbids us to be armed for self-protection. Lately—several months ago—whoever could bought guns (a consignment had been secretly received) and hid them in their houses, to be on hand in an emergency. I bought two, costing $30 each, and had them sunk into the floor under the tiles in my sitting room. There they rest quietly. . . . And yet I agree with you that we are "safer" here than in New York. In any case, I feel safe, because I am where I want to be.[87]

Unlike the kitchen knife, these guns were not for herself; they were to be given to the men of Jewish defense groups in case Rehovot was attacked: "I hope they may stay there forever," she said of the guns under her floor tiles. "Nevertheless, it is necessary to have them. We have a trained volunteer defense, and my guns are registered with them." Her essays and letters never mentioned those guns again.

Her letters also make clear that she didn't know how to use a gun. As she explained from Kibbutz Givat Brenner in 1938, "Everyone (but I) has learnt how to shoot."[88] Sampter felt that the kibbutz offered her a safer space, and she held fast to her pacifism even during the violence between Arabs and Jews. As Meir Chazan writes, her pacifism wasn't unheard of on the kibbutz, in part because it was also the political position of the kibbutz's most famous member, Enzo Sereni.[89] Sereni, one of the first Italian Zionists and a cofounder of Givat Brenner, vocally supported peaceful Arab-Jewish coexistence in Palestine. Later, during World War II, he served as an officer in the Jewish Brigade, parachuted into Nazi-held territory, and was ultimately killed in Dachau concentration camp. So, like Sampter, he was a provisional kind of pacifist, one who found some things worth fighting for.

Sampter published the kibbutz newsletter, a combination of regular community news and more philosophical reflections. During the spring of 1936, she reiterated her pacifist stance on all wars and acknowledged that violence created terrible losses on both sides. She recalled living with Tamar during the 1929 riots: a young Haganah man would walk from their small neighborhood to the heart of Tel Aviv each day to stand guard. "One evening," she wrote, "he returned in grief, threw his pistol down, and said he would not return to his job. 'Today, after the murder of the Goldberg son, young Jewish men not from the Haganah entered an Arab neighborhood, burst in and killed a house full of women and children. They shot and killed! This tragedy is worse than all the other tragedies! How can the Haganah defend Jews like this?'"[90] Sampter felt as this soldier did: to kill Arabs in their homes was indefensible.

She also grappled with pacifism and the need for self-defense, and the gendered implications of each, in the US press. In November 1936 the US-based *Jewish Frontier* published "Watchwomen," a Sampter essay that doesn't quite sound like true pacifism but also doesn't quite endorse fighting either. It began by extolling the bravery of the women of the *yishuv*— the name for Jewish settlement in Palestine—in moments of danger. Still, Sampter did not see women as natural fighters, which she took to be good. "There is no doubt whatever that woman by nature is not a warrior. But," she lamented, "unnatural times demand unnatural actions, and woman is as capable of self-defense as man."[91]

Even the culture of seemingly gender-equal kibbutzim assumed that men were the natural fighters, an assumption that created angst for the women. Sampter wrote about women kibbutzniks' response to defense: "When a shower of bullets poured in upon the *kvutza*, the men went out to reply to it with gun fire and drive away the assailants, but the women were ordered into the darkened dining hall and told to lie flat on the floor; and they obeyed. They obeyed with shame and protest and indignation swelling in their hearts."[92] A conflict of gender ideals caused this shame and indignation: how could they be womanly, gentle, nonviolent, and retiring and simultaneously strong kibbutz women who worked and contributed to the safety of the community? Kibbutz gender ideals did not always match up with the gendered assumptions reflected in kibbutz practice.

In 1938 Sampter wrote a letter to the editor of the *Jerusalem Post*, but soon after she "received a note from the editor that he dare not publish it," she wrote in longhand at the end of her own typewritten copy. She had written it in response to the British government's decision to carry out the execution of Shlomo Ben Yossef, a twenty-five-year-old member of Betar, a youth Zionist movement that advocated a Jewish state spanning both sides of the Jordan River, and the Irgun, Revisionist Zionists who rejected Jewish restraint from violence. In response to Arabs attacking and killing six Jews earlier in the spring of 1938, Ben Yossef and two other young men had planned to take revenge by ambushing a bus of Arabs. Their hand grenade, however, did not detonate, and when they shot at the bus, it terrorized but did not kill the passengers.

Sampter felt that the whole incident, from beginning to end, was a disaster. Arabs had killed Jews, Jews had tried to kill Arabs, and then the British-run government was going to kill two of the men who had tried to kill Arabs. (It confined the third to a mental asylum.) She worried, with good reason, that the government's execution of Ben Yossef would further embolden Revisionist Zionists and other groups that favored more violent tactics. Her letter began, "Now more than ever is needed the warning to the few hot-headed young people among us to abstain from all reprisals, to withhold their hands from revenge, from imitating the murderers who would provoke us to barbarism." She chastised Jews who wanted to meet violence with violence: they were dividing the Jewish community, whose "only effective weapon" was "solidarity," not guns.

The letter concluded with a plea for forgiveness: "It is easier to forgive the Arab terrorists acting in hot blood and ignorance than the calculated political cruelty of the Government. We have no more illusions now. That at least is good. Of both our open and disguised enemies we can only say in the words of one of the greatest of Jews: 'Forgive them, for they know not what they do.'"[93] It was classic Sampter: profoundly opposed to violence, critical of the colonial authorities, and religiously broad.

Zionism and Democracy

Should the State of Israel be a Jewish state, or should it be a state for all its citizens? Is it possible to be both? And who should decide? I hear these questions at dinner tables and in diplomatic speeches. Almost 20 percent of Israeli citizens today are non-Jewish Arabs, and yet they occupy a different social place than Jewish citizens. (For example, they are not required to serve in the military.) To me, some injustices seem clear and seem to have obvious solutions whose major obstacle is the political will of those in power. Other problems seem more complex. It is striking to me that almost a hundred years ago, well before the State of Israel became a reality, Jessie Sampter was grappling with almost the same questions. And, like today, she found no easy answers.

In the early 1920s, Sampter wrote and then crossed out, "~~Zionist poli-~~ ~~tics are smashed. Let them die; they were the acme of the unreal~~."[94] Many of the issues Sampter had in mind remain pertinent today: How could a society be both democratic and Jewish, especially if some of its members were not Jewish? What about Jews who didn't seem to share a culture with Ashkenazi Zionists, such as Yemenite Jews? And what space would there be for Jews whose bodies challenged Zionist ideals, such as disabled Jews? Sampter loved Palestine and the ideal of a Jewish life there, but she did not always love the real—the conflict, violence, and intolerance among Jews, Arabs, the British, and even factions within each group. But the "unreal" of some Zionists' politics, including the impulse to see Palestine as a "land without a people," was even more damaging.

Not long after Jessie arrived in Palestine in 1919, she wrote to her sister about her nagging sense of homesickness. But it was not homesickness for the United States; it was a metaphysical homesickness, which she hoped Palestine would alleviate.[95] Right from the start, she loved it: "I love to be here more than I have loved to be in any other place," she wrote.[96] "My feeling is that I want to, that I must, stay here indefinitely. . . . I feel at home here, as I have never felt anywhere since I was twelve years old. . . . If I ever return to the States, it will be to visit, not to go home. Of course I shall always love the ideal America—but not so much as I love the real Palestine and the living Jewish people, real and ideal."[97] So what was this homesickness? It was the nagging feeling that her idealized Zionism had prepared her for an idealized Palestine, but the realities of its society and politics were not quite the Zionist picture she had been sold.

Although she was an idealist, Sampter did not see the world through rose-colored glasses. She wrote to her sister, "Life is so wonderfully rich, varied, terrible, and beautiful here, and all in so small a frame! I am full of hope despite the truly overwhelming problems."[98] The particular problems that weighed on her most heavily were relations between non-Jewish Arabs and Jews, the poverty of Yemenite Jews, and larger health and sanitation issues. After living in Jerusalem for a little more than a year, she wrote to Mordecai Kaplan, "It is all much better and much worse than we could possibly have imagined."[99]

In addition to its political and economic problems, Palestine did not offer religious communities that provided the "at-homeness" she had hoped for. After an unexpected snowfall during her first winter in Jerusalem, for example, she railed against the young religious men who refused to work because they were "too fine" and insisted on leaving the shoveling of roofs to others—to teachers and engineers and Yemenites who lived in the city.[100]

"Life here is extremely uncomfortable—according to New York standards—and I love it," she wrote to her sister.[101] In this letter she resolved to settle in Palestine even after her work contract was complete. Not all American Zionists liked it in Palestine. She described her friend, the American Alice Seligsberg: "She hates to leave here, where she is very happy in her work, and yet she longs to go back (Do not spread this)."[102] Practical aspects of life were difficult, and the sporadic violence was emotionally wrenching. Several years later, Sampter wrote, "I could never again live anywhere else but in this blessed, beloved land of mine. And yet here life is bitter, bitter! I live now with my feet on earth; I have seen reality; I love it more than my dead iridescent dreams, and yet it is terrible."[103]

Citizenship in Palestine was, to put it euphemistically, in a state of transition during the early years Sampter lived there. Although after the collapse of the Ottoman Empire, Palestine's neighbors had a solid sense of who was a citizen and what the citizenship process was, Palestine had yet to sort it out. Article 7 of the British Mandate required "enacting a nationality law" so that Jews who resided in Palestine could gain "Palestinian citizenship." And so, on August 1, 1925, the Palestinian Citizenship Order set that process into motion. Before that, there had been several changes in rapid succession: from Ottoman to British rule in December 1917, from British occupation to the adoption of the Palestine Mandate in July 1922 and finally to the Palestinian Citizenship Order.[104] Sampter applied and got her Palestinian passport in 1926—and she gave up her American citizenship. She was now a Jewish Palestinian.

But what did it mean to be a Jew settled in Palestine? Zionist goals were complex: Should the new society be a Jewish society, and if so, what place did non-Jewish Arabs have in it? And what role would Jewish Arabs, such as Yemenites, play? The intellectual and social currents of Zionism were largely Ashkenazi, and neither the landscape nor the ideology of Jewish society in Palestine made their lives easy. And how should a new society based on the physical working of the land think about physically disabled people? In the end, Sampter's vision would crip Zionism such that it made space for Jews with disabilities; it did some work toward queering Zionism to include Yemenites and other Arab Jews, but it did not ultimately make space for non-Jewish Arabs on equal footing with others. In the early 1920s, she wrote, "I love my land. I shall live and die here, with this suffering people. But where is the vision? I see the past, pious, tragic, ineffectual.

I see a present arrogant, disillusioned, uncertain. I see no future." She revised her pessimism, but it still sounded desperate: "We ourselves are the future; I am the future. There must be a way."[105]

Cripping Zionism

"Here being a Jew is the norm, not the abnormal," Sampter declared several years after moving to Palestine.[106] She had spent most of her life being "abnormal," in part because she was Jewish but also in large part because she was disabled. If being Jewish suddenly felt normal, being disabled still did not. In fact, in some ways, her limited strength for walking and physical labor was more disabling in Palestine than it had been in the United States.

Not only did Palestine have less developed infrastructure than the United States did, but the Zionist culture there promoted physical health as noble and ennobling. Even Hadassah saw the task of Jewish state building and citizenship as manly—and as things for the able-bodied. Henrietta Szold wrote in 1921, "Our nerves need steadying, our muscles are flabby, our resilience weak, our morale and discipline infirm. . . . Everything must be brought in, until men of muscle, judgment, experience, expertise, and means come in and develop its resources. Men of muscle have begun to come—the young, energetic halutzim of whom you have heard. They are the brawn of the Jewish community."[107] With this kind of rhetoric, what space was there for people with disabilities in this new Jewish society?

Sampter spent several weeks in Hadassah's hospital in Jerusalem soon after she arrived in Palestine. When she recovered enough to write about it, she did not apologize for her inability to work, nor see herself as a drain on the Zionist cause. Rather, her essays framed her experience as a celebration of Zionism for her English-speaking audiences. She praised the hospital itself: "To me it was almost worth the discomfort of a serious illness that I might spend several weeks as a patient, in the ranks of patients, in our own Hadassah Hospital in Jerusalem—the Rothschild Hospital." She celebrated its democratic structure: "I had no special privileges, save the privilege of a pleasant personal acquaintance with many of the physicians and nurses. I lay in the general women's ward. In the Rothschild Hospital, there are no private rooms, and consequently there is no 'private' and 'ward' psychology on the part of the nurses—they are in fact sisters, as they are called in Hebrew 'Ahiot'—sisters to all their patients, with a friendliness, a kindliness, a comradely helpfulness that seems equal toward the Yemenite housemaid, the poor Askhenazic widow, the Hebrew school teacher or the physician's wife."[108] Her American Zionist audience could see the Zionism they hoped for: collectivist, democratic, philanthropic, and scientific.

Her readers in Hadassah, including the big yearly convention, loved it. A. H. Vixman, president of the Pittsburgh chapter, wrote it up for the *Jewish Criterion*. She closed her own with Sampter's words: "As for myself, I hope I may be pardoned for repeating again, the words of Jessie Sampter—who concluded her beautiful article entitled 'Bed Number Six' published in the last issue of the *B'nai Israel Bulletin* with the phrase 'God bless Hadassah!' 'and forgive me if I am proud of her.'"[109] Copies of "Bed Number Six" were subsequently sent to all chapters.[110]

And yet, even while "Bed Number Six" strongly supported Zionist ideas, it also cripped Zionism: its narrator and many other characters were physically or mentally disabled, and yet they played important roles in the new society. It even shows pioneers as potentially ill and disabled: "Two or three young pioneers, 'halutzim,' look down ill from the workingmen's camp. They are contented and quiet."[111] All bodies, even those of the hale pioneers, were susceptible to illness and disabilities—and that was nothing to be ashamed of. Unlike the Zionist narratives that celebrated overcoming malaria as a rite of passage, here the emphasis was not on overcoming or the masculinity of toughing it out.[112] Sampter herself, physically in pain and struggling with depression, told the story of her time in the hospital as illustrating not only Hadassah's Zionist ideals of building the state and providing medical care but also her own Zionist ideals of an inclusive Jewish culture that embraced Yemenite Jews, disabled women, and sick *halutzim* not as outsiders but as central figures. Even from her early days writing from Palestine, then, Sampter was cripping Zionism to make space for disabled bodies.

This commitment echoed beyond her writing. Sampter helped create the first Deaf school in Palestine. She raised money from both the United States and Palestine and worked on the committee that would ultimately create the school. For her, the project was part philanthropy but also part political work: she wanted to shape a Zionism that included these students. Although she followed along with the dominant mode of teaching Deaf students—oralism, in which students are encouraged to speak instead of using sign language—she still insisted that these students could and should be full members of the new Zionist society.

This is not to say that making space for disabled bodies was easy, and Sampter sometimes despaired. In May 1921 she wrote, "I dreamed the other night that I offered my life for the life of a halutz. Then I found myself turning into the halutz. I did not want that; I wanted to give him my life. I said so, and it happened. I died and he lived. A simple enough dream of desire."[113] Her dream suggested a society that valued the life of a pioneer over the life of a disabled woman. Though she called it "simple enough," it was not simple at all: Sampter struggled with the popular Zionism that valued strong and healthy Jewish bodies above all.

Several years later, she wrote of a similar sort of despondency in response to feeling as if there was no space for her:

> It seemed to me there was nothing for me to do here because I had not the working body. I thought I had lost all influence and power; I was wasted. Our gift of language must in large measure be wasted here. It may seem as if the best and deepest of us were wasted. But I think it is not true. There is a better and a deeper. . . . It is our vanity that is shattered, not our worth that is lost. . . . We shall unify at last the body and spirit, sanctify the work of our hands with the consecration to it of heart and head.[114]

The paragraph reiterated her metaphysical understanding of the unity of the mind, body, and spirit, but it also despaired that Zionism in Palestine valued only physical prowess while it "wasted" minds and spirits.

Creating space for a disabled body and appreciating the political value of minds and spirits were more than philosophical issues for her: without them, she questioned the value of her own life. "This paragraph was much more despondent, despairful as to my own powers," she admitted, but Leah and another friend had listened to her read the paragraph and supported her. "This conversation, in which they insisted on my worth as a friend, proved a turning point in my decision, for I was at this time resolved to kill myself as soon as I had finished the book [her unpublished autobiography]."[115] Her friends made her feel valued. And through their eyes, she could also see her own value to a crip Zionist project.

As she toured different parts of Palestine, she met pioneers and workers, and even as a tourist she saw gaps between the real and the ideal. The Jewish colonies in the Galilee were "inspiring and depressing," she wrote to her brother-in-law, Edgar Wachenheim.[116] She wrote that Jewish villages all have something in common: "They all have a fine, daring spirit, pioneer courage."[117] And yet they also at once glorified physical health and took it for granted: "They do not fear work but, with few exceptions, they do not understand its dignity. . . . A tendency to be arrogant, super-intellectual, to look upon themselves as heroes."[118] Her unpublished novel "In the Beginning" had "Jewish boys, bronze-legged, working in the fields" but criticized the narrowness of these same Zionists.[119]

She wanted a broader Zionism, one that recognized the unity of body and soul—and also recognized the diversity of bodies. To Mordecai Kaplan she wrote, "The problem of the Jewish soul can be solved only here, and through first hand knowledge of life here. Yet no one will solve that problem even here unless he comes truly in the spirit of the *halutz*, prepared to make material sacrifices and to take his chance in the 'labor market' here, whether in the highest or the lowest field."[120] For an engineer or a painter, that might mean willingness to work in the field. For Sampter, that meant the material sacrifices, from American toilet paper and her preferred woolen stockings to the nearness of family and the less disabling infrastructures of American urban environments. Spiritual regeneration and a "sound economic basis" were not two unconnected goals: "I believe the two must come together, that they are aspects of one vision."[121] Sampter echoed Kaplan's Zionist commitment to spirituality in addition to economic practicalities, but she did not share Kaplan's vision of the "viril[e], self-perpetuating Jew" at the center.[122]

Even some of her essays that do not explicitly discuss disability show the tensions between a Zionist ideal of able-bodiedness and the reality of a population whose bodies varied. In 1923, for example, Sampter penned an article about why Jews were leaving Palestine. The answer seemed mundane: they didn't have jobs. But it was more complicated: they also felt they had no place in the society if they were part of the "so-called non-productive element."[123] Sampter thought the problem could be fixed, but she recommended ways of increasing options for more productivity, such as creating fisheries or expanding loans to include Palestine-born Jews, not just new immigrants. Perhaps she felt that a plan that truly valued "the so-called non-productive element" was too radical to be accepted by other Zionists—but it is more likely she had also internalized some of Zionism's producer-minded ethos. The article shows how a nonnormative embodied life, in this case, that of someone who was not materially or economically productive, mattered deeply for Zionist politics.

Even a cripped Zionism, however, did not always mean a fully inclusive Zionism. In 1938, the year of Sampter's death, she published another personal essay about a hospital stay in which she was assigned bed number six. But the story was not about her: it was about the patient in the next bed over. "Bed Number Five" was less rosy, but it still portrayed Hadassah as a force for good, operating with a sense of noblesse oblige, and it still cripped

Zionism. Sampter opened the essay with a description of the girl in the bed next to her: she had "a lovely face, flower-like and delicate, with dark skin, framed by curling light brown hair with a braid over each shoulder, the sunburnt skin and the sunburnt hair of a daughter of Jerusalem. From each small well-shaped ear dangled a gold ring. To my mind, earrings give to the face a barbaric flavor; and in the girl, half-woman, half-child, they emphasized a wild sweetness. She did not look ill."[124]

Today we might say that the girl had an invisible disability: depression. She had attempted suicide, which many of the hospital employees attributed to the difficult conditions at her home. "All the housework for my little sisters and brothers and parents and everybody" fell to her, she explained. Sampter described Shoshanna's joy at reading and picking flowers in the garden. At the conclusion of the essay, the doctor spoke to Sampter in English so that the girl could not understand: "We have found a place for Shoshanna. She is going to 'work' for a childless woman who contemplates something like adoption. She can't be sent back to her real mother who is an irresponsible nervous invalid. Later her 'employer', who will pay her parents, by the way, for the privilege of keeping her, intends to send her to school or have her taught. We think that if Shoshanna gets a little bit of the milk of human kindness she will not try again to drink poison."

I'm sure the story made Hadassah readers feel good about the work of the hospital. And yet the doctor's words demonstrate a number of common exclusionary assumptions among Ashkenazi Zionists in Palestine. First, he claims that the Sephardi mother is an unfit mother. She does not care for her children using "modern" or "scientific" methods, and her child becomes ill because of it. Stereotypes of Sephardim, Jews who traced their ancestry to the Iberian Peninsula, overlapped with stereotypes of Yemenites: they might have oriental charm, but they lacked scientific knowledge. Second, and related, he suggests that a different woman will be a better mother and may "adopt" Shoshanna, even though we have no indication that her parents are willing to give her up. Third, he hints that the Sephardi way of having an older child work instead of go to school is culturally backward. It certainly is not "human kindness." There is no space in his ideal society for a "nervous invalid" as a mother—and particularly not one who is also Sephardi.

Although Sampter does not speak back to the doctor or challenge his Orientalist ideas about Shoshanna's mother, her essay nevertheless undermines some common Zionist assumptions. At the most basic level, Sampter's story makes a space for a girl with depression as part of the society.

She will contribute through both her own education and her labor. Her depression is not an obstacle to her inclusion in a Zionist project; the only obstacles recognized are the material ones of labor, economics, and bad parenting.

A cripped Zionism would recognize the interconnection of the body, mind, and soul and would see value in each—not a value limited to production or ability to work the land but the value of a "daring spirit" and willingness to sacrifice for the new society. But as "Bed Number Five" suggests, it was still a Zionism that allowed Orientalist stereotypes. Sampter's approach to Yemenite Jews shows how her Orientalism coexisted with deep commitment to inclusion.

Yemenites, the "Orient," and Zionist Society

When Sampter visited the settlement of Rehovot for the first time, she remarked on its Yemenite Jews: "All had their own gardens of vegetables and fruit. We conversed in Hebrew with these different Jews, these Arab Jews so separate from us. Can we not overcome that barrier?"[125] Her answer was yes, undoubtedly, that barrier could be overcome. Yemenite Jews already embodied a lot of her Zionist ideals: "They are a thrifty, sturdy folk, inured to hardship, learned and pious, and speaking a pure Sephardic Hebrew."[126] But her solution for overcoming the barrier made clear a lopsided power dynamic: Western Ashkenazi Jews would do the teaching, and Yemenites would have to do most of the changing. To become equal participants in the project for a Jewish society in Palestine, Yemenite Jews should adopt Western ways—education, gender roles, science, medicine, and rational religion.

Yemenite Jews moved to Palestine for both religious and political reasons. Most believed that Jews would return to the land during the messianic age, and so Palestine had a spiritual appeal. More materially, political instability in Yemen, which was then part of the Ottoman Empire, pushed many to move. Most Yemenite Jews had immigrated to Palestine after 1882—within just a couple of generations of Sampter's arrival. They spoke Arabic and Hebrew, and their religious practices were neither Sephardi nor Ashkenazi; today scholars put them under the heading Mizrahi, literally, "Eastern." At the time, however, the idea of a Mizrahi identity had not yet coalesced: Jews were Yemenite Jews, Moroccan Jews, or Egyptian Jews, rather than all members of a single group called Mizrahim.[127]

Sampter was one of the few writers, and the most prodigious, about Yemenite Jews for an American audience. The vast majority of American

Zionists largely ignored the presence of Yemenites in Palestine, unless it was to mention how Western Zionists should help them out of the persecution in Yemen or had helped uplift them from poor health or superstition.[128] Others also saw Sampter in this model of noblesse oblige, as author Marion Rubinstein wrote in *Adventuring in Palestine*, a book for older children and adults:[129] "The nursery was so fine that tourists came to visit it. It had been built with the help of an American writer, Jessie Sampter, who lived among the Yemenites and saw their straw-thatched homes where in one room the entire family lived with their sheep, goats, chickens, and donkey. 'Gveret Sampter went to America to ask all the people there to give money to build this nursery. Now she teaches us how to live like Americans. I dress my little girl like an American,' Laya said very proudly."[130] Sampter was doing a good thing by teaching these Yemenites superior culture, in Rubinstein's eyes, even though that was not Sampter's goal.

Unlike most of her contemporaries, Sampter wrote about Yemenite customs, culture, and people—and not merely as a reason for fundraising or self-congratulation. Her 1920 article about Jerusalem during the arrival of the British explained how each community celebrated this "redeeming" of the land. She discussed a Yemenite celebration as just another part of the list: "Old men sang, and little children. The men danced solos. Then the people came up and brought their offerings . . . a month's savings, a year's savings. Men brought a shilling to whom a shilling means more than a million dollars to Mr. Schiff."[131] She called the dancing "weird and beautiful," differentiating Yemenites from the more upscale neighborhood celebrations she described—though one of those upscale celebrations included a goat standing on a piano, so by comparison the Yemenites looked rather normal to her readers after all.

She also brought Yemenite Jews into her vision of Zionism for children. *The Key*, a story Sampter wrote for American children, celebrated Jewish settlement of the land (a common theme of Zionist propaganda), but it also foregrounded the equality of Ashkenazi and Yemenite Jews (a far less common theme). After Shama, a Yemenite Jewish girl, loses the key to the chicken coop she is tending, the Ashkenazi Akiba helps her out. "I am a Jewish boy," said Akiba, "and you are a Jewish girl. I think in Palestine it is time we understood that we are all Jews and Jews are all brothers. Only I wish you didn't have to cry about losing the key to someone else's chicken house. I wish you had your own, as I have in Nahalal," the agricultural settlement where he lived with his family.[132] Sampter also dedicated her time to organizing schooling for Yemenite children, especially girls.

But Sampter's love and goodwill did not mean she was exempt from Orientalism. And, like other Orientalist attitudes, hers had both positive and negative aspects. After complaining about how the elite Jewish set used Yemenites "as a cheap servant class," she turned around to romanticize them: "Oh, these beautiful Yemenites! The large-eyed, dark children, the prophetic men, the little, quaint women in beaded kerchiefs; I like them; I like their crisp, Arabian Hebrew. Their ignorance, their spooky superstition."[133]

Sampter loved much of Yemenite culture but saw them as needing uplift in Palestinian society. She saw aspects of Yemenite Jewish culture as premodern—in both romantic and negative ways. In her view, they needed three key things: first, education for girls; second, modern medicine; and third, fairer wage practices.

To fix the first of these problems, it seemed that the Yemenite community would have to change its ideas about gender. "Education is given only to boys, whose only study is the Bible and its commentaries," Sampter explained in *Modern Palestine*.[134] Having women and children work while men studied was patriarchal: "They have not yet developed public spirit and their attitude toward women and children is a possessive one. Girls are sent to do housework in the village homes when they are but eight or nine years old. They used to be married by contract at eleven or twelve, but now marriages under sixteen are rare. Polygamy, permitted by their customs, is also gradually disappearing under the pressure of social environment. Women, many of whom work as scrubwomen, washerwomen or in the fields, give all their wages to their husbands."[135] She wanted to spare Yemenite girls from the "benevolent slavery of domestic service."[136] Yemenite communities should change these antiquated ideas about women's educational and economic subservience to men, Sampter thought.

During the late 1920s, Sampter tried to support a kindergarten for Yemenite children in Rehovot, as well as some night classes for adults. They were always woefully underfunded, but she helped keep them going as long as she lived there. She founded a "club" of Yemenite girls who met at her home to read and write, but she knew things like that could never single-handedly solve the problem. "It is important that Yemenite youth should finally be assimilated with the rest of Jewish youth, although this must be effected without losing their distinctive values or respect for their own traditions"—they should be allowed to attend school with others, as some of the Yemenite fathers had done with their daughters in Rehovot.[137]

And yet she recognized that Ashkenazi Jews were also contributing to the problem. (This recognition, to Sampter's credit, was quite unusual. I haven't found another of her contemporaries making this critique in such a pointed way.) She was critical of those who excluded Yemenite children from village schools, whether by decree or just by social exclusion: "The teachers admitted to me . . . that the fault lay not altogether with the Yemenites and that the causes were social as well as economic. The Yemenite children would probably not be welcome in the school in Rehoboth."[138]

Sampter went along with Hadassah's general maternalistic (and paternalistic) idea of the inferiority of folk medicine. She lamented Yemenites' continuing belief in "the superstition of the evil eye," fetishizing of "neighborly advice," and "faith in magic cures."[139] If they would adopt Western medical norms, childbirth would be easier, women would be healthier, and they would have a better and truer understanding of the world. And yet Sampter was also charmed by their magical thinking. In her novel "In the Beginning," a Yemenite woman is awed by snow: "'Sugar! Salt from heaven!' she murmured. 'God is sending us a sign!'"[140]

Though Sampter wanted to westernize Yemenite life, she was far from the harshest critic. One Hadassah nurse wrote of "the rubbish of medievalism that still prevails in Eastern countries," and another derided "superstitions and foolish customs."[141] Nutrition, including eating vegetables, was unknown to many, Hadassah materials complained.[142] While Sampter tempered her language, she, too, thought that Yemenite communities needed to abandon their health-related customs in favor of Western medicine.

The third key need, however, demonstrated that integrating Yemenites into a Zionist society was not only a job for the Yemenites themselves. Sampter took Ashkenazi Jews to task for exploiting Yemenite labor. In several versions of her guide to Zionism and Palestine, the chapter "Social Justice in the Jewish State" explained this gently to its American audience: "The problem of the Yemenite or Arabian Jews, whose standard of living approaches that of the native Arabs," was they were "therefore contented to accept wages which are nowhere near a living wage for the Russian Jewish workman."[143] In the next edition, she would put this more bluntly: "Yemenite Jews were workers from the beginning, but they were exploited, receiving little more pay than the Arabs and less than the Ashkenazic Jew."[144] If Zionists wanted a democratic and collectivist society, Sampter averred, they were going to need to do better with respect to the economic treatment of Yemenites.

Thus, even while she trafficked in Orientalist stereotypes, she saw Yemenites as an essential part of the Jewish community and as partners in Zionism. Sometimes she could even do both in the same breath. She wrote about the "tragic tenderness of Jewish eyes, the sensitive nostrils. Medieval as those of the older Sephardic and Ashkenazic immigration, and more primitive, there is yet something new and different in these Arabian Jews. . . . The Yemenite definitely belongs to the New Settlement."[145] And in another article in the American Jewish journal *Menorah*: "For my part, this simple people with its Oriental folk ways attracts me strongly. I could gladly live in the Yemenite colony. And I have no doubt that the growing respect for labor and the power of labor will bring this people into its own and unify us in our own land."[146] Sampter's Zionism included Yemenite Jews, though it pushed for westernization in some realms. But her Zionism had less space for non-Jewish Arabs.

Exclusion from Democracy

How could Jews and Arabs live together? The question occupied Sampter from her earliest weeks in Palestine until her death. "I believe the burden of *noblesse oblige* lies upon us, and that we *can* solve this problem," she wrote to Henrietta Szold about the "anti-Zionist Arab press" and its objection to designating Hebrew the official language.[147] Though her experience with the situation deepened throughout the years, that sentiment could fairly characterize her lifelong stance: she thought that Jews and Arabs could and should live together as equals but that Arab culture had not yet advanced to the level of Jewish culture, and so Jews would need to help them get there.

Before Zionists settled in Palestine, it was not "a neglected and deserted country."[148] It was not, as Mark Twain would have it, a "waste of a limitless desolation."[149] Nor, as Zionist leader Theodor Herzl imagined in *Altneuland*, would Arabs celebrate the Jewish arrival because of the cultural improvements they would bring. These myths resonated with many American Zionists, including a young Sampter, who wrote, "Forty years ago the will of the Jewish People broke into the barren waste of Palestine."[150] When she arrived in Palestine, however, she felt quite differently.

There were other people who called the land home. The 1922 census of Palestine recorded the population of Palestine as 757,000, of whom 78 percent were Muslims, 11 percent were Jews, 10 percent were Christians, and 1 percent were Druze.[151]

Sampter's Zionism centered on creating a Jewish society in Palestine. Though she wanted to upbuild the land as a Jew, she vehemently rejected the idea of a Jewish state. In an unpublished piece originally titled "Nationalism" and then changed to "Arab," Sampter wrote about her hopes for the future of Palestine: "I want no special government; only that which is good for us all. I surely want no such anachronistic idol as a Jewish state, a racial state!" Nationalism could poison societies. World War I had proven that for the pacifist Sampter, and Palestine should not follow a similar path. "I want the Arabs to drop their outworn romantic nationalism as I have dropped mine. I want Jews to drop theirs, and—with all westerners—their silly airs of superiority." "Superior and inferior," she wrote, "is merely my taste against yours." For Sampter, the goals of Zionism were "to re-settle Palestine with Jews," many of whom would work the land. And part of this resettlement was designed to help "make life for the Arabs and other inhabitants a richer, cleaner, more exciting experience."[152] Though she never expected Arab gratitude for Jewish settlement—she recognized that Zionists impinged on their lives and livelihoods—Sampter insisted that a good Jewish Zionist was a good neighbor.

Like her admiring gaze toward Yemenites, Sampter's view of non-Jewish Arabs combined aesthetic pleasure with cultural denigration: "The Arab peasant is wonderfully picturesque and attractive, and utterly ignorant, dirty, and uncivilized," she wrote to her brother-in-law, Edgar. "For his sake, too, we are needed. For we are kin. Jewish civilization and agriculture would be shared by him."[153] Her visit to Rehovot left her utterly charmed, in no small part because of the nearby Arab settlements. "The Arabs about here are very primitive, picturesque and friendly," she wrote to her sister. Her letter described their work ethic, their crops, and their work in the village.[154]

In her autobiography she wrote candidly of this push and pull:

In my own land, in the land of Jew and Arab, I do not know the Arab. That is because I cannot speak his language. To me he is a structure, a moving, living statue, something which I hear and read and so form opinions. But his inwardness I cannot discover. I have an instinctive liking for the Arabs; Palestine without their folk beauty, their Bedouin tents, their wild, gypsy-like children, their free, vigorous barbaric men, their straight-backed light-stepping, gay-robed women, would lose half its charm. Without Arabs and camels, is east east? Their loud voices, their nasal monotonous songs, their pipings lure me. I try to picture the mind of a bare-footed, blue-robed young woman from an Arab village, filthy and wild, who carries a wide basket full of grapes on her head. She smiles and says "saida" or even the Jewish greeting, "shalom"; her white teeth glisten. I know she cannot read or write. Who is her God?[155]

In spite of her decades-long commitment to being a "seeker" and a "great adventurer" in terms of religion, Sampter knew little about the Islam of her neighbors. "Do you know or have you read any good books on Islam?" she wrote to Elvie in 1933. "Curiously, I know less about it, from the intellectual and spiritual side, than any of the other religions, and living in the midst of its influence, I ought to understand it more."[156] She later clarified, "About a book on Islam, I know the history, that is, the origins. What I don't understand is the philosophy, the beliefs, the sects, the ideology. I want to get a sympathetic aspect of Islam, and I find all the presentations repellent and written from an unsympathetic point of view."[157] Sampter wanted to know about the religion of her Arab neighbors from a sympathetic point of view—and yet, in fifteen years of living in Palestine, this is the first time she brought it up with her sister, her usual source of books and magazines. Arabs were a central concern for her and other Zionists, and yet their lives remained opaque, a matter of sympathetic curiosity at best.

Sampter's ideas about non-Jewish Arabs had much in common with her views of Yemenite Jews, though she saw non-Jewish Arabs as harder to understand. The similarities in her views about these two groups of Arabs—a strong romanticism, accompanied by a sense that her own culture was nevertheless more advanced—shouldn't surprise us since they are textbook Orientalism. And yet Sampter also saw them as quite different: Yemenite Jews, by virtue of being Jewish, seemed both closer to her and more important to integrate into Zionist culture in Palestine.

If non-Jewish Arabs were "kin" and neighbors, but their ways were "uncivilized," what should be their role in the socialist democracy she envisioned? "Democracy is a bold faith. It says: we deny that men may use each other as they use animals. There are no inferior races. . . . There are ^perhaps no inferior races but there are races in inferior conditions. We cannot deal with them as equals, though we must deal with them as an end in themselves."[158] A diluted Kantianism underpinned her commitment to treat Arabs as humans but not give them full civil rights. And yet she still recognized that non-Jewish Arabs could have a communal goal parallel to the Jewish goal: "Nationalism is the expression of freedom. Each wants it for himself. Why not for his neighbor?"[159] Though she was not ready to give Arabs equal participation, she was very much in favor of more paternalistic kinds of help: "Give the Arab work, sanitation and education. Then you can build a Jewish homeland here, and make a good neighbor."[160]

Some of this may have seemed naive to her Zionist readers when riots broke out in Jerusalem in 1920. The violence took a bloody toll on the Jewish community there, as Sampter reported: "Old men and women, little boys, stabbed in the back beaten on the head . . . young men, dead and dying . . . an old woman with her ear cut off. A girl of fifteen violated . . . one hundred and seventy-five wounded Jews and a half-dozen dead."[161] The riots inspired some to double down on Jewish defense, and even secret paramilitary organizations, but Sampter held fast to her pacifism.

In fact, after the riots she demonstrated an unusual commitment to the Zionist project—by 1926 she was a citizen of Palestine under the British Mandate. And, unlike other American Zionists in the yishuv, she also gave up her US citizenship. "I ought to resign myself to all the consequences of Palestinian citizenship," she wrote, in a rare moment of humor, when she was down to her last roll of fine American toilet paper.[162] She gave up something else too, something more precious than toilet paper: her right to vote. Mandatory Palestine did not allow women to vote in yishuv-wide elections until shortly after she became a citizen.

In August 1929 non-Jewish Arabs killed sixty-seven Jews in Hebron, in the culmination of a summer of violence and tensions. The formerly tranquil city, the centuries-old home to Sephardi Jews and Arabs, erupted in bloodshed. A group of Arabs killed both Ashkenazi yeshiva students and longtime Sephardi residents. Sampter was horrified about the violence and saw it as her role to get whatever information she could past the British censors: "It is a sacred duty to use this opportunity of writing freely of the events of the last ten days in Palestine and sending my testimony with a personal messenger, an American citizen who is sailing. All mails are censored. But indignation and horror and mental and emotional exhaustion are almost as great a barrier against words."[163] She blamed the British for allowing the Hebron massacre to happen, and, she thought, the world should know.

Though Sampter was shaken, she reiterated her commitment to society in Palestine to the exclusion of American citizenship:

> The American citizens in Jewish Palestine sent a cable to Washington asking the Government to protect against the criminal negligence of the local administration which, among other horrors, is responsible for the piecemeal butchery—to be precise—of eight American boys, defenceless [sic] students in the Academy at Hebron. Although I contributed a word or two to the cable, I was not able to sign it because I am no longer an American citizen but a Palestinian. Never was I glad as now of this change of citizenship. I have a right to the protection of my own government in my own country and I do not want to ask for special privileges.[164]

At first glance, this seems like an odd time to be glad that she was no longer an American citizen. Why take pleasure in a lack of support and safety? The answer lies in Sampter's commitment to the collectivism of a Palestinian Jewish identity. If she were still a US citizen, then she would have an out; she would be a part of the Zionist settlement, but she would also be exceptional. She wanted full inclusion without exception. Sampter sought a Jewish society that would deal with its own problems in its own ways, rather than relying on other nations.

Sampter saw this particular problem as one of Arab, Jewish, and British making. She traced the violence back to a dispute about the Western Wall, during which she faulted non-Jewish Arabs for having an irrational religious commitment, but she also faulted Jews for dragging themselves into the issue on those same irrational terms: "How debasing for us to find ourselves involved in a 'religious war' on a superstitious issue that levels us with our still-medieval neighbors!"[165] She also blamed Jews for their conduct at the Western Wall as one reason for the buildup to the Hebron massacre: "There is an irenic connection as of unintended cause and effect between the procession of these radical youths on the streets of Jerusalem and the flesh and blood of these other orthodox youths in the streets of Hebron left to the mercy of stray dogs and cats."[166]

Yet the most blameworthy group, in Sampter's view, was not the Arabs but the British. "Not that one can compare this censure [of the Arabs] with what should be dealt to the playful British officials in Palestine who constitute our present government. Call us the canary-bird, not over-wise, and the Arabs the cat, only normally cruel. What of the boy whose pet was the bird and who after letting the cat into the cage is careful to grant them equal freedom?"[167] After the 1920 Jerusalem riots, she had written about non-Jewish Arabs, "These people are not our foes." The British and the effendi were the real perpetrators: "Our foe is the foe of humanity, imperialism, dirty politics, militarism, pulling the strings for the farce, the tragedy that has been enacted in Jerusalem. The Arab hoodlum is only the unconscious dummy."[168] More than just turning away, the British were almost orchestrating this violence, and that was unforgivable.

And yet, though she was unrelentingly critical of the British Mandatory forces, her own position also bordered on the colonial:

> During these terrible days, there has been time for thought. I have completed my readjustment. But for striking individual exceptions in both groups, I see the Palestinian Arabs as in a lower stage of culture and

civilization from that of the Jews, which makes it impossible for them at present to understand our conceptions of national or personal ethics. We must live with them, or rather side by side with them, and be careful to maintain our level despite the natural inclination of all things—not only water—to the lowest mean level. . . . But part of that job and the last test of our ability is to deal with them in friendliness and mutual helpfulness, in honesty and in co-operation.

If the Arab objects to my diagnosis, he cannot improve it by murdering me or even by refuting me. There is only one answer he can give, and that may take time.

And as for our present answer to him, it can be only one, a three-fold one: More Jewish immigrants, more Jewish land and more Jewish constructive and creative work for our country.[169]

More immigrants on more land could surely sound like a colonial project. Was a Jewish colonization project necessarily colonialism? What if it created a Jewish society at the expense of Arab sovereignty? Sampter never quite confronted these questions head-on.

"Is Zionism anti-Arab?" Sampter had asked herself in the 1920s. "I try to answer frankly. It is hard, for on that answer our life depends. Zionism may be anti-Arab; it need not be so. My Zionism is not anti-Arab. Nor is the Zionism professed by the Zionist Organization," she declared, perhaps with a willful naiveté.[170] Sampter desperately wanted to have a society that was both democratic and Jewish, but she could never quite get beyond the unsatisfactory compromise of what historian Rafael Medoff calls "delayed democracy," in which non Jewish Arabs would be fully included in democracy only once they were sufficiently civilized—or sufficiently on board with the Zionist project.[171]

In the wake of the 1929 riots, she was particularly critical of Judah Magnes, though the two often agreed on other political matters. To her sister, she wrote that he was naught but a "handsome and attractive fool" who "would have had many chances for leadership and failed us entirely. At one time, I put hope in him, but he is no leader, only a glib talker who puts his foot in his mouth."[172] The two generally shared Zionist outlooks, and they had shared unpopular stances in the past, such as their shared opposition to the United States entering World War I. Magnes had been the rabbi at Temple Emanu-El in New York, which hosted the founding meeting of Hadassah, and he had also employed Sampter's friend Lotta Levensohn as his secretary until she, too, moved to Palestine. Given this shared past, what could he have done to alienate her so? "There are, in general, three types of active persons of goodwill," she explained, "(1) the saints or leaders who do the right thing at the right time (2) the heroes who do the wrong thing at the right time and (3) the fools who do the right thing at the wrong time." Magnes was a fool. Establishing a binational society was the right thing to do, she thought, but beginning those talks in response to the violence was the wrong move.[173] She also felt misrepresented: Magnes "makes it appear that the Jewish or Zionist attitude toward Arab questions is belligerent or aggressive." By accusing other Zionists of aggression, he was "maligning our peaceful intentions by setting himself up as a saintly pacifist." Sampter assured her sister that most Zionists were indeed "like Magnes and me," that is, generally pacifist and working toward a binational future. Although that seems historically inaccurate, Sampter clearly reacted against seeing her own Zionism portrayed as the exception.

After Rosh Hashanah, the Jewish new year, in 1931, Henrietta Szold wrote to Sampter, "May the new year bring enlightenment toward the solution of 'the Arab problem,' our problem. As the months go by I realize increasingly that we stand and fall with it. If we fail to solve it, we are lost, because we shall have denied our whole past and its aspirations; if we succeed we shall have vindicated the Zionist condition that Judaism is still an active, productive force of supernal value."[174] The two had been corresponding about this for years; in 1929 Szold had written to Sampter, "We cannot hold ourselves guiltless. Visit our schools and then say whether our teachers are educating our children to the solution of our race problem."[175] Neither Szold nor Sampter ever solved "our" problem.

Gender Ideals and Real Inequalities

In the summer of 2017, when leaving Ben Gurion, Israel's major airport, I passed an exhibit, "120 Years of Zionism," on the wall beside the electronic people movers shuttling people toward the gates. It celebrated the history of the Zionist movement seamlessly with the history of the State of Israel. It began, "The Zionist movement was one of the first national movements in history to give women the right to vote. Starting with the elections to the Zionist Congress in 1898, women enjoyed the equal right to vote and to be elected to public office. By comparison, women's suffrage was introduced in England only in 1918, in the United States in 1920, and in France in 1944." And later: "Since the first waves of immigration, women have been fully integrated into the activities and leadership of the Zionist enterprise.

Female kindergarten and elementary school teachers and educators played a central role in reviving the Hebrew language," it explained in Hebrew and English. "Women served alongside men in the early security and defense forces, Hashomer, Haganah, Palmach, Irgun, and Lechi," it claimed.

This story of women's equality is a popular one—and for good reason. It fits contemporary ideas about the proper political place of women as citizens, voters, and leaders. It is a story that, if true, a country would want to celebrate. But there is a problem: it's not really a true story. Women Zionist pioneers certainly did work the land, and many men and women wanted gender equality in politics, economics, and family life in the new society they were building. But they didn't achieve it. Women could not vote at the First Zionist Congress in 1897, and at the second congress, they were seated at a special "women's caucus" held before the congress itself.[176] Only a handful of women attended the early Zionist congresses, and even fewer ever spoke. (When I did an internet search for the terms *women* and *Zionist Congress*, several of the first hits appeared with the apt addendum "Missing: women.") During the First Aliyah, the name for the wave of Zionist (or proto-Zionist) immigration from 1882 to 1903, women could not participate in local governing councils or administrative bodies in moshavim. Women also could not vote in yishuv-wide elections until 1926, when the Union of Hebrew Women along with many individual women finally won their decade-long fight for women's suffrage.[177] And though women were crucial in the revival of the Hebrew language, to suggest, as the exhibit does, that "kindergarten and elementary school teachers" are positions of political leadership and power is a profound misreading. These women in the educational field played essential roles, but they did not see themselves as part of the "leadership of the Zionist enterprise." Nor were they seen in that way by either the Zionist leaders or the larger Jewish culture in Palestine. As one historian writes, "Discrimination against women in public life has been a component of Israeli identity from the start."[178]

And military ones too: defense organizations routinely excluded women from participating in some of the ways men participated. The Haganah, the underground Jewish defense force, officially included women only beginning in 1925, and the Tel Aviv branch tended to allow only one woman per platoon of men, though women worked with it from its inception in 1920.[179] When she remembered recruitment for the Jewish battalions of World War I, Rachel Janaith wrote, "For the men there was the front—and for the women, again, disappointment. There were hundreds of women who reported for duty with the [Jewish] Legion, just like men. Of course, they were not taken. That rebuff left us flat and wearied; *we* were not to participate in that great moment."[180]

Women had to fight for inclusion in economic spheres as well as political ones. "I went to the employment bureau of the colony to look for work. I was told that there were only three colonists who were prepared to take women workers, and none of them had a special place for me," wrote Techiah Liberson of her experience in the first decade of the 1900s.[181] When she explained that she didn't want "ladies' work" and had come because she had heard workers were needed, Judith Edelman was told, "I don't know. The colonists don't want girls."[182] Rebecca Danith remembered, "It was with the utmost difficulty that I, a woman, could persuade the comrades to take me along [on a contract roadwork job for which she had been hired]. There were all sorts of objections. The work was too much for a girl; it wasn't nice for a Jewish girl to be working on the open road. There was even one comrade who believed that it would be a national crime!"[183] Miriam Schlimowitz remembered of her time in a kvutza in the Galilee: "I was bitterly disappointed when I perceived how small the role was which the woman played, how weak their influence on the common system."[184] Married women joined the Federation of Labor as the "wife of Comrade So-and-So," rather than as primary members.[185] Women's fight for recognition and inclusion in work was about more than symbolism or idealism; it was about livelihood too. This aspect was highlighted when, in the midst of the economic crisis during World War I, the unemployed Miriam Greenfeld killed herself.[186]

All these women lived in Palestine at the same time as Jessie Sampter. They recalled their experiences, and they described a burgeoning culture that Sampter was a part of too. Those who were involved in communal living or working in particular tended to be more likely to aspire to gender equality. Although lots of these people wanted their new culture to be equal for both sexes, their good intentions and lofty ideals did not always translate into reality.

Sampter had high hopes for the promise of a new society in Palestine, especially through communal living on kibbutzim and kvutzot. Her 1925 story *The Key* told a didactic children's story about the unjust social inequality among Ashkenazi colonists and Yemenite Jews and the potential of kibbutzim.[187] One Ashkenazi boy explained his kibbutz life:

"We have to help at home with the cows and chickens—I always milk the cows—and of course we have a school garden and in vacation time we work with the grown folks in the field. Even the kindergarten teacher goes out with the little children to show them how to work. You should see my little brother Simon, who is only four years old, handle a hoe. There is nothing soft about us." Akiba did not look soft. Though only thirteen years old, he was almost as tall as Dad, he had strong muscles, his blond hair and his bare legs—for he wore breeches almost up to his thighs and sandals without stockings—were sunburnt the color of his khaki suit.[188]

When she told this story for American Jewish children, the kibbutz was a place of strong muscles and health where one worked the land. Idealism also characterized her writing for adults. The kibbutz was to bring "the ambitions of the communal settlements in Palestine—a new life and a nobler life," she and her coauthor and fellow kibbutznik Dorothy Ruth Kahn (later Dorothy Bar-Adon) wrote in their volume about Kibbutz Givat Brenner.[189]

She believed in the kibbutz as an ideal. And she and Leah decided they wanted to make their lives there. The kibbutz member Eliezer Regev wrote, "In my memory, on one of those days, Moshe Tzemach came to me and talked to me about the desire of a rich American woman, living in a house surrounded by a magnificent garden, a mansion in every way, to establish a conversation with a few of the members of Givat Brenner about the possibility of joining our group."[190] Regev, Tzemach, and another man went to Jessie and Leah's house in Rehovot. There they found the beautiful house and garden. They drank tea, and the five people discussed Jessie and Leah's desire to move to the kibbutz. But it wasn't an easy decision.

Regev and his fellow kibbutzniks had heard things about Sampter, and so they hesitated to offer her and Leah a place on the kibbutz. "Contrary to the rumors—nonsense that came to our ears about a capricious and spoiled woman," Sampter appeared to them as "a woman with a bent face and good eyes, and a mouth and chin that said 'will and firmness.'" She had a forceful spirit that contrasted with her "frail body." Tzemach remembered his first meeting with her: she was "thin, pale-faced, big-eyed, clever, and restless. I felt that I was facing a woman whose greatness was accompanied by sincere simplicity, and in the course of a conversation with her, you became more enchanted."[191] Yet they tried to dissuade Jessie and Leah. The two discussed it, and they persisted. They would visit the kibbutz to get a more complete feeling for life there. Givat Brenner's leadership was full of questions: Weren't Jessie and Leah as old as the oldest founding members? "Where on our kibbutz can these two elderly women stay? And one of them is disabled!"[192] Leah didn't know if a single kibbutz out of all of them had two women in their fifties—and one "disabled and frail." But as the kibbutz minutes noted, Sampter would bring about 3,500 Palestine pounds with her (about 1,400 months' worth of skilled labor!).[193] However, she insisted that some would be used to set up the rest home. "At the general meeting there was certainly a lively debate, and there were members who opposed it," recalled Leah. "After all, two women of this age, given the work and living conditions of the time were not so desirable." The members also doubted a vegetarian rest home would succeed. Privately, Jessie and Leah also worried what would happen if it didn't succeed. Maybe they would "turn it into a cultural center or children's home," but if that happened, they wondered, "Would we be allowed to continue living on the kibbutz?"[194] They created their own insurance policy, giving 3,000 lira to the kibbutz but loaning 1,000 lira to nonmembers for the creation of a well. That way, if they were forced to leave, they could recoup the 1,000 lira and live on their own again. Some combination of their commitment and Jessie's money won over the kibbutzniks, and they made plans to move there. They entered their contract with the kibbutz together, and it named Leah as the head of the household.[195] They sold Jessie's house in Rehovot to Leah's sister.

The kibbutz had 280 adult members, 50 children, 30 cows, and hundreds of chickens when she and Leah joined. Tamar spent much of her time away at school, but she also joined the community. Sampter pledged her money (apart from a small sum for Tamar's schooling and other needs) to build a vegetarian rest home for workers who were ill or disabled or otherwise just needed a rest. (Givat Brenner's rest house would be the first kibbutz sanatorium of many—a trend that became a fixture for Israeli vacationers for decades to come. Workers even received a small "sanitorium payment" designed to let them take these simple vacations with their families.[196]) Living on the kibbutz brought Sampter back to her earlier experiments in collective living: "It reminds me of my settlement and YWHA days," she wrote to her sister fondly.[197] But life on the kibbutz was even better than those past communalist experiments because of the integration of body and soul at the heart of the kibbutz enterprise, she thought. "Everyone works. One could not live and not work; it would be a spiritual impossibility."[198]

She wrote to her sister shortly after she and Leah had finally been able to move onto the kibbutz. "Yes, all work is done without remuneration. All pay to individual workers goes to the common fund. Leah just got a pair of sandals which cost her a walk to our shoemaker's, behind the dining hall."[199] Leah's main job was kitchen duty: "I would get up at six in the morning, and I would go to work in the kitchen," she recalled.[200] Jessie was very much in favor of a communalist project, though she recognized that the real did not always fully match the ideal: "Life here is very free, and there is a great deal of personal consideration. Each is treated according to his needs. In that sense, there is not equality because needs, health, and strength differ. The ideal which guides us is, as far as possible, to give to each according to his needs and get from each whatever he can give. As you say, it does not always work out so well. Still I should decidedly call this experiment a great success, not in relation to the ideal, but in comparison with life in other places."[201] As Sampter suggested, reality was more complicated than some utopic communalist vision. Yes, the kibbutz was communal, and so cooperating and helping others were central to its ethic. But despite the community's aim of "a nobler life," they could not escape the reality of conflict. Givat Brenner itself was founded in 1928 and named after the writer Yosef Haim Brenner, who was killed in May 1921 in the Jaffa riots. So in this sense, even the name of the communalist kibbutz evoked a history of conflict, violence, and land disputes.

Even the ideal of collectivism was not entirely inclusive. Jessie was both of the kibbutz and not of it. Her primary contributions were monetary and literary. She founded the rest home for workers, and she wrote for the kibbutz newsletter while others worked with their hands. For example, one day in 1934, Leah bought materials for couch cushions in Tel Aviv, and she sewed them the next day.[202] During these two days, Sampter was quite weak and unable to do much apart from a small amount of typing. These days were not atypical. Sampter never labored manually on the kibbutz. An older member brought Jessie breakfast and lunch, cleaned the room, and "helped her with whatever she needed" while Leah was working.[203] When Leah received an offer to manage a farm for a year, "Jessie was afraid to remain at Givat Brenner without me," Leah remembered. Dorothy Ruth Kahn wrote after Sampter's death, "Jessie never knew kibbutz life in its entirety, in its simple reality. She was not really familiar with that hard life movement which turns quite a few among us into cogs in the machine."[204] In addition to signaling Sampter's partial exclusion from the heart of the kibbutz, Dorothy Ruth Kahn also suggested that the collectivist producer ethic was not all it was cracked up to be. Like capitalism, it, too, could make people feel reduced to their ability to work.

And, as Sampter wrote about in a widely translated article (including into Hungarian!), gender equality was not yet a reality. "Married Women in Kevutzot" explained, "Women, for lack of training, are still weak on the public and administrative side; and in the completely democratic govern-ment of the kvutzah, where the town meeting is the responsible body, women are not yet taking their share of public work."[205] She lamented that fewer women than men entered leadership positions and that women often voted for men rather than other women during these elections. Yet she was hopeful for the future: "The younger the group, the more active the women are in public affairs," and so the next generation would do bet-ter.[206] She also expressed her displeasure when women had to cook instead of work the fields:

> It's a pity
> The girls who cook had learnt no skill abroad
> Hard to cook in huge cauldrons for a hundred
> With nothing good to choose from, and a longing
> To plow and plant the earth."[207]

A kibbutz was a place where traditional gender roles should not be fol-lowed, Sampter insisted, but it would sometimes be a struggle to live up to those ideals.

Conclusion

Telling Sampter's life as a theological and political one raises a question for me: How do we choose the people we write about? Should we write about good people? Interesting people? What happens when we write about sym-pathetic people with some unethical commitments? And how does the pre-sent matter to the past?

We come to know our subjects intimately. I know Jessie Sampter—her family, her politics, her religious ideas, her aches and pains. I followed her garden. When she planted portulaca, I remembered my grandmother's por-tulaca, as I do every year when I plant my own. I thought about her nastur-tiums and how she wondered with her sister if the nasturtiums in Palestine were different from those in the United States. When mine looked awful, I wondered if the ones from Palestine were more drought tolerant. I sympa-thized when she felt as if the work in the garden was never done.

But her gardening was also different from mine. Though she had always loved plants, in Palestine her gardening took on a new meaning. She sowed and pruned as part of a project to build a nation, "to make the desert bloom," as a popular Zionist slogan would have it. She eulogized the Zionist, bota-

Sampter at Kibbutz Givat Brenner, 1934. Courtesy of Givat Brenner
Archives, Yesha Sampter papers.

nist, and spy Aaron Aaronsohn with a poem weaving together plants and the Jewish people.[208] My garden will never be a political project the way hers was.

Jewish nationalists wanted their own land and their own right of self-determination. Palestine was their ancestral land according to religious texts. And in 1917 Britain "gave" it to them via the Balfour Declaration. A Zionist victory.

Except herein lies part of the complication: the desert was not deserted before Sampter or even the earliest wave of Zionist immigrants got there. Though small Jewish communities also lived there throughout history, before the Zionist immigration movements of the late nineteenth century, the majority of the inhabitants of the land were non-Jewish Arabs. Some of them were nomadic, so they didn't have the same relationship to land-ownership that the arriving Zionists did, but much of the land of Palestine was their land.

This, alongside certain British governing styles and policies, set the stage for conflict between Jews and Arabs in Palestine. Sampter herself often defended "the Arabs." I've heard her described as a binationalist. I think there are valuable aspects of her Zionism that are worth considering, even though—or especially because—they are roads not taken.[209] But she also readily trafficked in Orientalist stereotypes, and she wanted a home-land for Jews even if it cost Arab communities. This, then, is not merely a recovery project designed to show that Sampter got Zionism perfectly right. It is the tale of a fascinating and flawed life, a life marked by seeming contradiction, and, for all these reasons, a life worth our consideration.

CHAPTER FIVE

Afterlives

Mary Antin's last letter was still in transit when Jessie Sampter died, and so her dear friend would never read it. Antin often went many months without answering Jessie's letters, and so there were quiet times in their correspondence, but this new silence between them meant something else entirely. There would be no more letters. Antin was bereft. She sent a letter to Jessie's sister. "Death has visited me many times," she wrote. "I thought I knew how it felt to lose a friend. But this is—Jessie. Elvie dear, I have been lost in a cloud of selfish grief. I can't *spare* Jessie."

Her only consolation was that there was still more Jessie to be had in the world. Mary declared that she would learn Hebrew so that she could know another Jessie, the one she would find in Jessie's Hebrew poems and writings: "I think I'll sit down and learn Hebrew just for the sake of tasting Jessie's expression of herself in that grand language. There, I am sure, I'd find still another Jessie."[1]

I, too, have tried to catch glimpses of many Jessies by thinking about Jessie in the language of queerness, in the language of disability, and in other languages too. She didn't write in those languages, precisely, but through them I could see more of her.

Mary Antin and I are not the only seekers. Others have also sought and found other Jessies. Even after her death, she shaped how her family, her friends, and her Zionist colleagues saw the world. And so, in a way, the story of her life did not end when her life ended. A reception history might discuss how Sampter's readers interpreted her, but I am interested in more intimate but also more far-reaching questions: how people who knew her thought about her life, how they used her life to see something more about their own ideas and ideals, and how people who never met her created their own interpretations of her life for their own ends—the ways she has affected others and the ways others have used her to their own effects.

"I, for one, believed, yes, knew, that I had been forever, that I was not 'made' in these few years," Sampter wrote in *The Seekers*. "If we believe in the vast Self of life, and if we are a part of that awakening Self, how can we die?"[2] From her childhood, Sampter pondered human immortality, and she always held that human minds and bodies do not live on in any material sense. But throughout her life she toyed with the concepts of immortality and transmigration—the idea that something of the spirit could be reborn. "I think the results of life are eternal, even if not the precise memories," she wrote.[3] Whereas I personally remain agnostic about various kinds of immortality and transmigration, as a life-writer I can confidently say this: Sampter has lived on.

Her afterlives include variations on her own story. They also include the role she played in other people's stories, including mine. She has lived on as an ideal Zionist (in the years just after her death), as a Jewish educator and children's poet (in the 1950s), as a songwriter (in the 1950s), and as a quotable philosopher appearing in Weight Watchers inspirational books, on websites, and on a road sign in India (in the 1990s).

Perhaps you will see, as I do, larger questions hovering in the background as I tell these afterlives: What access do we have to the experience of others, especially those who have died? Can we really tell someone else's story, or are we always telling a version of our own? I see history as a practice of the present. It asks questions that reflect the relevance and interest of our own times—and our own selves. Biographies and narrative histories are not just a series of facts; they are stories. And those stories have much of the author in them.

And so the past lives on. But it is not that simple: when someone tells a story of the past, that past is not merely preserved; it is both revivified and changed. In a telling, the past lives new lives, and life-writing becomes a path to immortality. Sampter wrote, "Were it not for the immortality of the self, the world itself might shrivel up and disappear."[4] She wasn't thinking of life-writing, but she could have been.

Remembering the Dead in Our Own Image

The obituary is its own distinctive genre of life-writing. The life of the deceased often becomes a series of snapshots of joys and accomplishments, like a carefully curated Instagram feed of photos of happy moments. For almost everyone, apart from serial killers and genocidal dictators, obituaries contain facts but border on eulogy. In an obituary, no one mentions a person's propensity to interrupt, loud snoring, or unreliability as a friend. When, in 2018, a Minnesota woman's children submitted her obituary to the local paper with the closing sentence, "She will not be missed by Gina and Jay, and they understand that this world is a better place without her," it went viral.[5] Although we all know that family relationships can be complex, such scathing sentiment in an obituary titillated readers. We expect obituaries to praise.

In addition to saying something about the deceased, obituaries also have something to say about the culture they come from. Americans began to publish death notices even before the early republic, and with historical distance we can see how their themes often reflected broader cultural moments. They were sentimental and religious during and after the Civil War, and by 1900 personal wealth and work habits dominated the stories.[6] Across these eras, obituaries often emphasized gendered characteristics: women were loving, caring, and kind, and men were strong providers. But which particular characteristics each author thinks will paint the deceased in a positive light tell us something about larger cultural values—and about the obituary writers themselves.

When Sampter died, newspapers, magazines, and newsletters printed obituaries for her. *Israël*, a Cairo-based French-language Zionist paper, called her a "true pioneer" and an "inspired poetess who devoted many poems to Eretz Israel [the land of Israel], its inhabitants, and its landscapes."[7] The American *Bnai Brith Messenger*, the publication of a non-Zionist-leaning organization that had just elected a Zionist president, noted the end of her "colorful career" and recalled her organizing of "one of the first Zionist schools of the world in New York City."[8] An English-language Jewish newspaper in Bombay mourned the passing of the "leading American poetess and pioneer."[9]

The day after she died, the *Palestine Post*, the Jerusalem-based English-language newspaper for which she sometimes wrote, painted her as a martyr for the Zionist cause. It called her life "an epic poem": "It [w]as an epic of suffering: of physical suffering, for good health was denied her from girlhood, and of spiritual suffering. For she, like Miranda, could have said, 'O, I have suffered, With those I saw suffering.' And latterly she was compelled to learn how enormous could be 'man's inhumanity to man,' until life, as it were, defeating her aim to raise mankind ever higher, became almost unbearable."[10] The *Post* was founded in 1932 by Gershon Agron (then Agronsky), who would later become the mayor of Jerusalem. In addition to publishing some of her articles, Agron had praised Sampter's books and propaganda.[11] His newspaper reported on life in Palestine for English-language readers, including the ruling British, but it also promoted labor Zionism. And from at least this one labor Zionist perspective, Jessie Sampter had suffered—and died, maybe even died for the cause.

Even in these earliest recollections, I see a familiar pattern. When, in the early twentieth century, the theologian Albert Schweitzer reviewed the scholarship about the historical life of Jesus, he found that each writer's Jesus looked an awful lot like the author. Some of Sampter's obituary writers seem to have taken the cue. As a child, Sampter had wondered "what it would be like to be like that man Jesus Christ."[12] Sampter did not "found a religion," as she imagined Jesus had, but like the Jesus scholarship, Sampter's obituaries and her friends' remembrances often reflected the writers as much as they did Sampter.

For many Zionists, after her death she became the ideal Zionist. *Davar HaPoelet*, the women's-interest offshoot of the labor-focused *Davar*, devoted five pages to her. It included Leah Berlin's brief description of Sampter's life, especially her work with children, from her creation of institutions for Yemenite education to her hosting of HaNoar HaOved, a youth Labor Zionist organization.[13] "Jessie Sampter Dead: Poetess and Veteran Pioneer," read the headline of an obituary in the *Palestine Post*. The obituary made her out to be an upbeat and even perky woman: "Early on Friday morning Jessie Sampter walked out of the Rest House which she had built in the Communal Settlement of Givat Brenner. In good spirits she bade her friends good-bye until she would return on Sunday. An hour later she died in the Beilinson Hospital in Petah Tikva. This was a fitting end to a life of rare courage and uninterrupted activity."[14] The obituary was signed by "D. K.," likely Sampter's friend Dorothy Kahn, for whom the *Palestine Post* was a "second home," according to her biographer.[15] Kahn had lost a colleague and a fellow Zionist writer, but given this description, had she lost a friend? Sampter's activity was hardly "uninterrupted." And how was dying in the hospital "a fitting end to a life of rare courage"? How well could she have known Sampter if she painted her in this light?

Sampter at Kibbutz Givat Brenner, 1930s. Courtesy of Givat Brenner Archives, Yesha Sampter papers.

In fact, Kahn and Sampter knew each other very well. Kahn was an accomplished newspaperwoman, knowledgeable in genres and conventions. And so Kahn painted Sampter as a good Labor Zionist, a good woman, and a good Jewish pioneer, all while she also painted her friend Sampter's life as similar to her own.

For Kahn, Sampter was an intellectual inspiration. Sampter was Kahn's senior by twenty-four years. Both women were born in the United States and moved to Palestine as single women hoping to make a career of writing, and they became friends at Givat Brenner, where they read each other's drafts. "Uninterrupted activity" described Kahn's own life: when her father died, the sixteen-year-old Kahn went to work for the *Atlantic City Press* in New Jersey; she moved to Palestine a decade later to continue her career as a journalist and had enough fascinating material to publish an autobiography before she was thirty. While she was living at Givat Brenner, she covered the riots, life on kibbutzim and in Arab villages, and a host of politically volatile situations. The two women collaborated on a book-length manuscript about kibbutz life, in which each woman combined personal experience and political critique.

She wrote about Sampter's steadfast commitment to the Zionist movement through writing: "The life of Miss Sampter, poetess and pioneer, has been as dramatic as the Zionist movement to which she had been attached for 35 years. Although crippled by paralysis at the age of 12, she played her part in the building of the country until the day of her death, when she was concerned about a manuscript on the Collective Settlements completed a few weeks ago and now in the hands of the publishers."

Kahn's obituary also touted Sampter's feminine virtue of selfless care for the less fortunate: "Born in America in 1883, Miss Sampter began her good works by living and working among East European immigrants in a New York Settlement House when in her early twenties. Until the last day of her life she was receiving and ministering to refugees—but now they came from Germany, Austria, and Italy." As a fellow American, Kahn would have known about the feminine aspects of Progressive Era politics. Women were accepted, and even celebrated, in settlement house work because it was close to the familiar tasks of the domestic sphere, such as housekeeping, cooking, and cleaning, but also genteel activities like reading culturally significant books. Yet, apart from the books, these were never the things that excited Sampter. And though Sampter spoke clearly in favor of admitting European refugees to Palestine and even incorporating them into life at Givat Brenner, she herself did little "ministering" to them.

Kahn, herself a labor Zionist, emphasized that part of Sampter's life too: "The essence of her life was her devotion to the cause of Labour," Kahn wrote. "Five years ago she renounced her private possessions and became a member of Givat Brenner, building a rest home and garden primarily for workers. Here she lived and worked among people whom she believed had started on a path toward the life abundant." Hinting at the increasingly dangerous political situation in Europe, Kahn continued, "Miss Sampter was a pacifist. Although destined to be cut off at a time of international turmoil she held to the end an unalterable belief that the sword would be turned into ploughshare. Hers was a valiant, unalterably gracious soul in a particularly weak body."[16] Kahn's portrait of Sampter managed to be a lot like Kahn: a brave, feminine labor Zionist. And her obituary painted a portrait of a labor Zionist's life that praised Sampter while it simultaneously reinforced the idea of the nobility and courage of the labor Zionist cause.

Shortly after the news of her death, Sampter's friends and colleagues in New York gathered together in tribute, sharing their memories of her as a strong Zionist with serious intellectual influence. They met at Shearith Israel, New York's oldest synagogue, and the rabbi there, David de Sola Pool, served as chairman and began the gathering by inviting one of Sampter's friends to read three of her poems. "The meeting was unlike the usual memorial meeting because Jessie was unlike the usual run of human being," Sampter's friend Margaret Doniger recalled.[17] Louis Lipsky, former editor of the *Maccabaean* and longtime Zionist official, spoke, but he, too, found himself giving a personal rather than institutional account of Sampter's life. "There was that about Jessie that refused to be confined within conventional organized patterns in any movement, and he could only speak as a fellow human being moved by deep respect for her rare qualities of spirit," Doniger wrote of his tribute.[18] In a letter to her friend and fellow Zionist Rose Jacobs, Doniger described the gathering: her husband "said that there was something about that meeting that held him under a spell for days and days. I think all of us felt more or less that way, and if I tell you that it was a religious experience much more than a tribute, you will know just what I mean."[19] To Sampter's friends in New York, even more than a worker for the Zionist cause, she had been a religious adept, a spiritual paragon, and an inspiration.

The January 1939 *Hadassah Newsletter* featured the tributes of Margaret Doniger and Julia Dushkin. Each of them remembered Sampter much as they saw themselves: intellectually strong and committed to Zionism. Doniger wrote, "So often I have heard persons on first meeting Jessie Sampter to say of her, 'What a sweet and gentle soul.' Sometimes they would add in kindly fashion, 'If only she were stronger.'" But, Doniger countered, they were mistaken. Sampter was a strong soul, even if she were not a strong body: "That delicate, sensitive, almost saint-like face and frail body with its telltale marks of an attack of infantile paralysis, hid from view a strength of character and courage which most of us who are 'strong' can only vaguely understand." Doniger admired her intellect and commitment to bringing ideals to life: "She could never tolerate a cleavage between ideals and practice. . . . She knew no half-way measures."[20]

Dushkin remembered Sampter through the natural world at her memorial service: the flowers, the plants, and the trees took the main stage. But they appeared as ways to tell Sampter's life, not as distractions from it. Nature, which Sampter saw as part of a great unity including people, became a way to see Sampter. "In full poetic justice, Nature and New Palestine combined to make our parting from her a spectacle of unforgettable beauty, a stirring spiritual experience! Rolling hills, a gentle breeze, white fleecy clouds over sea and sand dune and the warm golden light of a late November noon sun. Trees heavily laden with grapefruit and oranges; here and there a flowering acacia tree with its drooping boughs of yellow, all blended into one shimmering stretch of light, dazzling yet soothing! Such was Nature's setting when we all gathered to bid Jessie farewell." The gathered mourners threw "countless white asters and chrysanthemums, all from Jessie's own garden," onto her grave.[21]

Was Dushkin a gardener? Did she love plants? I can't say for sure. I suspect she was; her vivid descriptions are the sort that come from the eye of someone who has spent long hours with plants. Her daughter dedicated a book of poetry to her parents, and those poems, too, are rich in natural and horticultural imagery that sees the details of leaves, of flowers, and of the light around them. But I can't know for certain because, although Julia Dushkin was a pioneer in Jewish education, in the archives she is overshadowed by her husband, Alexander Dushkin. Both were friends of Sampter, both were intellectuals, and both worked hard and traveled far and wide to bring the latest scientific education methods to Jewish communities. But only one has an archive.

Julia Dushkin's recollection of the memorial also captured something of the intimacy of female friendship and, I think, of the love that Leah and Jessie shared. When they arrived at Givat Brenner, guards directed Dushkin and Henrietta Szold to the study house, where Jessie's body lay. "Keeping watch at her side stood the devoted Leah Berlin, pioneer like Jessie, and friend who had watched over her for nearly twenty years and carried joint responsibility with Jessie for their common undertakings." Dushkin described the candlesticks, the ones Sampter had used for Sabbath candles, burning near the head of the table. Flowers sent by Yemenite children from Rehovot covered her coffin. "Silent and alone stood Leah Berlin until we entered with Miss Szold. Suddenly the gates of her grief broke open, she cried out for a moment and then that tall strong woman dropped her weeping head on Miss Szold's frail shoulders and for the first time we saw Miss Szold weeping too." When it was Leah's turn to place flowers on her grave, "she murmured, 'Nuhi ktsat, Jessie,' ('rest a little, Jessie') just as she was wont to say oftentimes each day in urging rest upon her." These women were Sampter's family.

Dushkin concluded by telling how Szold had spoken to the Youth Aliyah group. She told them the story of Jessie's life, how she freed herself from the bondage of her crippled body; how through proper internationalist understanding she arrived at an acceptable Jewish nationalism; how through the medium of a Christian minister she learned of Zionism and through it of Judaism; how not satisfied only to worship at the altar of the idea, she came from America to Palestine to help embody the ideal; how in the quest for truth and justice she came to accept Labor's ideals. Here then, in the hearts of these newly exiled children from Austria and Germany, did Miss Szold plant the first seeds of Jessie's immortality.

Dushkin told Sampter's story as the story of an American Zionist woman and a champion of children.

As the months ticked on, others wrote their own Jessie Sampters into being. Judith Ish Kishor eulogized Sampter in the syndicated column The Sabbath Angel, a children's feature in the Anglo-Jewish press. There Sampter became a Jewish fairy-tale princess living the dream of heteronormativity and Zionism. "At least once a week, when the hot days of summer come, I think about a lovely poem called 'Summer Sabbath,' which I want to show you now," she wrote to her young readers. "Jessie Sampter, who wrote this and so many other songs and verses for Jewish children, passed away several months ago."[22]

In Ish Kishor's story of Sampter, she was a pioneer of Jewish children's poetry in a way that made her into a founding mother. Ish Kishor wrote, "It was her idea that there ought to be poems for Jewish children, as natural and as interesting and as easy to read as the poems that Robert Louis Stevenson wrote for all children. There were very few like that, before Jessie Sampter began to write them. By now, there is really a Jewish 'Child's Garden of Verses,' just as she had wished."

More a fairy-tale princess than a dashing heroine, in Ish Kishor's telling, Sampter lived in a timeless moment in a delightful "cottage" with her grateful daughter:

Miss Sampter, ever since she began to write for you, wanted to go to Palestine. Her wish came true. She had a little cottage in the colony of Rehovot, not far from Tel Aviv, and there I spent a day or two with her, when I visited the Holy Land. She was very happy, for she had adopted a little girl who had no parents of her own. This happily-ever-after picture was my last view of her, but I always remember her whenever I read her verses. And you must remember her too. For her beautiful poems are an everlasting present to all Jewish children.

Ish Kishor urged Sampter's immortality through writing. Sampter would be joyful and nurturing, mothering all future Jewish children who read her uplifting and educational poetry. Ish Kishor did not mention that Jessie had Leah or that she had no Prince Charming. As a fairy-tale princess, this Jessie Sampter was hardly queer.

Ish Kishor herself also wrote Jewish children's literature and poetry. In 1895 she had been born into a Zionist family; her father, Ephraim Ish Kishor, attended the First Zionist Congress in Basel in 1897. Though she spent her life in the United States and England, Ish Kishor presented a beautiful and romanticized Palestine to her young readers. She found a Jessie Sampter whose life had been saved by Zionism, who provided the image of "happily-ever-after" in Palestine.

Ish Kishor told Sampter's story to her young audience. Henrietta Szold told Sampter's story to the children at her memorial service. Julia Dushkin told Sampter's story to *Hadassah Newsletter* readers. Dorothy Kahn wrote her story for *Davar* readers. And as each woman told Sampter's story, she also told something of herself.

As the years passed, others who had not known her began to tell Sampter's life story—and not all of these were idealized Sampters. The journalist Robert St. John used her story in his 1949 *Shalom Means Peace*. He had written about the Middle East, three biographies of David Ben-Gurion, and ten other books about Jews, Judaism, or Israel. When he died in 2003, his own obituary in a Jewish weekly called him "journalist, author and tireless supporter of Israel." Ben-Gurion, Israel's first prime minister, had called him, glowingly, "our goyisher Zionist."[23]

St. John loved strength, bravery, and self-determination—things he saw in Zionism. As a sixteen-year-old, he had lied about his age to enlist in the US Navy and fight in World War I. A few years into his journalistic career, Al Capone's men beat him up for his exposés about the gangster. In 1949 St. John published *Shalom Means Peace* after he spent time in Israel/Palestine covering the war and the foundation of the state during the previous year. Written for a largely American audience, it dramatized the dangers and victories of the new nation of Israel.

Between observing political strife and violence, he also visited kibbutzim, including Givat Brenner. The place impressed him. He saw strong men building a nation and plowing the land. He saw willingness to fight.

And though she had been dead for a decade, he also thought he saw something of Sampter. With her, however, he was not impressed.

In his tale Jessie Sampter played the role of the spoiled brat, an also-ran Zionist who was too prissy to do the real work of nation building. Though Sampter's money was good for the kibbutz, he thought, she was frail and spoiled and didn't really fit kibbutz life.[24] "Jesse [sic] Sampter was an American spinster. She was an ardent Zionist, a vegetarian, and a retired artist. When she first came to Palestine, she knew nothing about the kibbutzim. She came to open a school for Yemenite Jews from the East," he wrote, liberally glossing the tale. "She even adopted a Yemenite girl as her own daughter. Then, fifteen years ago, she met some of the Givat Brenner people and got an urge to be a member."[25] In truth, Sampter had admired kibbutzim since before she moved to Palestine, and she had been impressed with the nearby Kvutzat Schiller for many years and frequently visited it when she lived in Rehovot. But in St. John's story, Sampter played the role of the rich and spoiled American who joined a kibbutz on a lark. Her money and her physical weakness meant that she wasn't real kibbutz material; her character served as a counterpoint to the true pioneers of the kibbutz.

St. John explained what one kibbutz member had said about Sampter: "There was only one trouble. Unfortunately Jesse Sampter was very wealthy. At least by Palestinian standards. She had several thousand pounds. Ten or twenty thousand dollars. But under our rules no member is allowed to possess money. It doesn't often happen, but if a candidate has money he must dispose of it before we will take him as a member. When we explained the rule to Jesse Sampter she said: 'But what if Givat Brenner fails? I'm an old lady and I'm a cripple and an invalid and I'm quite frail. What happens to me if your settlement fails?'"[26] This tale is dubious on some accounts, but it was still the story of Sampter's life. Sampter wasn't an "old lady"; she was not yet fifty when she moved to Givat Brenner. And she and Leah had chosen Givat Brenner in large part because it was both established and growing. They had done their homework and were confident about its future. Yet some kibbutz members reported that she had a reputation of being a spoiled American. Like the wicked son in many traditional Passover Haggadot (texts read during the Passover seder), here Sampter asks about "your" settlement.

In St. John's story, Sampter was self-centered and demanding, and the kibbutzniks gave her a stern talking to but ultimately acquiesced because of her money:

We told her that joining a kibbutz is like getting married. One has to gamble a bit. She'd have to take us for better or for worse. Finally she made her decision. She said she wanted to join and she would give all her money to Givat Brenner, but there would be certain conditions. We would have to use the money to build a rest home on a certain hilltop she had picked out, and we must agree that meat would never be served in the place, because she didn't believe in meat. We debated the matter for a long time. The site she had picked was a bare rock hill. Earth would have to be carried to the top by horses and humans. As for the rule about meat, we aren't vegetarians. But we finally agreed. Then Jess[i]e Sampter gave us her money, and became a member, and lived to see the rest home completed.[27]

St. John's facts were (mostly) true, but he marshaled Sampter's story in service of a Zionism quite different from her own—a muscular political movement suddenly embedded in the new and embattled nation-state of Israel. And her life story served as a contrast, not an inspiration.

Other characters fit St. John's Zionist vision better. "The man next to me was in his twenties," he reported immediately following his discussion of Sampter. "He said he was Solomon Mitchell from Winnipeg and he'd gone to college at Grinnell in Iowa. He'd been a Palestinian for just six months and liked it."[28] St. John called Mitchell "a Palestinian" after he had been in Palestine for only six months, while he still branded Sampter "an American" even though she had lived in Palestine for most of her adult life. His romanticized vision of Zionists as Jews with guns and political power was a good fit for a strapping college man but an uneasy fit for a disabled pacifist woman.

But like many of her eulogies, St. John's story of Sampter reveals his own ideas as much as hers. His narrow view was not lost on contemporary readers. The American Jewish sociologist Nathan Glazer reviewed the book in *Commentary*, the magazine of American Jewish political thought, where he wrote, "Mr. St. John was very impressed with the new Jewish state and its people and institutions, and writes about them enthusiastically, thoughtlessly, and somewhat inaccurately, in the way most journalists visiting foreign parts generally do." Glazer noticed St. John's gendered visions of Zionism and Israel: "The women are all beautiful and nurse unspeakable mysteries, the children are blond and curly-haired, the men brave and bronzed and impassive, the Mediterranean 'inscrutable,' and so on: everything is in exasperatingly familiar categories, processed for 'easy reading.'"[29] This Sampter, whose story served a Zionism of "easy reading" and manly soldiers, existed only at the very margins of that Zionism.

A similar, though far more detailed, Sampter appeared as Shelly Steiner in the Israeli novelist Moshe Shamir's 1973 book *Yona MeHatzer Zara* (From a different yard).[30] Shamir was related to Leah Berlin, and the novel's main character is modeled closely on Berlin and her life after moving to Givat Brenner. Shelly shares a great many biographical details with Sampter, from emigrating from the United States and having money to small details such as having Chaim Weitzman move into her Rehovot house after she left and having played the violin. Shamir even describes photographs of Sampter that I have seen. Yet Shelly is a relatively unsympathetic character: she is needy, complicated, and a little disconnected from reality, and she clings to the main character (named Leah). Several scenes involving Shelly and Leah have sexual undertones, including what seem like sexual fantasies, charged conversations around saying "I love you," and a comparison of making the decision to live on the kibbutz to getting married.[31] The other kibbutz members tolerate Shelly for her money but see her more as an American interloper than as a real Zionist.

Yet another 1949 book created quite another Jessie. Sampter became the "Skipper of the Schooner *Courage*" in a book called *America's Triumph: Stories of American Jewish Heroes*. Its author, Dorothy Alofsin, wrote books for children and Jewish communities. Born in 1898 in Michigan, she had lived through many of the same events as Sampter—World War I, the growth of Zionism in the United States, and the rise of Adolf Hitler, though Alofsin also saw the devastating effects of the Holocaust and the founding of the State of Israel. She found a Jessie whose life, she hoped, would inspire American Jewish children.

This Jessie's life was a story of overcoming: the doctor diagnosed young Jessie with "infantile paralysis," the curvature of her back and "deforming" of her fingers and thumb, but she would not let these hold her back from her dreams. When she narrated Sampter's declaration of her intention to go to Palestine, Alofsin embellished the reaction of friends and family: "You're not strong enough," they insisted, "to brave the discomfort and primitive life you would have to endure." Henrietta Szold said, "Even if you were a Samson, I should not approve of your going to Palestine. Zionism in America needs your gift, the power of the written word."[32] Yet she went. In Palestine she faced more hurdles: "There were days when Jessie Sampter was ill and unable to carry on the work she had undertaken as her special task, teaching Yemenite children who, with their parents, had escaped from the persecution of Yemen, in Arabia," Alofsin wrote.[33]

Yet this Jessie never despaired. Depression and psychoanalysis, both significant parts of Sampter's life, made no appearance here. Alofsin reprinted Sampter's poem "Winter Sunshine," which painted both Palestine and optimism as the cures for what ailed her. When the speaker's "life was ebbing low with pain," she let the Jerusalem sun "melt my pain away."[34]

Alofsin's Sampter also fulfilled the womanly ideals of caring for children, again against all odds. "She went frequently to an orphanage to tell stories to the children. With fingers only partially under control, she painted faces on stuffed stockings so the children could have dolls." (The following page of *America's Triumph* is a full-page drawing of a grinning man with a plow in the bare earth. Two women with kerchiefs and scythes walk by in the background. The contrast to Alofsin's Sampter is striking.) When she decided to adopt Tamar, Alofsin explains that everyone told her not to. "Even Leah Berlin, Jessie's friend and roommate, who waited on her so tenderly when she was in pain, said: 'You're not strong enough to undertake the care of an active child. It will put an end to your writing.' Jessie Sampter continued smiling. She would not permit herself to make decisions based on fear."[35] She also became a savior for the German youth who came to Palestine in the late 1930s: "Here, they knew, they were wanted. They had found a home at last."[36] Alofsin, like Ish Kishor, made Sampter's gender far more conventional: she smiles, she wants a child, and she is naturally maternal.

This Sampter, though she had gone to Palestine, also told her own story as an American story. Palestine was like a new America, her young readers learned:

> She told herself: "A long time ago the Puritans brought to America their heritage from the Hebrew Bible and wove it into new laws and a democratic way of life. Now, I, and others like myself, through our religion and through the ideals of the land of our birth, have brought our double heritage of democracy back into democracy's birthplace. Palestine, like America, will become a beacon of light to the surrounding countries. I'm grateful that I can have even a tiny part in this."
>
> She recalled the doctor who so many years before had told her mother, "Help Jessie to want only what she'll be able to achieve." Well, she had achieved a fuller, richer life than many people who hadn't ever known a day's illness. . . .
>
> She thought with a smile of her childhood make-believe, when as Skipper Jessie she had sailed in her schooner *Courage*. She wished she had a schooner now, so she could really sail wherever girls and boys are

found, to bring them a message of victory over pain—to tell them that they, too, could achieve their heart's desire in spite of difficult circumstances, as long as their aim is high, their patience does not falter, and their courage never ends.[37]

The last part makes me smile too, mostly because of how foreign it seems to me, how far it seems from the Sampter I know. Yes, she cared deeply about children's education. But she never declared "victory over pain" and certainly would not preach such a lesson to children. In fact, she found the idea misguided. She was also acutely aware of the differences between the United States and Palestine and would have rejected any easy parallels between Puritans and Zionists. At a more personal level, she spurned saccharine phrases, and though I'm sure she smiled, she is rarely doing it in photographs. But Alofsin's Jessie was a role model for children: upbeat and optimistic, American and Jewish, strong and persevering.

A New Heroine

"I have now selected a new heroine," wrote Bertha Badt-Strauss to her friend Jacob Pickard in 1950.[38] Born into a family of educators in Breslau in 1885 and highly educated herself, Badt-Strauss had already written significant works on other Jewish women writers: her PhD dissertation on the German writer Annette von Droste-Hülshoff and a book on Rahel Varnhagen, as well as literary translations of many others. She had learned of Sampter through Dorothy Alofsin.

Badt-Strauss's Jessie Sampter was a Zionist and an educator, but perhaps most of all she appears as a woman on an intellectual quest to understand and improve the world around her. At times almost a bildungsroman, Badt-Strauss's story of Sampter is one of education and discovery. Unlike in Robert St. John's story, she did not play the role of a stock character but pursued knowledge and willingly changed her life according to what she learned. If, as the old saying goes, there are really only two stories: a man goes on a trip, and a stranger comes to town, then the story of Sampter was certainly the former. Or, more accurately: a woman goes on a trip. It mattered to Badt-Strauss that Sampter was a woman; she recognized the obstacles, expectations, and experiences that came with being a woman.

Badt-Strauss knew from the start that she had chosen a little-known figure for her heroine. As her own biographer Martina Steer writes, "It is hard to understand today how Bertha became aware of Jessie, for despite Jessie's merit for the Zionist movement in America, she shared the fate of many women who had done a great deal in public: hardly anyone knew her."[39] Badt-Strauss knew that she would have to "revive" Sampter, as she wrote to a friend.[40]

But why "revive" Sampter at all? In part, Badt-Strauss wanted to present more complex and compelling portraits of Jewish women. She had studied literature, languages, and philosophy in Breslau, Berlin, and Munich and was one of the first women to earn a doctoral degree in Prussia. She worked as a researcher and a publicist, and she identified with a cultural Zionist movement called the Jewish Renaissance. But, as Steer explains, "the predominantly male protagonists of the Jewish Renaissance had a very simple image of the Jewish woman: the bad Western European Jewess versus the good East European Jewess. As a religious German-Jewish woman Badt-Strauss was not only unable to find herself in either of these images but also considered this strategy as not very useful in motivating women to rethink their attitude towards Judaism."[41] Her doctoral dissertation, as well as her work on Varnhagen, had already presented Jewish women as sophisticated intellectuals as well as multifaceted humans, not just the sinners or saints that her male colleagues wrote about.

Badt-Strauss was particularly interested in people with complex relationships to Judaism. She edited and published the letters of Hermann Cohen and Moses Mendelssohn, each of whom, in his own way, tried to reimagine Judaism and its place in the modern world. She wrote about Rahel Varnhagen and Fanny Lewald, both of whom converted to Christianity but still reflected on Judaism and Jewishness. She recognized that women in particular could have fraught relationships with a tradition whose most public displays of piety as well as intellect were the province of men. She knew about the social advantages of conversion and the ways they could differ for men and for women. And she took seriously the question of how to be Jewish religiously in a rapidly changing social and political landscape. In addition to her books, Badt-Strauss published articles in German magazines, the *Encyclopedia Judaica*, and a host of other venues. She translated and edited scores of letters and shorter writings of German intellectuals. The biography of Sampter, published in English, would be her last major work.

Early in Badt-Strauss's adult life, she became a Zionist, though, unlike in Sampter's case, her siblings shared her political commitment. Her husband, Bruno, never did. As the 1930s wore on, it became clear they would have to leave Germany. The two moved to the United States in 1939 when

Bruno, also a PhD and an expert in Moses Mendelssohn, received an offer to teach at Centenary College in Shreveport, Louisiana.

It wasn't easy writing a biography of Jessie Sampter from Shreveport. Badt-Strauss had also learned she had multiple sclerosis in the 1920s, and by the 1940s it was progressing.[42] She did her research for her Sampter book almost entirely by mail. She corresponded with Elvie Wachenheim, Mordecai Kaplan, and some of Sampter's other friends and colleagues. She tried to get hold of Sampter's published and unpublished materials, and for the most part, she did. In 1956 she published *White Fire: The Life and Works of Jessie Sampter*.

In his introduction to *White Fire*, the rabbi Eugene Korn wrote, "Wisely keeping herself in the background, Dr. Badt-Strauss tells the story of Jessie's life, principally in her heroine's own words."[43] Yet once you know about Badt-Strauss, you can see her on almost every page. Just as her Jessie Sampter balks at being pitied because of her disability, so did Badt-Strauss. She wrote to a friend, insisting that she did not want to be perceived as the "poor little cripple" even as her multiple sclerosis worsened.[44] Badt-Strauss's young Sampter "objected to more spoiling and became a fighter," and Badt-Strauss speculated, "Perhaps her indomitable will to go her own way in matters spiritual as well as in everyday life enabled her in later years to become the advocate of ideas which all her family opposed; this will grew up in the days of her illness."[45] She declared "Jessie's fateful illness" to have been a "blessing in disguise."[46] Later she declared that "illness and bodily handicaps could not curb the indomitable spirit of the young poet."[47] Throughout her story Badt-Strauss suggested that something about illness, including mental illness, was generative for Sampter. "She would never have been able to minister to the many ailing young souls if she had not herself experienced the dangerous affinity of vision and mental crisis."[48] It is hard not to imagine that Badt-Strauss herself had experienced both the frustrations of illness and also the way it could facilitate human connection or be conducive to insight. In her own letters, she is far more interested in being "a fighter" than in any "spoiling."

In some ways, Sampter's life story represented roads not taken for Badt-Strauss: Sampter had moved to Palestine and started a life there, even without the support of a husband or parents and certainly without the formal higher education that Badt-Strauss had. Sampter had lived with chronic physical illness but still worked in the Zionist movement. When Badt-Strauss and her husband sought to leave Germany, they ruled out Palestine because of the inferior living conditions and poor job prospects for both of them. But Sampter had gone two decades earlier, when there was even less infrastructure and no clear long-term job prospects for her. Badt-Strauss also admired American Jewish women more generally, calling them the "purest embodiment of the Jewess" in her 1937 *Jewish Women*.[49] European Jewish women might learn from their American counterparts how to think of Jews as a people in order to prepare for nation building in Palestine.

"The life of Jessie Sampter, tragic though it was, also reflects the undying quality of the Jewish soul, which insists on being reborn again and again and flinging into the teeth of an incredulous world the truth, not only of Jewish vitality but of Jewish creative genius," one reviewer of Badt-Strauss's book wrote.[50] Both Zionist inspiration and inspiration porn, the story of this Jessie Sampter impressed on its readers the idea that to suffer was Jewish, but so was to overcome.

Badt-Strauss's Sampter was a heroine of women and a heroine of the Jewish people. She represented American Zionism and American Jewish women, who should be a model for other modern Jews. She moved to Palestine because of her ideals, even though it wasn't practical and her future there was unclear. And she represented strength in spite of adversity. She had polio, she sometimes struggled to walk significant distances, she needed physical help from others, and yet she left the imprint of her spiritual ideals on those around her. Most of all, it seems, Jessie Sampter was a heroine for Badt-Strauss.

The Forgettable Voice of a Poet and Songwriter

Since the late 1940s, Sampter has also lived a low-key life as a poet, particularly in the Reform movement in the United States. A short 1957 article in the *Association of Jewish Refugees Journal* declared, "There is hardly a modern Reform Prayer Book or collection of hymns for Jewish children that does not include one or several poems by her. Thirteen years after her death three of her hymns were included in the Union Hymnal, edited by the Central Conference of American Rabbis, and are sung in the Service in the Synagogue."[51] Sampter had become institutionalized as a contemporary Jewish writer of poems, hymns, and songs.

The kosher wine company Manischewitz printed two of her poems, "Passover" and "The Questions," in its Passover booklet beginning in 1947. The booklet, "The Story of Pesach," contained stories, essays, and songs related to Passover, which had been compiled by a five-man editorial team with expertise in Jewish education. It had a printing of 300,000. Like the ubiquitous midcentury Maxwell House Haggadah that accompanied the brand's coffee purchases, these booklets came with Manischewitz's matzos. Countless families encountered her poetry there on the last page of the booklet after short stories by literary icons Sholom Aleichem and Y. L. Peretz.

Not everyone found her inspirational, however. The children's literature critic Leonard Mendelsohn complained that the bulk of existing Jewish children's literature was, well, basically garbage, and Sampter's work was no exception. He wrote, "Even a sophisticate like Jessie Sampter failed to create any suitable lyrics for Jewish children."[52] The Reform movement, he explained, selected three poems from "Sampter's collection, *Around the World in Rimes* [sic] *for the Jewish Child*, for inclusion in its Union Hymnal. Later these poems with their musical setting were reprinted in the *Union Songster: Songs and Prayers for Jewish Young*. Two of these poems are banal, if not misleading, translations of traditional blessings. The third is presumably a child's view of the Sabbath."[53] He liked none of them. "English speaking Jews, whatever their education, have immense tolerance for the aesthetically precious. Bad quality is so commonplace in the market for Jewish children's literature that it is often not recognized for what it is. All critical faculties of the Jewish reading public have been discretely anesthetized."[54] For Mendelsohn, Sampter's poetry was just another example of the pallid aesthetics of the Reform tradition. He remembered that she was a children's author, but he would have been just as happy to forget.

But the majority of American Jews who encountered Sampter's work in the middle of the twentieth century probably thought little about her at all. For most of the people who read from the *Union Songster* or the Manischewitz Passover booklet, Jessie Sampter was just a name. In both of those collections, Sampter appeared not as her own person or as a standout author but as one voice of a collective Jewish tradition.

A Misfit of American Jewish History

The historian Jacob Rader Marcus found another Jessie—a tragic one. Born in 1896, Marcus became a Reform rabbi and then the first professional historian to dedicate his career to studying Jews in the United States. In 1981 he published *The American Jewish Woman*, which included a brief entry on Sampter:

JESSIE ETHEL SAMPTER: ARDENT JEWISH NATIONALIST

Zionism, Jewish Palestine, the State of Israel—these have appealed to a number of Jewish women who had found little comfort in Judaism, but finally made their way back to their people through a love for Zion. Influenced by Henrietta Szold, the left-wing traditionalist Mordecai M. Kaplan, and Emma Lazarus's brilliant sister Josephine, Jessie Ethel Sampter (1883–1938) became a devoted member of the people who gave her birth.

Her family on both sides were of antebellum stock, well-to-do, cultured, on the road to assimilation. Her father was an early follower of Felix Adler, the founder of the Ethical Culture movement. Jessie, a semi-invalid all her life—unhappy, lonely, unattractive—was a "seeker," constantly searching for spiritual peace and a rewarding purpose in life. She found it first in Unitarianism and then, at long last, in Zionism, in poetry, and in a dedication to the challenge of the new Palestine, where she settled in 1919. There the special object of her attention was under-privileged Yemenite newcomers.

She wrote on Zionism and published several modest volumes of poetry. The following rhymes are for children. Her purpose in these poems was essentially didactic; she was eager to make Jews, their customs, their history, their beliefs, attractive to the children who, she hoped, would be the stalwart Jews of tomorrow.[55]

Marcus was remarkably thorough for such a small space: he mentioned her class background, relationships, writing, Yemenite education projects, and more. Yet the Jessie Sampter that Marcus found was also tragic. She was "unhappy, lonely, unattractive." What Jessie had he found? One, I soon discovered, who fit into his larger understanding of gender and Jewish history.

In his introduction Marcus reflected on the past histories of Jews in the United States: "This omission of women was unwitting, for it is patent that if American Jewish history is the record of its communities, its institutions, and its achievements, it owes almost everything to the family, and the family is the wife, as well as the husband and children."[56] At first, this seems quite enlightened: history is also the story of women. Yet it also prescribed a narrow role for women. American Jewish history is about families, and families are about a husband, a wife, and children.

Sampter's story did not feature her as a wife in a heterosexual nuclear family, so she did not fit easily as a success in the story of American Jewish history. Marcus did strike a positive note about Sampter's book of poetry for children, *Around the Year in Rhymes for the Jewish Child*, which he deemed "particularly charming."[57] If history is about families, and families are also about wives and children, as Marcus would have it, Sampter's published writing for Jewish children became a highlight of her life.

Marcus includes ten pages in the introduction to his book to describe "her story"—that is, the story of "the Jewish woman" in the United States. Five of these pages are about marriage, and Marcus often described women primarily in relation to their husbands. "The typical Jewess of that day was the wife of a craftsman-retailer or a storekeeper," he wrote, for example.[58] Grammatically as well as conceptually, the Jewish woman appeared in the singular and often in relationship to men.

Marcus presented the desirability of marriage as self-evident; he assumed that all women wanted it too. About the period 1893–1919, he wrote, "Most girls, natives or newcomers, were looking for a husband, not for an education."[59] He noted, "A few even opted for a career rather than domesticity, though it is probable that they would have sought both if the two could have been reconciled."[60] He also wrote, "In those days there was no future for a young woman except in a home of her own with a husband and children."[61] This sentence took me aback when I first read it: it directly contradicted the stories of the accomplished single women that appear throughout his volumes. Why would a historian as careful and knowledgeable as Marcus write such a sentence? I can't know for certain, but it seems that the gender norms and expectations of his time had so permeated his understanding of American Jewish history that they overrode the documents in front of him. Given the strength of these ideas about women as wives and biological mothers, Jessie Sampter must have seemed either strange or very sad to him. Perhaps both.

And neither strange nor sad fit the often celebratory tone Marcus adopted for his story of "the American Jewish woman." Sampter appears fleetingly in other academic histories—as an example of an American Jewish woman educator, a pacifist kibbutz member, an American Zionist, or an American Zionist woman.[62] But for both biographical reasons and narrative ones, historians have not seen Sampter as a center of American Jewish history.

Through all of these small narrative appearances and fleeting mentions, I noticed something curious: the few authors who disparaged her were all men. St. John presented a spoiled and sneer-worthy Sampter; Marcus saw a tragic figure; Shamir imagined a rich and needy American. (Not all, however: some male authors, like the historian Meir Chazan, told stories about Sampter that are neither disparaging nor tragic.[63]) Some female authors, like Dorothy Alofsin and Bertha Badt-Strauss, held her up as a hero. Maybe what seems like a gendered difference is only coincidence. But maybe women authors were more likely to see Sampter as a hero because they knew more intimately the demands and restrictions that the world puts on women, their minds, and their bodies. Maybe the men didn't know, and maybe some didn't even know they should try to understand. Maybe they had other things to say, things they thought were more important, like about politics. Maybe every Jessie these authors found is more than just a little of each writer telling their own story.

Kashmir, Weight Watchers, and Me

There is another Jessie I could never quite get hold of. But seeking her and catching glimpses of her reminded me of all the stories that are lost, the ones that go untold, and the ones that slip through our fingers as we try to hold onto them.

For the time I was writing this book, and even as I write now, Jessie Sampter has a short Wikipedia page with a small photo.[64] Though quite a few images of her exist, this photo wasn't of Sampter. It was of a roadside sign in Ladakh—a region of India known for the Himalayas and its political unrest, near the borders with Pakistan and China/Tibet. The sign is painted bright yellow with black block lettering, and it reads, "Border Roads Organisation" and below, "Simplicity is the peak of civilization.—Jessie Sampter."

Yes, that is a Sampter quote. It's from the middle of a poem in the middle of *The Emek* that describes kibbutz life.[65] But how odd! A phrase from the middle of poem in the middle of a book that seems not to have sold enough copies even to be profitable.

The online photo had no GPS coordinates, and the person who uploaded the picture to Wikipedia never answered my emails. No other photos, save retouched versions of this one, existed on the internet. The photo's data said it was taken in the Nubra Valley, but the valley has two branches and well over two hundred kilometers of main roads. Although one of the branches is technically the Shoyo Valley, locals call the whole area Nubra, I learned.

I decided to go see the sign.

Finding it would require some sleuthing. My partner is a historian of India and an experienced motorcyclist, and I needed both his language skills and his driving experience in my quest for the sign. We flew into Leh, a town that sits more than eleven thousand feet above sea level in Jammu and Kashmir. The altitude forced us to plod along the streets at roughly the same speed as the local cows and donkeys. I took altitude sickness pills. My hands and feet tingled almost all the time. To get to the Nubra Valley, we would need to go even higher—to navigate Khardung La, the "world's highest motorable pass," as the sign at its summit declares. The 18,379-foot height it claims might be a small exaggeration, and there might now be a recently built road in the Himalayas that surpasses even that, but the cold, thin air and the glaciers don't lie. The mountain pass is extraordinarily high.

The road itself is terrible. There are no guardrails. It's cut into a nearly vertical slope, which means that when there are curves, sometimes you cannot see more than twenty feet of the road ahead around the mountain. Drivers should honk loudly to avoid head-on collisions, the rules of the road dictate. A hand-painted black horn on a bright yellow background appears on many of these curves, reminding drivers to honk. "Lane Driving is Safe Driving," a sign reminds Indian drivers who rarely heed lanes and often drive in the place Westerners think of as the lane for oncoming traffic. But more often than not, on Khardung La, the road is barely a single lane wide. The melting glaciers break up and carry away the pavement and deposit huge rocks onto the path. Road crews, who are actually military units, sometimes blast rock formations above the road to preempt any landslides. Holes in the road fill with the streaming glacier water, so you can rarely guess how deep they will be.

We rented a Royal Enfield 500, a classic Indian motorcycle still manufactured in Chennai, and embarked on the trip over Khardung La to the Nubra Valley. I learned that the former supervisor in charge of the Khardung La area was named Jangiti Krishna Murthy. A good omen, I thought, for him to share a name with one of Sampter's favorite thinkers even though it was of no historical relevance, just a family name. To get up and over the pass and into the valley would take us all day. Cold and queasy from the altitude and nursing a sore back from the incessant bumping and banging of the Royal Enfield over the road, I still gaped at the mountains and valleys and rock formations. They were like none I had ever seen.

I also looked at every road sign. The Jessie Sampter sign, as I had come to think of it, had been painted by HIMANK, a project team of the Border Roads Organisation. "Border Roads" hints at the complexity of these projects:

they take place in contested regions like Jammu and Kashmir. Road construction and upkeep are military projects, and the men who work for them are military men. The HIMANK team goes by the nickname "the Mountain Tamers," which is also spelled out in rocks on the face of the mountain near their headquarters in Leh. (When we stopped at the gate of the headquarters to ask if they had any records of signs, we were told no. How about an archive? No. Was there anyone we could talk to? No. A dead end.) Before embarking on the trip, I had tried networking: a colleague had a friend in the army. Could he help me find out the history behind this sign? No, he answered, he could not meet with me because he would not be able to explain why I would be in the building. And that was that. To go across the world in search of a roadside sign was strange, apparently so strange as to be suspicious to career military men.

But I went anyway. Several hours after we descended from the pass, I recognized part of the valley from the photograph: this should be where the sign is! The mountains were the right color and the right distance from the road, and the valley was the right shape, flat and wide for hundreds of meters before it gave way to mountain. And there were signs, yellow HIMANK signs, even the right shape and size, but no Jessie Sampter sign. Could I have been wrong about the landscape matching the photo?

We took the Royal Enfield all the way up the western fork of the Nubra Valley to the last HIMANK sign before Pakistan. The India-Pakistan border, like the Israel-Palestine partition, postdated Sampter. In her time, I thought, British power shaped this land too. The inhabitants also resented the British and their maps and their guns. Nine years after Sampter's death, the British partitioned India in 1947, the year before they partitioned Palestine. In disputed Kashmir, like parts of Israel, the border has never settled. Both borders have carried the weight of religious difference, sometimes creating the feeling of more difference—and more distance—than before those lines were drawn.

Another border, and a different religious difference, dwells near the eastern fork of the valley. On that side, the valley is near Tibet, now under the controversial rule of China and also including a border region whose unrest goes back at least to the 1830s. When we were there, the Dalai Lama was visiting. He and his entourage drove through each of the villages, stopping at the monasteries in a few of them to speak and greet the people. Prayer flags in their white, blue, yellow, green, and red sequence flapped in the wind above the roads near where people lived. The villagers lined the road with colorful rugs and potted plants they brought from home.

Some dressed in traditional celebratory clothes, and others in more everyday pants and skirts.

But it was not just Buddhists: Muslims, too, brought their potted plants to hear the Dalai Lama speak. The Nubra Valley's population is mostly Buddhists and Muslims but with far more of the former. When we stopped at a roadside food stall, we stood in a line of Buddhists and Muslims chatting while they waited for biscuits and tea. There was a moment when I could hear both the call to prayer and the metallic jingle of the big red Buddhist prayer wheel just across the street. On the morning we left the village of Hunder, just before the Dalai Lama did, we went up the eastern fork of the valley, taking the same route he would, unbeknownst to us. As we came into one town, a giant green hand-lettered sign hung over the road: "Heartiest Wel come from Muslim Committee Sumyur." We stopped, and as we drank our tea, we watched villagers stream by. Buddhists, yes, but also Muslims, happy to spend their afternoon hearing the Dalai Lama's words. Jessie Sampter would have approved, I thought as I sat there, in search of one of her afterlives.

After an hour or so, we turned and left, motoring under the prayer flags. The joyous crowds and their plants lining the streets had gone. We returned down the eastern fork of the valley, heading back toward the pass.

I never found the sign.

As we passed back over the part of the valley where I had expected to find the sign, I had a sinking feeling. We stopped in front of each sign to get a closer look. These signs had been painted over. They said 1445RCC, but I knew the Sampter sign had been painted by the 54RCC crew. "Driving faster, cause disaster!" read one—one that I had found amusing earlier but that now only disappointed me. When I looked closely, I could see at the bottom of the sign that yellow had been repainted over black lettering. This had been a 54RCC sign. So had the next one, the one in just the right spot according to the photo I had seen. New crews must have repainted these signs. Perhaps the valley flooded, and even if it didn't, the gravel and sandy mountain bits would surely erode a sign like this over time. Jessie Sampter had been erased.

But her absence from the Nubra Valley also prompted me to see something else about her—about all of us, really. Some lives are lost to history. Others we can recover partially. But no lives are lives we can fully know. It feels right that after spending so much time researching Sampter, some things are still a mystery. No life is fully transparent, not even one's own. The partial story I have is only partially about Sampter. Some of it is about me: the strange moments of explaining to Nubra Valley dwellers who a long-dead Zionist woman was and why I had come all this way to find a boring road sign. Every act of life-writing is an exercise in taking partial knowledge and then setting down an even smaller sliver of that. In the end, I do not know what the person who chose that Sampter quote thought when they chose it. I do not know how they convinced others to agree. I do not know who painted the letters on the sign or whether they contemplated its meaning while they did.

I have a theory about how that Jessie Sampter sign got there, though. In late 2018 I found myself requesting that my university borrow *Weight Watchers Success Everyday* for me.[66] I wasn't trying to lose weight, but I was anxious to see it. It's a paperback page-a-day book with one quotation at the top of each page and then a couple of inspirational paragraphs below it. The quotations are attributed to familiar writers and politicians, such as Johann Wolfgang von Goethe and Winston Churchill. It also has less well-known figures, such as the former Major League umpire Bruce Froemming, whose name you would only know, as I did, if you watched entirely too much baseball in the 1980s and 1990s. The quotations have no citation of sources, and none of the authors is described (so nonaficionados are left wondering who Froemming is). Quite a few of the quotations are attributed to "anonymous" or described as national proverbs. The December 31 page says, "Simplicity is the peak of civilization." It credits Jessie Sampter. Fittingly—and enigmatically—that is the end of the book.

I have to admit that I had to look through six books and countless essays again before I found where she had written it. While it sounds like something she might write, it was never the main theme of any of her books or longer essays. I slowly went through my stack of Sampter books and essays, scanning each page. Finally, I found it, in the middle of a line in the middle of a poem that she published in *The Emek* in 1927. How did a Weight Watchers writer find it?

The first appearance of the quotation I have found is unattributed in Herbert Samuel's *Leisure in a Democracy*, published in 1949, well after Sampter's death.[67] Samuel had been the high commissioner of Palestine from 1920 to 1925. He and Sampter knew each other, and although she wasn't always comfortable in the high-class British social gatherings he and his wife held, their social circles overlapped significantly. Samuel quotes the phrase in a way that suggests it is a saying people just know. Maybe, then, it wasn't utterly original for Sampter. Or maybe Samuel borrowed it from her, either consciously or not. But whatever the case, since then it has been identified with Sampter.

Today that particular quotation—"Simplicity is the peak of civilization"—appears in quite a few other places. It is in all the online quote aggregators, the vast majority of which attribute it to Sampter, though a small number attribute it to Henry David Thoreau. Authors use it as an epigraph in the books *The Simplicity Shift: Innovative Design Tactics in a Corporate World* and *Empower the Leader in You!* and the workplace advice article "Top 3 Ways for IT Managers to Keep IT Simple."[68] It appears in *The Quotable Jewish Woman* and the *Zen Habits Handbook for Life*.[69] What do these authors and editors think when they see Jessie Sampter's name? What does it mean to them? In many cases, probably not much. The online quote aggregators make any thematic quote available at the touch of a keyboard. No need to learn about the long-dead woman who wrote those words. But even if they don't know about her, her words take on new meaning with regard to design, innovation, leadership, information technology, and Americanized Zen habits.

But where did these quote aggregators get the line in the first place? Collections of quotations often feed on earlier collections, and Sampter's line is no exception. The Wisconsin-based Reform rabbi Joseph Baron first included it in his 1956 *Treasury of Jewish Quotations*, along with two other quotations of Sampter's work (both from *Book of Nations*).[70] Baron had lived in New York from 1907 to 1916, and during that time he was active in Young Judea and other Zionist organizations. I have no direct evidence that he knew Sampter, but it seems highly likely that their paths crossed. He might have read *Book of Nations* when it came out: he, too, was affected by the war. He served Temple Sholom of Chicago because Rabbi Abram Hirshberg was serving as a chaplain in the army.

Whether or not Baron ever met Sampter, whether or not the compiler of *Weight Watchers Success Everyday* knew anything about her, and regardless of the fact that quote aggregators are not even human and so it's questionable whether they know anything at all, they played a role in creating one of Sampter's afterlives. Writing is funny like that. So are memories.

Conclusion: Remembering and Not Remembering

There are also ways that Sampter isn't remembered, at least not now: people have not lauded her as a rediscovered national writer. Maybe this is because people think her poetry isn't very good; maybe it's because she was never the president of Hadassah; maybe it's because she didn't have children in the United States to proclaim her legacy. But maybe it's also because she was a woman, and many people in the Zionist movement (and many American men) thought of women as extras in that drama.

Some of Sampter's contemporaries might have been surprised to know that she did not live on as a celebrated Jewish writer. In 1922 Elma Levinger wrote that many saw Sampter as "the legitimate successor of Emma Lazarus." Her poems and prose were "possibly the finest expression of Jewish nationalism voiced by an American writer."[71] In 1934 a reviewer in the *American Israelite* praised her: "Miss Sampter is the Emma Lazarus of our day. When the literary historians of the future search out the best poetry and travel-essays of this period in Jewish history, Miss Sampter's works will stand at the very summit."[72] He was wrong. Her poetry is read little, the *Union Songster* excepted, and her essays and books are read even less. Even in the *Union Songster*, people rarely pay attention to her as an author but instead approach her poetry as a nearly anonymous contribution to Jewish communal tradition.

We remember some writers more than others because of the way their words speak to us. We have personal favorites, and we also have a national canon: Robert Frost, Mark Twain, William Faulkner, and others. Some aspects of memorializing have to do not only with words but also with gender. What if the national canon in that list said, instead, Emily Dickinson, Zora Neale Hurston, Sylvia Plath, and Maya Angelou? Are these women remembered in the same ways as the men? Are Black writers remembered in the same ways as white ones? Do bodies matter as well as words? Are the two separable? To take a specific example, James Joyce (1882–1941) was almost exactly Sampter's contemporary. He, like Sampter, wrote as part of a nationalist project. In a brilliant reflection on gender and writing, Ann Enright discusses the relationship of national memory and the use of writers:

> In order to become properly iconised, as he was on the Irish Writers poster, it was necessary that Joyce be dead. An awareness of writers' gravesites, the impulse to build statues and monuments, all of this was useful when it came to the national work of building a better past for ourselves. The deadness of the writer is especially interesting because they feel so alive on the page: this makes their books a talisman not just against shame but also against mortality. Which makes me wonder— and I have no answer to this—whether women will ever seem dead in the same way.[73]

Can Jessie Sampter ever be dead in the same way that the storied Zionist Theodor Herzl is? I, too, have no answer.

Yet it is not my goal to find Jessie Sampter the national writer and make her into an icon. It is not my quest to have her memorialized like Herzl, with a town named after him and a giant sketch of his head on its water tower. It is to tell a messier story of a complex human being—a human being whose life seems so particular and unusual and yet has lessons for a broader understanding of humans. It is also to suggest that a messier story, including attention to embodiment as a central part of that story, might be a new way to tell the stories of iconic thinkers and writers.

As I wrote this book, I gave lectures about Sampter's life and writing. After almost every presentation, someone would come up to me and say that I should look into having a movie, play, or television special written about her. This is an unusual experience for someone who spends much of her research time in archives. Most of the materials I read register as dull and esoteric to the general public. Yet there is something compelling about Sampter. In the introduction to her 1920 book of poetry, *Around the Year in Rhymes for the Jewish Child*, she addressed her young audience about "our great wish, yours and mine, to do things that make it interesting to be Jewish."[74] Whether or not young readers managed to do such things, Jessie Sampter got her wish.

Some of the people I talked to found Sampter so interesting because of contemporary politics. Israel/Palestine continues to be wracked by conflict, and so people wonder about how things could have gone otherwise. Could "the situation," as it's sometimes known in Hebrew, be less intractable? Might a different vision of Zionism, like Sampter's, have been better for Mizrahim and for disabled people and queer people? What about the relationships between Jews and non-Jewish Arabs? Were there other possibilities? Are there now? These questions animate people across the political spectrum.

Although the historical possibilities of politics interest me, I don't think they alone would have been enough to make me go across the globe and try to chase down a road sign just to find another trace of a woman. The Jessie Sampter I was seeking also has a story that is much more personal, more intimate. Her religious seeking and her recombining were profoundly hers but also made me see better the processes through which so many people create their own worldviews. Her defiance of easy categories of sexuality and family reminds me that relationships and human bonding don't always follow set patterns, and how deviance from those patterns may make a life less obvious but never less meaningful. Her body—its pains and its disabilities but also its ability to grow and nurture plants—felt as if it held deep truths about the human body. We all have bodies, and those bodies don't always do what we want. They don't always behave in ways that we expect; sometimes they are unruly. And they don't always match up with our ideologies or our politics.

These stories of Jessie Sampter's life are not neat and tidy, but they are compelling. Since those first cold moments in the archive, I have been compelled by the question of what her life meant to her and at the same time aware that I could never fully know. I have also been driven by the question of what her life could mean to me and to you, my reader. Yet even reading the same documents I did, you could find "still another Jessie," to use Mary Antin's words. Bodies, families, sexuality, politics, religion: these affect us all but not always in the same ways. It is my hope that telling the stories of Sampter's life will help us see each of these more clearly in our own lives and that we take to heart the lesson that a meaningful life does not require perfect alignment among them.

Notes

Introduction

1   In 1918 Henrietta Szold lamented that only three hundred copies of *A Course in Zionism* had been sold. Henrietta Szold to Jessie Sampter, April 18, 1918, box 30, folder 1, RG13 Executive Function Records, Henrietta Szold: Correspondence subseries: Associates and Friends, Hadassah Archives, American Jewish Historical Society (AJHS), New York.

2   Lepore, "Historians Who Love," 133.

3   These are made-up examples, so as not to single out particular writers. Many books never return to that scene of self-disclosure; it appears in the introduction, never to be heard from again. They seem to assume that the relationship between the author and the work is either self-evident and so requires no explanation or unknowable and so makes explanation impossible.

4   I include just a few scholarly inspirations here. On bodily senses, see Neis, *Sense of Sight*; Nabhan-Warren, "Embodied Research and Writing"; and Weiner, *Religion Out Loud*. On affect, see Schaefer, *Religious Affects*; and Thandeka, *Learning to Be White*. For widely read authors on materiality, see Morgan, "Materiality"; and Keane, "Materiality of Religion." A brief but suggestive discussion also appears in Stewart Diakité and Hucks, "Africana Religious Studies."

5   Lakoff and Johnson, *Philosophy in the Flesh*, 1.

6   Lakoff and Johnson, *Philosophy in the Flesh*, 3.

7   Jacqueline Rose, "Who Do You Think You Are?," *London Review of Books*, May 5, 2016, http://www.lrb.co.uk/v38/n09/jacqueline-rose/who-do-you-think-you-are.

8   Sampter, "Speaking Heart," 92a, May 25, 1921, Jessie Sampter Papers (A219), Central Zionist Archives (CZA), Jerusalem, Israel. (The "Speaking Heart" manuscript spans A219\11 and A219\12.)

9   She landed in the United States on November 3, 1925. Her arrival made the *Bnai Brith Messenger*, November 27, 1925, 3.

10 Sampter, "In the Beginning," 139. A219\3, CZA.

11 Jessie Sampter to Elvie Wachenheim (henceforth JS to EW), May 24, 1920, A219, CZA. All citations of correspondence between Jessie and Elvie are from A219, CZA.

12 Eiesland, *Disabled God*, 22.

13 Eiesland, *Disabled God*, 31.

14 Yuknavitch, *Book of Joan*, 101.

15 Yuknavitch, *Book of Joan*, 101.

16 For more on the tendency to view those with disabilities as "inspirations," see Stella Young, "We're Not Here for Your Inspiration," *The Drum*, ABC News, July 3, 2012, http://www.abc.net.au/news/2012-07-03/young-inspiration-porn/4107006.

17 Judith Butler, "A 'Bad Writer' Bites Back," *New York Times*, March 20, 1999.

18 For more on gender in the archive, see Scott, *Feminism and History*; Smith, *Gender of History*; and Lerner, "Women's History Sources."

19 JS to EW, January 23, 1930.

20 JS to EW, Edgar Wachenheim, and "kiddies," October 1, 1919.

21 JS to EW, March 12, 1920.

22 Sampter, "Speaking Heart," 247.

23 See, for example, Ahad Ha'am, "An Open Letter to My Brethren in the Spirit," 1891, Jewish Virtual Library, http://www.jewishvirtuallibrary.org/quot-an-open -letter-to-my-bretheren-in-the-spirit-quot-ahad-ha-am.

24 Urofsky, *American Zionism*, 344, 40.

25 Quoted in de Haas, *Louis Dembitz Brandeis*, 163.

26 Isaac Mayer Wise, editorial, *American Israelite*, July 4, 1882.

27 N. Cohen, "*Maccabaean's* Message," 163; and the cover image of *Maccabaean* 32, no. 5 (May 1919).

28 Boyarin, *Unheroic Conduct*, 273–74; and Imhoff, *Masculinity*, 181–82.

29 Both of these lines of thinking about Jewish bodies and the Zionist project can be seen in Nordau, "Physical Intellectual and Economical Amelioration." This article, in particular the discussion of a statistical survey of the Jews, is one example of how some Zionists attempted to apply the era's ideals of "scientific rationality" to their national mission. This discourse did not originate in Zionism but rather was part of a wider context in the fin de siècle in which many scholars believed science proved empirical truths about races and nations.

30 Quoted in Margalit, "Social and Intellectual Origins," 153.

31 Quoted in Weiss, *Chosen Body*, 2.

32 Weiss, *Chosen Body*.

33 Nordau, "Muscular Judaism," 435.

34 Shapira, *ha-Halikha 'al kav ha-ofek*, 28.

35 Boyarin, *Unheroic Conduct*, 222.

36 On the United States, see Imhoff, *Masculinity*, 180–98. On Europe, see Presner, *Muscular Judaism*; and Stanislawski, *Zionism*, 93–96, 107–8.

37 McCune, *Whole Wide World*, 38.

38 Quoted in McCune, *Whole Wide World*, 39. *Proceedings and Speeches at the 14th Convention*, p. 4, RG 3, box 6, folder 2, Hadassah Archives, AJHS.

39 JS to EW, November 7, 1933.

40 Divrei HaKnesset, 9:2004, quoted in Berkovitch, "Motherhood," 611.

41 Rosenberg-Friedman, "David Ben-Gurion"; and Presner, "Clear Heads."

42 Maxa Nordau, "Pioneer Types: The Women Workers of Palestine," *New Palestine*, October 15, 1926, 203, quoted in Simmons, "Playgrounds and Penny Lunches," 285.

43 Szold, "Palestine Realities: A Letter from Palestine to Hadassah," *New Palestine*, March 10, 1922, 147.

44 Z. Carmi, "Penny Lunches in Palestine: Letter Sent to Miss Sophia Berger by Z. Carmi of the Public Schools of Haifa," *Hadassah Newsletter*, November–December 1927, 9, quoted in Simmons, "Playgrounds and Penny Lunches," 278.

45 Andrew Kahn and Rebecca Onion, "Is History Written about Men, by Men?," *Slate*, January 6, 2016, http://www.slate.com/articles/news_and_politics /history/2016/01/popular_history_why_are_so_many_history_books_about _men_by_men.html.

46 Little, *Many Captivities*, 9.

47 Halberstam, *In a Queer Time*, 3. On the flexibility of time, see also Edelman, *No Future*; and Muñoz, *Cruising Utopia*.

48 Halberstam, *In a Queer Time*, 3.

49 Muñoz, *Cruising Utopia*, 96.

50 Halberstam, *In a Queer Time*, 7. Jasbir Puar has also considered time in relation to queerness in *Terrorist Assemblages*, xxv–xxx.

51 Zola, "Language of Disability"; and Gill, "Disability Culture." Also, Ellen Samuels frames it six different ways in "Six Ways of Looking at Crip Time."

52 Belser, interviewed in "Crip Time: Finding Your Own Rhythm," *Guide Gods Digital Collection*, accessed September 15, 2019, http://www.clairecunningham.co .uk/guide-gods-digital-collection/beautiful-disabilities/.

53 Kuppers, "Crip Time," 29.

54 St. Pierre, "Distending Straight-Masculine Time," 56. St. Pierre defines *straight-masculine time* as follows: "This judgment of his temporality as abnormal or deficient is structured by what I term the straight-masculine time order: a future-directed linearity abstracted from the flux of bodily time," 50.

55 Sampter, "Three Hours," 10.

56 Belser, interviewed in "Crip Time."

57 Kafer, *Feminist, Queer, Crip*, 27.

58 Sampter, "Speaking Heart," 76.

59 See, for example, some of the things in A219\5, CZA.

60 Merleau-Ponty, *Phenomenology of Perception*, 249.

61 Sampter, *Seekers*, 79.

62 Margaret Doniger to Rose Jacobs, January 25, 1939, F32\39\1, "Hadassah: Jessie Sampter Material."

Chapter 1. A Religious Life

1 Sampter, "Speaking Heart," 14.
2 I use the phrase *American religion* carefully. I do not mean to conflate the United States with the American hemisphere. Rather, I use the phrase to refer to the discursive "America" and "American religion," with knowledge of how it has trafficked in exceptionalism and relied on claims to diversity and religious freedom. For a more detailed essay on this kind of use, see Harriss and Imhoff, editorial.
3 Sheskin and Dashefsky, "Jewish Population."
4 "Hester Lynn," one of Sampter's unpublished novels. Badt-Strauss, *White Fire*, 9.
5 Sampter, "Speaking Heart," 15.
6 Sampter, "Speaking Heart," 4.
7 Sampter, "Speaking Heart," 22.
8 See, for example, Sampter, "Confession (Part 2)," 12.
9 Sampter, "Speaking Heart," 23.
10 Sampter, "Speaking Heart," 60.
11 Sampter, "Speaking Heart," 25.
12 "Rudolph Sampter," *New York Times*, February 26, 1895, 7.
13 Adler, *Creed and Deed*.
14 James, *Immigrant Jew in America*, 153–54.
15 Sampter, "Speaking Heart," 73.
16 Sampter, "A Confession (Part 2)," 2.
17 Sampter, "Speaking Heart," 12.
18 Sampter, "In the Beginning," A219\2 and A219\5, CZA.
19 Sampter, "Speaking Heart," 12.
20 "A Portrait of Jewish Americans," Pew Research Center, October 1, 2013, 7, 8, https://www.pewresearch.org/wp-content/uploads/sites/7/2013/10/jewish -american-beliefs-attitudes-culture-survey-overview.pdf.
21 For some examples, see TallBear, *Native American DNA*; Selka, "Cityscapes and Contact Zones"; and Imhoff and Kaell, "Lineage Matters."
22 Weisenfeld, *New World A-Coming*.
23 Sampter, "My School," 638.
24 Sampter, "Summer Sabbath," in Sampter, *Around the Year in Rhymes*, 73.
25 Sampter, "Speaking Heart," 84.
26 Sampter, "Speaking Heart," 84.
27 Doyle, *History of Spiritualism*.
28 Albanese, *Republic*, 182. See also Holloway, "Enchanted Spaces," 182–87.
29 Sampter, "Speaking Heart," 84.
30 Sampter, "Speaking Heart," 84.
31 Sampter, "Speaking Heart," 89. Later she lived in a YWHA (Young Women's Hebrew Association) settlement house.
32 "Report of the Social Settlement Committee," *Proceedings of the Twenty-Third Annual Meeting of the NCCC* (Grand Rapids, MI: NCCC, 1896), 167, quoted in Crocker, *Social Work*, 113.

33 Lillian Wald was concerned about "the difficulties of readjustment for the pious Jew" in the move from the Pale of Settlement to the United States, and she saw her Henry Street settlement house as one place to ease this transition. Wald, *House on Henry Street*, 253. Wald even began her involvement in Henry Street through religious means: the house hosted a Sabbath school for immigrants, and it asked Wald to come teach about nursing one day. Buhler-Wilkerson, "Bringing Care."

34 Sampter, "Speaking Heart," 66.

35 Sampter, "Speaking Heart," 67.

36 Mary Antin to Horace Kallen, April 14, 1917, MS #1, box 2, folder 4, Horace Kallen Collection, American Jewish Archives (AJA).

37 Antin, *Promised Land*, 40.

38 For more details on Antin's religious journey, see Mindra, "Evangelical and Progressive Inscriptions," 173–74; and McGinity, *Still Jewish*, 28.

39 Antler, *Journey Home*, 25.

40 See Antin, *Selected Letters*, 121–50.

41 Lazarus, *Spirit of Judaism*, 63.

42 Antler, *Journey Home*, 112.

43 Gilder, *Critic* 26 (1887): 293–94, quoted in Young, "Emma Lazarus," 291.

44 Sampter, "Speaking Heart," 92.

45 Lazarus, *Spirit of Judaism*, 19.

46 "An Affirmation of Self-Faith," *New York Times*, March 13, 1909.

47 Sampter, "Into the Depths," in *Great Adventurer* (unpaginated, under the heading I). Subsequent quotations from this similarly use the section title (here "Into the Depths") and the roman numeral headings.

48 Sampter, "Into the Depths," in *Great Adventurer*, II.

49 Sampter, "Into the Depths," in *Great Adventurer*, IV: II.

50 Sampter, "Into the Depths," in *Great Adventurer*, V.

51 Haskins, *Ralph Waldo Emerson*, 48, quoted in Tolles, "Emerson and Quakerism," 142.

52 Sampter, *Seekers*, 1.

53 Sampter, *Seekers*, 4.

54 Sampter, *Seekers*, 3.

55 Sampter, *Seekers*, 5–6.

56 Sampter, *Seekers*, 9–11.

57 Royce, introduction to *The Seekers*, ix.

58 Royce, introduction to *The Seekers*, viii.

59 Royce, introduction to *The Seekers*, xi.

60 Royce, introduction to *The Seekers*, xi.

61 Sampter, *Seekers*, 12.

62 Sampter, *Seekers*, 26–27. The students "liked it so well," she wrote, that she wrote it out for them. The review in *Current Literature* remarked that these students were not, as Sampter suggested, merely average. See "Teaching Children," 630. Sampter saved a clipping.

63 Even Advaita Vedanta and its proponents had elements of recombination: it emerged as the dominant form of Hindu theology in the late nineteenth and early twentieth century, in part as a way to respond to Christian missionaries' critiques of Hinduism. On this, see McKean, *Divine Enterprise*, 282–83.

64 On New Thought, see Satter, *Each Mind a Kingdom*.

65 Sampter, *King Asoka*, undated manuscript, A219\9, CZA.

66 Sampter, *King Asoka*, 1.

67 Sampter, "Speaking Heart," 264.

68 Sampter, "Speaking Heart," 264.

69 Eugene Crowell, "Christian Spiritualism," *American Spiritual Magazine*, December 1877, 368. For the intimate links and crossings between American Christianity and Spiritualism, see Braude, *Radical Spirits*; Taves, *Fits, Trances, and Visions*; and Schmidt, *Restless Souls*.

70 Sampter, "Speaking Heart," 287.

71 Sampter, "Speaking Heart," 320.

72 Sampter, "Speaking Heart," 322.

73 See, for example, Ariel, "Christianity through Jewish Eyes"; and Rabin, "Jews in Church," 237. Some examples of sermons and other writings are collected in G. Berlin, *Defending the Faith*.

74 Sampter, "Speaking Heart," 355.

75 Sampter, "Passover 5680," 172.

76 Sampter, "Speaking Heart," 402.

77 Kaplan, *Communings of the Spirit*, 107. Sampter discussed the inspiration and the process of translating Krishnamurti into English in JS to EW, March 18, 1934.

78 Kaplan, *Communings of the Spirit*, 108.

79 Pianko, *Jewish Peoplehood*, 45–48.

80 For two separate accounts, see Sampter, "Snowbound in Jerusalem" in A219\1, CZA; and Sampter, "Speaking Heart," 444.

81 "The Scouts of Zion," *Review*, September 22, 1922, 18. Sampter saved a copy, now in A219\5, CZA.

82 Sampter, "In the Beginning," 151.

83 Sampter, "In the Beginning," 178.

84 Sampter, "In the Beginning," 180.

85 "Mission," Pluralism Project, accessed February 21, 2018, https://web.archive.org/web/20151220110647/http://pluralism.org/about/mission.

86 Silk, "Defining Religious Pluralism."

87 Albanese, *A Republic of Mind and Spirit*; Ahlstrom, *A Religious History of the American People*.

88 For some examples across disciplines, see Eck, "Prospects for Pluralism"; Hutchison, *Religious Pluralism in America*; and Chaves and Gorski, "Religious Pluralism."

89 Hutchison, *Religious Pluralism in America*.

90 Lori Beaman's insights about the sociology of American religion also support this critique. Beaman, "Myth of Pluralism."

91 Porterfield, "Religious Pluralism, the Study of Religion, and 'Postsecular' Culture," 190.

92 For just a few examples of more recent work using the category of diversity, see Kidd, *America's Religious History*; Bremer, *Formed from This Soil*; and Laderman and León, *Religion and American Cultures*.

93 Rabbi Maurice Lefkovits, "The Attitudes of Judaism Toward Christian Science," *Central Conference of American Rabbis Year Book* 22 (1912): 300–318; and Appel, "Christian Science."

94 Braude, *Radical Spirits.*

95 See Frank, "'Bought with a Price."

96 Bender, *New Metaphysicals*, 134.

97 Bender, *New Metaphysicals*, 6.

98 Cressler, *Authentically Black*, 84.

99 Michael Lipka and Claire Gecewicz, "More Americans Now Say They're Spiritual but Not Religious," Pew Research Center, September 6, 2017, https://www.pewresearch.org/fact-tank/2017/09/06/more-americans-now-say-theyre-spiritual-but-not-religious/; and Art Raney, Daniel Cox, and Robert P. Jones, "Searching for Spirituality in the U.S.: A New Look at the Spiritual but Not Religious," PRRI, November 6, 2017, https://www.prri.org/research/religiosity-and-spirituality-in-america/.

100 Parsons, introduction, 2.

101 Mehta, *Beyond Chrismukkah*, 127.

102 Jain, *Peace Love Yoga.*

103 This isn't to say that these worldviews—or any worldviews at all—are *actually* fully cohesive and coherent, merely to say that this is how they are imagined.

104 Rabin, "Jews in Church," 237.

105 See, for example, Brinkmann, *Sundays at Sinai*, 206.

106 Hoffman, *From Rebel to Rabbi*; and M. Cook, *Modern Jews*, 7–11.

107 Hagood, *Secrecy.*

108 Best, *Langston's Salvation.*

109 Weisenfeld, *New World A-Coming.*

110 Wenger, *Religious Freedom*, 128–29.

111 Mehta, *Beyond Chrismukkah*; Ariel, "Hasidism"; and Lucia, *White Utopias.*

112 Sampter, "Speaking Heart," 72d.

Chapter 2. A Life with Disability

1 The phrase *out of time* is a reference to one articulation of the notion of "crip time," what disability studies scholars sometimes call the notion that time moves differently for the disabled body. See, for example, St. Pierre, "Distending Straight-Masculine Time."

2 Sampter, "Speaking Heart," 28.

3 Sampter, "Speaking Heart," 28.

4   Jacobson, *Life before Post-polio Syndrome*, 3.

5   Sampter, *King Asoka*, 15.

6   Sampter, "Speaking Heart," 28–29.

7   Wendell, *Rejected Body*, 18.

8   Johanna Hedva, "My Body Is a Prison of Pain So I Want to Leave It Like a Mystic but I Also Love It and Want It to Matter Politically," transcript of reading and audience discussion, Sick Woman Theory, February 1, 2016, https://sickwomantheory.tumblr.com/post/138519901031/transcript-of-my-body-is-a-prison-of-pain-so-i.

9   Shotwell, *Against Purity*, 4.

10 Imhoff, "Why Disability Studies," 186.

11 Wendell, *Rejected Body*, 165–80.

12 Meghan O'Rourke, "What's Wrong with Me?," *New Yorker*, August 26, 2013, https://www.newyorker.com/magazine/2013/08/26/whats-wrong-with-me.

13 O'Rourke, "What's Wrong with Me?"

14 Elvie Wachenheim to Mrs. Emmanuel Halpern, F32\39\1, Hadassah: Jessie Sampter Material, CZA.

15 Sampter, "Speaking Heart," 29.

16 Sampter, "Speaking Heart," 26.

17 A lot of ink has been spilled about Jews and whiteness. As a relatively affluent English-speaking daughter of Ashkenazi German American parents, Sampter experienced very little race-based discrimination. Her ancestors, had they lived in the United States, could not have been enslaved. Then, as now, race was a complex subject, but to deny that Jews like Sampter were white misreads the dominant historical record. For a more detailed discussion, see Imhoff, "Race, Religion, and Jewish Sexuality."

18 See, for example, Baynton, *Defectives in the Land*.

19 Sampter, "Speaking Heart," 30.

20 Sampter, "Speaking Heart," 34a.

21 Sampter, "Speaking Heart," 35a.

22 Sampter, "Speaking Heart," 37.

23 Sampter, "Speaking Heart," 40.

24 Charmaz, "Loss of Self."

25 Sampter, "Speaking Heart," 37.

26 Siebers, *Disability Theory*, 5. This move is structurally similar to the idea that women's experiences merit attention not just because they may lack aspects of a man's experience but also because they bring distinctive ways of knowing about the world.

27 Sampter, "Speaking Heart," 60.

28 Sampter, "Speaking Heart," 60.

29 Badt-Strauss, *White Fire*, 14.

30 S. Young, "We're Not Here."

31 Sampter, "Speaking Heart," 31.

32 Sampter, "Speaking Heart," 31.

33 Sampter, "Speaking Heart," 33.

34 Bone, "Trapped behind the Glass," 1297.

35 Eulberg, "What Having Polio Causes," 3.

36 Diamond, *Full Circle*, 4.

37 JS to EW, November 17, 1927.

38 Daudet, *In the Land of Pain*, 19.

39 Sampter, "Speaking Heart," 391.

40 JS to EW, December 13, 1937.

41 JS to EW, December 13, 1937.

42 JS to EW, December 20, 1937.

43 JS to EW, January 26, 1938.

44 JS to EW, June 17, 1921.

45 Jessie Sampter, "Eternal Values," August 1938, A219\1, CZA.

46 JS to EW, August 22, 1938.

47 JS to EW, August 28, 1938.

48 JS to EW, August 28, 1938.

49 Wendell, *Rejected Body*, 14.

50 See Imhoff, "Why Disability Studies."

51 L. Davis, *End of Normal*, 85.

52 Petro, "Race, Gender, Sexuality, and Religion." For a wonderful book-length study, see White, *Reforming Sodom*.

53 Eiesland, "Barriers and Bridges."

54 Robert Orsi describes a heady mix of pity, condescension, and theological power assumed of "shut-ins" and other disabled folks in "Mildred, Is It Fun to Be a Cripple?"

55 Thomson, "Eugenics," 78; and Davis, *End of Normal*, 98.

56 Keller, *World I Live In*, 85–86. Throughout this book, I use Deaf (with a capital D) to refer to the people, identities, and communities associated with Deaf culture. With a lowercase d, deaf refers to the audiological condition of not hearing or people who do not identify with Deaf culture. See Padden and Humphries, *Deaf in America*.

57 Sanford, *Waking*; A. Cohen, *What I Thought I Knew*; and Coggins, "Fake It Until You Make It," 200.

58 Sampter, "Speaking Heart," 252.

59 Schumm, "Disciplining Normalcy."

60 A significant majority of Americans define themselves as religious. For an overview of one large recent study, see "America's Changing Religious Landscape," Pew Research Center, May 12, 2015, https://www.pewforum.org/2015/05/12/americas-changing-religious-landscape/.

61 Adams, *Raising Henry*, 27.

62 Linton, *My Body Politic*, 33–34.

63 Sampter, "Speaking Heart," 78b, 78d.

64 See Lelwica, *Shameful Bodies*.

65 JS to EW, December 18, 1919.

66 Advertisement, *Photoplay*, February 1919, 105.

67 Thomson, *Extraordinary Bodies*, 11.

68 Mackelprang and Salsgiver, "People with Disabilities and Social Work," 8.

69 Wilson, "Trouble with Disability."

70 Barnes and Mercer, "Disability Culture: Assimilation or Inclusion?," 528.

71 JS to EW, June 10, 1921.

72 JS to EW, August 23, 1937.

73 Siebers, *Disability Theory*, 64.

74 Kafer, *Feminist, Queer, Crip*, 6–10.

75 Szold to Kallen, November 9, 1918, MS #1, box 29, folder 19, Horace M. Kallen Papers, AJA.

76 Jessie Sampter to Henry Hurwitz, March 1, 1915, MS #2, box 51, folder 8, Henry Hurwitz Papers, AJA.

77 JS to EW, January 16, 1927.

78 JS to EW, August 17, 1927.

79 JS to EW, August 10, 1936.

80 JS to EW, August 17, 1936.

81 JS to EW, April 5, 1932.

82 JS to EW, May 23, 1932.

83 JS to EW, August 21, 1921.

84 JS to EW, December 26, 1919.

85 JS to EW, February 20, 1921.

86 JS to EW, November 20, 1936.

87 JS to EW, August 10, 1937.

88 JS to EW, April 20, 1927.

89 JS to EW, April 10, 1928.

90 Sampter, "Holy Days in the Holy City," November 4, 1919, 16, A219\1, CZA.

91 Sampter, "Speaking Heart," 374a.

92 Sampter, "Speaking Heart," 378.

93 JS to EW, June 23, 1932.

94 JS to EW, June 16, 1931.

95 JS to EW, February 13, 1929.

96 L. Berlin, "Be-Kav HaYashar," 30.

97 JS to EW, July 26, 1927.

98 Regev, "HaEsh HaLavanah," 3.

99 Breckenridge and Vogler, "Critical Limits of Embodiment," 350.

100 Sampter, "We Learn from Our Children," 3–4, A219\1, CZA.

101 Sampter, "We Learn from Our Children," 3.

102 Sampter, "They Have Ears, but They Hear Not," 1, A219\1, CZA.

103 Ezekiel 18:2.

104 Sampter, "They Have Ears," 11.

105 JS to EW, June 17, 1930.

106 JS to EW, July 25, 1929.

107 Sampter met with part of the committee on June 25, 1931, and on July 22, 1931; she visited the school itself on December 18.

108 "The Deaf in Other Lands," *Volta Review*, January 1932, 599.

109 JS to EW, June 10, 1931.

110 JS to EW, July 29, 1935.

111 Sampter, *A Course in Zionism*, 7.

112 Thomson, *Extraordinary Bodies*, 161. Thompson's engagement with theological tropes and ideas is rich, though it remains a secularization narrative of the kind that most religious studies scholars critique as a naive understanding of history.

113 Orsi, "Problem of the Holy," 88.

114 Schumm, "Misfitting."

115 "Without a Country," 131.

116 Sampter, "Validity," A219\1, CZA.

117 JS to EW, August 17, 1936.

118 Sampter, "Joy," A219\1, CZA.

119 JS to EW, January 23, 1934; and JS to EW, February 6, 1934.

120 Scarry, *Body in Pain*, 52. Talal Asad offers a critique of pain solely as unmaking and isolating: "What a subject experiences and how, are not simply mediated culturally and physically, *they are themselves modes of living a relationship.*" Asad, *Formations of the Secular*, 84. Thank you to the anonymous reader for pointing me back to this generative text.

121 Sampter, "Joy."

122 JS to EW, February 28, 1938.

123 JS to EW, March 14, 1938; and March 21, 1938.

124 JS to EW, March 28, 1938.

125 JS to EW, April 3, 1938.

126 JS to EW, September 28, 1938.

127 Sampter, "Body Is Soul," A219\1, CZA.

Chapter 3. A Queer Life

1 Jakobsen, "Queer Is? Queer Does?," 516.

2 Furey, "Body, Society, and Subjectivity," 8; and Furey, *Poetic Relations*.

3 Crosby, *Body, Undone*.

4 One terrific recent example is Cleves, *Charity and Sylvia*.

5 There is a vast literature on the history of homosexuality, including Foucault, *History of Sexuality*; Chauncey, "From Sexual Inversion to Homosexuality"; and Stevens and Hall, "Critical Historical Analysis."

6 Dinshaw, *Getting Medieval*.

7 Smith-Rosenberg, "Female World of Love and Ritual," 8.

8 O'Neill, *Everyone Was Brave*, quoted in Cook, "Historical Denial of Lesbianism," 60.

9 Nara Schoenberg, "Outing Jane Addams: Was the Founder of Hull House a Lesbian? And Does It Matter?," *Chicago Tribune*, February 6, 2007. Some other writers also mention the possibility, though Allen Freeman Davis declares that whether she was a lesbian or not was "essentially irrelevant": see A. Davis, *American Heroine*, 306n45; and Brown, *Education of Jane Addams*, 361n60.

10 Sampter, "Speaking Heart," 158.

11 On medieval Christian mystics, see Hollywood, *Sensible Ecstasy*; and Rambuss, *Closet Devotions*. On Sufi love mysticism, see Hoffman-Ladd, "Mysticism and Sexuality." On Krishna as lover, see Bhattacharya, "The Transgendered Devotee."

12 Eli Clare explains his own experiences of feeling desexualized in *Exile and Pride: Disability, Queerness, and Liberation* (151). For a specific medicalizing example, in which others assume the desexualization of disabled bodies, see discussions about "pillow angels," including Kafer, 47–68.

13 See, for example *Parents* magazine's February 2003 cover, which featured a girl with spina bifida, or its October 2016 cover with a woman and a child with Down syndrome. In *Runner's World*, see, for example, the December 2004 cover, which features "Sarah Reinertsen, triathlete, marathoner, inspiration."

14 One example of mainstream inclusion is ESPN *the Magazine*'s featuring of paratriathlete Sarah Reinertsen in the nude on one of its "Body Issue" covers in 2009 (October 20, 2009). The reluctance of people to send "swimsuit photos" is described in this online article: Jordan Davidson, "This Is What It Looks Like When You Feature Disabled and Chronically Ill People in Magazines," *The Mighty*, August 1, 2016, https://themighty.com/2016/08/magazine-covers -featuring-disabled-people/.

15 Sampter, "Speaking Heart," 10b.

16 Sampter, "Speaking Heart," 10a.

17 Sampter, "Speaking Heart," 21.

18 Sampter, "Speaking Heart," 22–23.

19 Sampter, "Speaking Heart," 57.

20 Sampter, "Speaking Heart," insert stapled to 80.

21 Sampter, "Speaking Heart," 233.

22 Sampter, "Speaking Heart," 68

23 Sampter, "Speaking Heart," 68.

24 Antin's best-selling book *The Promised Land* would be published in 1912, but she had already published her first memoir, *From Plotzk to Boston*, in 1899, when she was eighteen years old.

25 Antin's poem "Snow," written when she was twelve, was published in *Primary Education*, March 1895, 91.

26 See, for example, Lazarus, "Zionism and Americanism."

27 Nadell, introduction, xiii–xiv.

28 Sampter, "Speaking Heart," 105.

29 Sampter, "Speaking Heart," 76.

30 Sampter, "Speaking Heart," 105.

31 Sampter, "The Face of Life," *Great Adventurer*, I.

32 Sampter, "Speaking Heart," 92.

33 Sampter, "The Face of Life," *Great Adventurer*, IV.

34 Lee Edelman most forcefully articulates a critique of what he calls "reproductive futurism" in *No Future: Queer Theory and the Death Drive*. José Esteban Muñoz, in response, posited a queer futurity that need not center on the figure of the child in *Cruising Utopia: The There and Then of Queer Futurity*. Jack Halberstam offers a sense of queer time that focuses less on a critique of reproduction and more on the existence of nonnormative queer kinship arrangements—an analysis that is closest to the reading I am offering here; Halberstam, *In a Queer Time*. All three show how the human sense of time and its orientation is profoundly shaped by sexuality.

35 Badt-Strauss, *White Fire*.

36 Halberstam, *In a Queer Time*, 1.

37 Sampter, "Speaking Heart," 37.

38 Sampter, "Speaking Heart," 39.

39 Sampter, "Speaking Heart," 53.

40 Sampter, "Speaking Heart," 195.

41 Sampter, "The Face of Life," *Great Adventurer*, V.

42 Sampter, "The Face of Life," *Great Adventurer*, V.

43 Sampter, "Speaking Heart," 77.

44 Henry Hurwitz to Jessie Sampter, May 10, 1915, MS #2, box 51, folder 8, Henry Hurwitz Papers, AJA.

45 Jessie Sampter to Henry Hurwitz, May 14, 1915, MS #2, box 51, folder 8, Henry Hurwitz Papers, AJA .

46 Sampter, "Speaking Heart," 97.

47 Sampter, "Speaking Heart," 123.

48 Kane, "'She Offered Herself Up.'"

49 Sampter, "Speaking Heart," 78a.

50 Sampter, "Speaking Heart," 232.

51 Sampter, "Speaking Heart," 201.

52 Sampter, "Speaking Heart," 208.

53 Sampter, "Speaking Heart," 208.

54 Sampter, "Speaking Heart," 209.

55 Clare, *Exile and Pride*, 151.

56 Sampter, "Speaking Heart," 252.

57 Sampter, "Speaking Heart," 261.

58 JS to EW, June 5, 1930.

59 JS to EW, July 16, 1919.

60 Sampter, "Speaking Heart," 294.

61 L. Berlin, "Be-Kav HaYashar," 26–27. It seems that when she met Sampter in 1919 in Jerusalem, she was working for the Smaller Action Committee of the Women's Zionist Organization.

62 Tamar de Sola Pool, "Old Wine in New Bottles," *American Hebrew*, June 25, 1937, 25.

63 Henrietta Szold to Elvie Wachenheim, May 30, 1920, quoted in Badt-Strauss, *White Fire*, 65.

64 February 20, 1921, quoted in Badt-Strauss, *White Fire*, 78.

65 Alofsin, *America's Triumph*, 258.

66 Sampter, "Speaking Heart," 302 insert.

67 Sampter, "Speaking Heart," 303.

68 JS to EW, November 13, 1919.

69 JS to EW, November 13, 1919.

70 JS to EW, November 27, 1919.

71 JS to EW, December 11, 1919.

72 JS to EW, December 18, 1919.

73 JS to EW, March 12, 1920.

74 JS to EW, March 12, 1920.

75 JS to EW, March 12, 1920.

76 JS to EW, March 19, 1920.

77 JS to EW, May 24, 1920.

78 JS to EW, June 8, 1920.

79 JS to EW, July 1, 1920.

80 Sampter, "Speaking Heart," 331a.

81 Sampter, "Speaking Heart," 332b.

82 Kath Weston brilliantly describes the conflicts, complexities, and constraints of queer families in *Families We Choose: Lesbians, Gays, Kinship*.

83 JS to EW, July 7, 1920; JS to EW, September 15, 1920; and JS to EW, October 14, 1920.

84 JS to EW, October 14, 1920.

85 JS to EW, December 20, 1920.

86 de Sola Pool, "Old Wine in New Bottles," 25.

87 de Sola Pool, "Old Wine in New Bottles," 25.

88 JS to EW, October 14, 1920.

89 Sampter, "Watchwomen," 47, 49.

90 Sampter, "Watchwomen," 49

91 Sampter, "Speaking Heart," 358.

92 JS to EW, December 20, 1920.

93 Sampter, "Speaking Heart," 369.

94 Sampter, "Speaking Heart," 369.

95 Sampter, "Speaking Heart," 370.

96 Sampter, "Speaking Heart," 374.

97 Sampter, "Speaking Heart," 374a.

98 JS to EW, April 29, 1923.

99 JS to EW, January 3, 1921.

100 JS to EW, November 5, 1922.

101 Sampter, "Speaking Heart," 379.

102 JS to EW, May 22, 1923.

103 Sampter, "Speaking Heart," 387.

104 Sampter, "Speaking Heart," 396.

105 JS to EW, March 6, 1921. "Little Nancy Samuel," the daughter of High Commissioner Herbert Samuel, also helped out with the troop on occasion.

106 JS to EW, November 17, 1922, quoted in Badt-Strauss, *White Fire*, 90.

107 Whether or not children were stolen or adopted out remains a matter of significant controversy. See, for example, Yolanda Knell, "Missing Babies: Israel's Yemenite Children Affair," BBC *News Magazine*, June 21, 2017, https://www.bbc.com/news/magazine-40342143; Yaacov Lozowitz, "Israel's Missing Yemenite Kids Were Abducted, Families Believe. The Archives Tell a Different Story," *Haaretz*, May 6, 2019; and Madmoni-Gerber, *Israeli Media*.

108 Jessie Sampter to Alberta Hall, February 20, 1926, quoted in Badt-Strauss, *White Fire*, 104–5.

109 Sampter, "Speaking Heart," 59.

110 JS to EW, May 22, 1927.

111 JS to EW, June 7, 1927.

112 JS to EW, September 21, 1927.

113 JS to EW, April 19, 1928; JS to EW, May 2, 1928; JS to EW, May 9, 1928; JS to EW, August 16, 1928.

114 JS to EW, November 21, 1928.

115 JS to EW, September 5, 1929.

116 JS to EW, August 20, 1931.

117 JS to EW, September 24, 1931.

118 JS to EW, February 6, 1933.

119 JS to EW, January 12, 1933.

120 JS to EW, January 24, 1933.

121 JS to EW, January 29, 1933.

122 JS to EW, July 27, 1933.

123 JS to EW, August 14, 1933.

124 JS to EW, February 12, 1934.

125 JS to EW, February 6, 1934.

126 JS to EW, April 8, 1935.

127 JS to EW, May 24, 1935.

128 JS to EW, October 5, 1936.

129 See *Bet Yesha: 30 Shana*.

130 JS to EW, March 14, 1934.

131 JS to EW, December 27, 1932.

132 JS to EW, February 20, 1933.

133 JS to EW, January 27, 1936.

134 Leah Berlin to Elvie Wachenheim, November 28, 1938, F32\39\1, Hadassah: Jessie Sampter Material, CZA.

135 Sampter, "Plow Deep," 225.

136 Sampter, "Soap Bubble City," 239.

137 JS to EW, July 9, 1921, quoted in Badt-Strauss, *White Fire*, 85.

138 Sampter, *Emek*, 4–5.

139 Sampter, *Emek*, 17.

140 Sampter, *Emek*, 57–58.

141 Sampter, *Emek*, 52.

142 JS to EW, November 6, 1929 (letter out of order in archive folder).

143 JS to EW, January 29, 1930.

144 Sampter, "Speaking Heart," 68.

145 JS to EW, March 12, 1929.

146 Woodhull, "Principles of Social Freedom," 42.

147 Kahn, "Yesha Sampter," 31.

148 Chazan, "Wise Woman," 83–96.

149 Thank you to Peter Nemes, who very kindly translated the title and first few sentences from Hungarian back into English so I could figure out which article it was.

150 Sampter, "Married Women in Kevutzot," 1, A219\1, CZA.

151 Sampter, "Married Women in Kevutzot," 4.

152 "Confession," 10.

153 "Confession (Part 2)," 15.

154 Jessie Sampter to Mordecai Kaplan, September 4, 1934, Record Group 1, Record Series 1, Eisenstein Reconstructionist Archives, Wyncote, PA.

155 JS to EW, December 5, 1933.

156 Sampter, "Holy Days."

157 Sampter, "Watchwomen," 54.

158 Sampter, "Married Women in Kevutzot," 3.

159 Dolfi, "Christian Domestic Discipline," https://sfonline.barnard.edu/queer -religion/christian-domestic-discipline-and-queer-religious-studies/.

160 Originally recorded by Darrell Evans, "Your Love Is Extravagant" has become a widely known Christian song. Darrell Evans, "Your Love is Extravagant," track 9 on *Freedom*, Vertical Music, 1998.

161 Hellner-Eshed, *River Flows from Eden*, 68–69; Wolfson, *Circle in the Square*; and Haskell, *Suckling at My Mother's Breast*, 102–6.

162 Sampter, *Seekers*, 104.

Chapter 4. A Theological-Political Life

1 Sampter, "Speaking Heart," 417.

2 Hochman, *Ugliness of Moses Mendelssohn*.

3 For one example of a central text of Jewish philosophy, see Ivry, *Maimonides' "Guide of the Perplexed,"* 34–39.

4 For one articulation of this philosophy, see Kaplan, *Judaism as a Civilization*.

5 Jessie Sampter to Mordecai Kaplan, September 4, 1934, Record Group 1, Record Series 1, Eisenstein Reconstructionist Archives. Two years later, she reiterated, "Today, after seventeen years in Palestine and after much thought and experience, I find myself only in part in agreement with you but nonetheless following your ideas with the keen appreciation of a student." Sampter to Kaplan, September 6, 1936, Record Group 1, Record Series 1, Eisenstein Reconstructionist Archives.

6 Sampter, "Confession (Part 2)," 12.

7 Sampter, "I Told You So," 81.

8 Antler, *Journey Home*; and Badt-Strauss, *White Fire*, 32.

9 Segal, *Book of Pain-Struggle*, 80.

10 Segal, *Book of Pain-Struggle*, 71.

11 Segal, *Book of Pain-Struggle*, 71.

12 Segal, *Book of Pain-Struggle*, 60.

13 Segal, *Book of Pain-Struggle*, 66.

14 Segal, *Book of Pain-Struggle*, 66–67.

15 Segal, *Book of Pain-Struggle*, 70–71.

16 "New Books," *New Catholic World*, April 1919, 120.

17 Segal, *Book of Pain-Struggle*, 7, 48.

18 Sampter, "Speaking Heart," 170.

19 Sampter, "Speaking Heart," 160.

20 Sampter, "Speaking Heart," 173.

21 Sampter, "Speaking Heart," 162.

22 Sampter, "Speaking Heart," 162.

23 Sampter, "Speaking Heart," 191.

24 Sampter, "Speaking Heart," 192.

25 Badt-Strauss, *White Fire*, 42.

26 Sampter and Kallen met in late 1913. Henrietta Szold to Horace Kallen, November 9, 1913, MS #1, box 29, folder 19, Horace M. Kallen Papers, AJA.

27 For an excellent exploration and contextualization of Sampter's thought alongside other Hadassah thinkers, see Rock-Singer, "Hadassah and the Gender of Modern Jewish Thought."

28 Szold, Letter to Jessie Sampter, July 15, 1913, quoted in Fineman, *Woman of Valor*, 80.

29 Quoted in Fineman, *Woman of Valor*, 80.

30 Henrietta Szold to Horace Kallen, January 28, 1914, MS #1, box 29, folder 19, Horace M. Kallen Papers, AJA.

31 For more on the Hadassah School of Zionism and Sampter's role in the wider Hadassah project, see Wolf, "Jessie Sampter."

32 Dushkin, *Living Bridges*, 139–40.

33 Henrietta Szold to Jessie Sampter, March 27, 1917, quoted in Lowenthal, *Henrietta Szold*, 97.

34 Sampter, "Hadassah School of Zionism," 3.

35 Sampter, "Speaking Heart," 193.

36 Sampter, "Speaking Heart," 221.

37 Henrietta Szold to Horace Kallen, October 18, 1914, MS #1, box 29, folder 19, Horace M. Kallen Papers, AJA.

38 For just a few examples, see Jill Lepore, "Don't Let Nationalists Speak for the Nation," *New York Times*, May 25, 2019; and Lewis Hyde, "How Nationalism Can Destroy a Nation," *New York Times*, August 21, 2019. The blowback after Donald Trump labeled himself a nationalist is one example of the wariness around nationalism. For example, see William Cummings, "'I Am a Nationalist': Trump's Embrace of Controversial Label Sparks Uproar," *USA Today*, October 24, 2018, https://www.usatoday.com/story/news/politics/2018/10/24/trump-says-hes-nationalist-what-means-why-its-controversial/1748521002/.

39 For a broader discussion of the tensions between nationalism and internationalism within Zionist thought, see Pianko, *Zionism*, 4–6, 11–18.

40 Sampter, *Nationalism and Universal Brotherhood*, 2.

41 Sampter, *Nationalism and Universal Brotherhood*, 3.

42 Sampter, *Nationalism and Universal Brotherhood*, 7.

43 Sampter, *Nationalism and Universal Brotherhood*, 7. She had put forth this conception in earlier writing too. In 1915 she had written that if we look in the Bible, "we shall find there the Jewish conception of nationalism." Sampter, "The Ideal of Peace in Jewish Thought and Life," 1915, A219\14, CZA.

44 Sampter, "I Told You So," 80.

45 Sampter, "I Told You So," 81.

46 Sampter, "What Our History Means," 15. A copy resides in A219\5, CZA.

47 Quoted in de Haas, *Louis Dembitz Brandeis*, 163.

48 Sampter, "Teacher," 4.

49 Sampter, "Jewish Position," 74.

50 Sampter, "I Told You So," 80. On racialism, see Appiah, *My Father's House*, 13.

51 Sampter, "I Told You So," 81.

52 Sampter, "Jewish Position."

53 Sampter, "Speaking Heart," 255.

54 Sampter, "Speaking Heart," 258.

55 Ludwig Lewisohn, "The World's Window: Anti-Semitism Once More," *Sentinel*, October 6, 1937, 5.

56 Sampter, "Cure the Causes," 77.

57 Sampter, "Speaking Heart," 72.

58 Sampter, "Speaking Heart," 79.

59 Albert Einstein, foreword to Sampter, *Modern Palestine*, v.

60 JS to EW, October 3, 1933.

61 Sampter, "War and the Jews," 124–25.

62 Sampter, "Ideal of Peace."

63 Sampter, *Book of the Nations*, 24.

64 Sampter, "Speaking Heart," 240.

65 Mary Antin to Horace Kallen, May 23, 1917, box 2, folder 4, Horace M. Kallen papers, AJA.

66 Zangwill, *Voice of Jerusalem*, 235.

67 Jessie Rittenhouse, review of *Book of Nations*, *Bulletin of the Poetry Society of America*, December 1917.
68 Quoted in Levensohn, "*Book of Nations*," 296.
69 Quoted in Badt-Strauss, *White Fire*, 49.
70 "Looking through the New Books," *Lyric*, December 1917, back cover.
71 Sampter, *Coming of Peace*, 18.
72 Sampter, "Healing of Peace," 8. The poem is dated "Jerusalem, Dec 4, 1919."
73 Sampter, "Speaking Heart," 244.
74 Sampter, "Speaking Heart," 250.
75 Wilcock, *Pacifism and the Jews*, 45.
76 Sampter, "Speaking Heart," 256.
77 Sampter, "Speaking Heart," 242.
78 Sampter, "Mother," 36.
79 Sampter, "Mother," 67.
80 Sampter, "To the Jewish Teacher," 227.
81 Sampter, "To the Jewish Teacher," 227.
82 Sampter, "Passover 5680," 172.
83 Sampter, "Passover 5680," 172.
84 Sampter, "Passover 5680," 172.
85 Sampter, "Passover 5680," 172.
86 Sampter, "Passover 5680," 172.
87 JS to EW, April 11, 1932.
88 JS to EW, October 24, 1938.
89 Chazan, "Wise Woman."
90 Yesha [Sampter], "Tkhunat hahaganah haivrit," Alon Givat Brenner, May 22, 1936. See also Chazan, "Wise Woman," for another description of this document.
91 Sampter, "Watchwomen," 53.
92 Sampter, "Watchwomen," 53.
93 Sampter, unpublished letter to the editor of the *Jerusalem Post*, June 30, 1938, found in A219\1, CZA.
94 Sampter, "Speaking Heart," 412.
95 JS to EW, August 28, 1919.
96 JS to EW, October 1, 1919.
97 JS to EW, January 3, 1921.
98 JS to EW, October 14, 1919.
99 Jessie Sampter to Mordecai Kaplan, December 30, 1920, SC-6102, Mordecai Kaplan Papers, AJA.
100 Sampter, "Snowbound in Jerusalem," 231.
101 JS to EW, December 18, 1919.
102 JS to EW, June 1, 1920.
103 Sampter, "Speaking Heart," 398.
104 On this, see Qafisheh, *International Law Foundations*.
105 Sampter, "Speaking Heart," 296.
106 Sampter, "Speaking Heart," 298.

107 Henrietta Szold to Hadassah chapters, October 26, 1921, A125\23, CZA.

108 Sampter, "Bed Number Six," 12–13.

109 Mrs. A. H. Vixman, "A Word about the Convention," *Jewish Criterion*, December 2, 1921, 20.

110 "Organization Activities," *Jewish Criterion*, January 13, 1922, 16. "Bed Number Six" also appeared in the *Hadassah Newsletter* in April 1922.

111 Sampter, "Bed Number Six," 13.

112 For a discussion of these, see Neumann, *Land and Desire*.

113 Sampter, "Speaking Heart," 387.

114 Sampter, "Speaking Heart," 417.

115 Sampter, "Speaking Heart," 417.

116 Jessie Sampter to Edgar Wachenheim Sr., October 30, 1919, A219\41.

117 Sampter, "Speaking Heart," 305.

118 Sampter, "Speaking Heart," 305.

119 Sampter, "In the Beginning," 114.

120 Sampter to Kaplan, December 30, 1920.

121 Sampter to Kaplan, December 30, 1920.

122 Sampter, "Speaking Heart," 192.

123 Sampter, "Causes of Emigration," 1.

124 Sampter, "Bed Number Five," 88–89.

125 Sampter, "Speaking Heart," 345.

126 Sampter, *Guide to Zionism*, 160.

127 Much of Mizrahi identity gets invented around the time of the founding of the state of Israel. See Khazzoom, "Great Chain of Orientalism."

128 Max Heller and Judah Magnes, for example, submitted a resolution to the Federation of American Zionists' 1912 conference to help Yemenite Jews emigrate to Palestine. See "Fifteenth Annual Convention of the Federation of American Zionists," 8. The organization sent a similar appeal to "all American Zionists" in November of the same year. See "Appeal on Behalf of the Yemenite Jews," 163.

129 "Book on Palestine," *Jewish Post and Opinion*, January 24, 1936, 1.

130 Rubinstein, *Adventuring in Palestine*, 45.

131 Sampter, "Jerusalem Gives," 80.

132 Sampter, *Key*, 30.

133 Sampter, "Speaking Heart," 297.

134 Sampter, *Modern Palestine*, 103.

135 Sampter, *Modern Palestine*, 103.

136 Sampter, "Children's House," 8.

137 Sampter, *Modern Palestine*, 104.

138 Sampter, "Oasis," 87.

139 Sampter, "Babies in Palestine," 122.

140 Sampter, "In the Beginning," 171.

141 Arthur, "Child Welfare"; and Rachel Pesah, "What a Nurse Sees," *Hadassah Newsletter*, October 1928, 7; both quoted in Simmons, "Playgrounds and Penny Lunches," 249, 270.

142 Simmons, "Playgrounds and Penny Lunches."

143 Sampter, *Guide to Zionism*, 133.

144 Sampter, *Modern Palestine*, 100.

145 Sampter, "The Forerunners: Sketches of the Old and New Settlements in the Holy Land," September 22, 1922, 11, A219\1, CZA.

146 Sampter, "Oasis," 87.

147 Jessie Sampter to Henrietta Szold, October 13, 1919, A219, CZA\41.

148 Bentwich, *Progress of Zionism*, 4. Quoted in Medoff, 11.

149 Twain, *Innocents Abroad*, 606–7.

150 Sampter, "In Any Case," 19. On Zionist myths, see Medoff, *Zionism and the Arabs*, 9–20.

151 Baron, *Palestine*.

152 "Arab," A219\1, CZA.

153 Jessie Sampter to Edgar Wachenheim Sr., October 30, 1919, A219\41, CZA.

154 JS to EW, April 30, 1920.

155 Sampter, "Speaking Heart," 324–25.

156 JS to EW, January 3, 1933.

157 JS to EW, March 21, 1933.

158 Sampter, "Speaking Heart," 409.

159 Sampter, "Speaking Heart," 310.

160 Sampter, "Speaking Heart," 409.

161 Sampter, "Passover 5680," 172.

162 JS to EW, January 2, 1930.

163 Sampter, "Testimony," 1, A219\1 CZA.

164 Sampter, "Testimony," 2.

165 Sampter, "Testimony," 4.

166 Sampter, "Testimony," 4.

167 Sampter, "Testimony," 5.

168 Sampter, "Speaking Heart," 325, 339.

169 Sampter, "Testimony," 13.

170 Sampter, "Speaking Heart," 325.

171 Medoff, *Zionism and the Arabs*.

172 JS to EW, December 12, 1929.

173 For a description of Magnes's responses to the 1929 riots, see Kotzin, "Attempt to Americanize the Yishuv."

174 Henrietta Szold to Jessie Sampter, September 20, 1931, A219\39, CZA.

175 Szold to Sampter, September 13, 1929, quoted in Medoff, *Zionism and the Arabs*, 56.

176 Gmur, "It Is Not Up to Us Women."

177 Izraeli, "Zionist Women's Movement."

178 Fishbayn Joffe, foreword, x. For an excellent history of women and their stories in this period, see Kark, Shilo, and Hasan-Rokem, *Jewish Women in Pre-state Israel*.

179 Boni-Davidi, "Haganah."

180 Janaith, "Stages," 138.

181 Liberson, "Those First Years," 26.

182 Edelman, "In the War Years," 59.

183 Danith, "Kvutzah of Shepherds," 57

184 Schlimowitz, "Women's Farm," 159.

185 Bar Droma, "Comrade So-and-So's Wife," 182–85.

186 Gordon, "The Kvutzah of Twenty," 90.

187 See, for example, Sampter, "Propaganda among Children," n.d., and "Children's Propaganda," February 27, 1925, #1132, Central Bureau of the Jewish National Fund (KKL5), CZA.

188 Sampter, Key, 16.

189 Jessie Sampter and Dorothy Ruth Kahn, "Collective" (unpublished book manuscript, undated but from 1938), 1, A219\17, CZA.

190 Regev, "HaEsh HaLavanah," 3.

191 Tzemach, "Brit HaHayyim SheNahtama," 7.

192 Regev, "HaEsh HaLavanah," 3.

193 "Tsiunei Derech," 31. This is marked as July 22, 1930, in the memorial volume, but it should be 1934. Leah recalls it was 4,000 lira.

194 Berlin, "Be-Kav HaYashar," 26–27.

195 Berlin, "Be-Kav HaYashar," 27.

196 For a quick and accessible history, see Naama Riba, "How Israel's Socialist Retreats for Workers Turned into Luxury Hotels," Haaretz, May 19, 2016, https://www.haaretz.com/israel-news/business/.premium.MAGAZINE-how-wellness-retreats-for-workers-turned-into-luxury-hotels-1.5385543?v=1610484450941.

197 JS to EW, February 19, 1934.

198 JS to EW, February 12, 1934.

199 JS to EW, March 18, 1934.

200 Berlin, "Be-Kav HaYashar," 28.

201 JS to EW, March 18, 1934.

202 JS to EW, July 6, 1934.

203 Berlin, "Be-Kav HaYashar," 29.

204 Kahn, "Yesha Sampter," 31.

205 Sampter, "Married Women in Kevutzot," A219\1, CZA.

206 Sampter, "Married Women in Kevutzot," 3.

207 Sampter, "Holy Days."

208 Sampter, "Aaron Aaronsohn," 153.

209 Noam Pianko, Arie Dubnov, and Hanan Harif have also used Robert Frost's phrase in connection to male Zionist thinkers. Pianko, Zionism and the Roads Not Taken; and Arie Dubnov and Hanan Harif, "Zionisms: Roads Not Taken on the Way to the Jewish State," Maarav: Online Israeli Art and Culture Magazine, April 29, 2012, http://maarav.org.il/english/2012/04/29/zionisms-roads-not-taken-on-the-journey-to-the-jewish-state-arie-dubnov-hanan-harif/.

Chapter 5. Afterlives

1 Mary Antin to Elvie Wachenheim, November 29, 1938, A219\38 CZA.

2 Sampter, *Seekers*, 79.

3 Sampter, *Seekers*, 78.

4 Sampter, *Seekers*, 77.

5 Cleve Wootson Jr., "'This World Is a Better Place without Her': A Family's Savage Final Send-Off to Their Mother," *Washington Post*, June 5, 2018.

6 Hume, *Obituaries in American Culture*.

7 "Eretz Israel Vouz Parle," *Israël*, December 22, 1938, 3.

8 "Jessie Sampter, Noted Poet, Dies in Palestine," *Bnai Brith Messenger*, December 2, 1938, 1. On B'nai B'rith, see Raider, *Emergence of American Zionism*, 184.

9 Clipping saved in F32\39\1, Hadassah: Jessie Sampter Material, CZA.

10 "Passing of a Poet," *Palestine Post*, November 28, 1938, 4.

11 CZA: KKL5\1132, Central Bureau of the Jewish National Fund papers.

12 Sampter, "Speaking Heart," 14.

13 Leah Berlin, "Her Path," *Davar HaPoelet*, December 30, 1938, 241.

14 D. K. [likely Dorothy Kahn], "Jessie Sampter Dead: Poetess and Veteran Pioneer," *Palestine Post*, November 27, 1938, 2.

15 Esther Carmel-Hakim and Nancy Rosenfeld, "Biography of Dorothy Kahn Bar-Adon (1907–1950)," in *Writing Palestine*, 10.

16 D. K., "Jessie Sampter Dead," 2.

17 Margaret Doniger to Rose Jacobs, January 25, 1939, F32\39\1, Hadassah: Jessie Sampter Material, CZA.

18 Doniger to Jacobs, January 25, 1939.

19 Doniger to Jacobs, January 25, 1939.

20 Margaret Doniger, "Remembering Jessie Sampter," *Hadassah Newsletter*, January 1939, 86, saved in F32\39\1, Hadassah: Jessie Sampter Material, CZA.

21 Julia Dushkin, "Farewell to Jessie Sampter," *Hadassah Newsletter*, January 1939, 86, saved in F32\39\1, Hadassah: Jessie Sampter Material, CZA.

22 Judith Ish Kishor, "Jessie E. Sampter," *Sentinel*, July 27, 1939, 25.

23 "Robert St. John, Non-Jewish Zionist, Mideast Journalist," *J. the Jewish News of Northern California*, February 14, 2003.

24 St. John, *Shalom Means Peace*, 128–30.

25 St. John, *Shalom Means Peace*, 128.

26 St. John, *Shalom Means Peace*, 128.

27 St. John, *Shalom Means Peace*, 128.

28 St. John, *Shalom Means Peace*, 130.

29 Nathan Glazer, "*Shalom Means Peace*, by Robert St. John," *Commentary*, May 1949, https://www.commentary.org/articles/nathan-glazer-2/shalom-means-peace-by-robert-st-john/.

30 Special thanks to Jacob Beckert for researching the novel and its subsequent interpretations. There is an awful lot to say about this book—and its two sequels that feature Leah as a major character. Little has been written about it in English

or Hebrew scholarship. However, those discussions would take us far afield from Sampter.

31 See, for example, Shamir, *Yona MeHatzer Zara*, 92, 93.

32 Alofsin, *America's Triumph*, 247–48.

33 Alofsin, *America's Triumph*, 252.

34 Alofsin, *America's Triumph*, 252.

35 Alofsin, *America's Triumph*, 254.

36 Alofsin, *America's Triumph*, 268.

37 Alofsin, *America's Triumph*, 268–69.

38 Bertha Badt-Strauss to Jacob Picard, October 9, 1951, Jacob Picard Collection, Leo Baeck Institute, Center for Jewish History, New York, quoted in Steer, *Bertha Badt-Strauss*, 275.

39 Steer, *Bertha Badt-Strauss*, 275.

40 Bertha Badt-Strauss to Jacob Picard, February 21, 1952, Jacob Pickard Collection, quoted in Steer, *Bertha Badt-Strauss*, 275.

41 Steer, "Bertha Badt-Strauss."

42 Steer, "Bertha Badt-Strauss (1885–1970)."

43 Korn, foreword, n.p.

44 Steer, *Bertha Badt-Strauss*, 275ff.

45 Badt-Strauss, *White Fire*, 13.

46 Badt-Strauss, *White Fire*, 14.

47 Badt-Strauss, *White Fire*, 21.

48 Badt-Strauss, *White Fire*, 58.

49 Bertha Badt-Strauss, *Jüdinnen*, 1937, 98, quoted in Steer, *Bertha Badt-Strauss*, 280.

50 Review of Bertha Badt-Strauss's *White Fire*: David Polish, "A Common Spirit Pervades Three Unrelated Books," *Sentinel*, September 26, 1957, 26.

51 M. Eschelbacher, "Recent Publications," *Association of Jewish Refugees Journal*, November 1957, 6.

52 Mendelsohn, "Jewish Children's Literature," 50.

53 Mendelsohn, "Jewish Children's Literature," 50.

54 Mendelsohn, "Jewish Children's Literature," 51.

55 Marcus, *American Jewish Woman: Documentary History*, 728.

56 Marcus, *American Jewish Woman, 1654–1980*, 15.

57 Marcus, *American Jewish Woman, 1654–1980*, 202.

58 Marcus, *American Jewish Woman, 1654–1980*, 17–18.

59 Marcus, *American Jewish Woman, 1654–1980*, 69.

60 Marcus, *American Jewish Woman, 1654–1980*, 69.

61 Marcus, *American Jewish Woman, 1654–1980*, 22.

62 Ingall, *Women Who Reconstructed*; Chazan, "Wise Woman"; Medoff, *Zionism and the Arabs*; and Klapper, *Ballots, Babies, and Banners*. The historian Joyce Antler tells part of Sampter's story—mostly through her relationship with Henrietta Szold—in her history of twentieth-century American Jewish women. But Antler's book, like so many other histories of women, is often seen as a specialty

interest rather than the primary story of American Jews and Judaism. Antler, *Journey Home*, 109–25.

63 Chazan, "Wise Woman."

64 "Jessie Sampter," *Wikipedia*, last edited July 29, 2021, https://en.wikipedia.org /wiki/Jessie_Sampter.

65 Sampter, "Civilization," *The Emek*, 60.

66 *Weight Watchers Success Everyday*.

67 Samuel, *Leisure in a Democracy*, 17.

68 Jenson, *Simplicity Shift*; Marques, *Empower the Leader*; and Jim Wong, "Top 3 Ways for IT Managers to Keep IT Simple," Brilliant, April 22, 2015, https://www .brilliantfs.com/top-3-ways-for-it-managers-to-keep-it-simple/.

69 Partnow, *Quotable Jewish Woman*, 60; and Babauta and Ra, *Zen Habits Handbook*, 72.

70 Baron, *A Treasury of Jewish Quotations*, 454.

71 Elma Levinger, "Jewish Woman as Author," *American Israelite*, October 26, 1922, 1.

72 Louis Newman, "Telling It in Gath," *American Israelite*, January 1, 1934, 4.

73 Ann Enright, "Diary," *London Review of Books*, September 21, 2017, 35.

74 Sampter, *Around the Year in Rhymes for the Jewish Child*, 6.

Bibliography

Archival Sources

American Jewish Archives, Cincinnati, OH
American Jewish Historical Society, Manhattan, New York
Archives for the History of the Jewish People, Jerusalem, Israel
Central Zionist Archives, Jerusalem, Israel
Givat Brenner Archives, Givat Brenner, Israel
Ira and Judith Kaplan Eisenstein Reconstructionist Archives, Wyncote, PA
Leo Baeck Institute, New York, NY

Selected Published Works by Jessie Sampter

"Aaron Aaronsohn." *Maccabaean* 32 (June 1919): 153.
Around the Year in Rhymes for the Jewish Child. New York: Bloch, 1920.
"Babies in Palestine." *New Palestine*, August 3, 1923, 122.
"Bed Number Five." *Hadassah Newsletter*, February 1938, 88–89.
"Bed Number Six." *Bnai Israel Bulletin* [Pittsburgh] (1922): 12–13.
"Causes of Emigration from Palestine." *American Israelite*, August 30, 1923, 1.
"The Children's House." *Hadassah Newsletter*, January–February 1931, 8.
The Coming of Peace. New York: Publishers Printing Company, 1919.
"A Confession." *Reconstructionist* 3, no. 4 (March 1937): 6–11.
"A Confession (Part 2)." *Reconstructionist* 3, no. 5 (April 1937): 12–16.
A Course in Zionism. New York: Federation of American Zionists, 1915.
"Cure the Causes." In *How to Combat Anti-Semitism in America*, edited by Stephen
      Wise, 72–79. New York: Jewish Opinion Publication Corporation, 1937.
The Emek. New York: Bloch, 1927.
The Great Adventurer. New York: Kerr, 1909.

"The Hadassah School of Zionism." *Hadassah Bulletin* 13 (August 1915): 1–6.

"The Healing of Peace." *Maccabaean* 33, no. 7 (July 1920): 8.

"In Any Case." *Maccabaean* 26, no. 2 (February 1915): 19–20.

"I Told You So." *Maccabaean* 31, no. 3 (March 1918): 79–82.

"Jerusalem Gives." *Maccabaean* 34, no. 3 (September 1920): 80.

"The Jewish Position (A Formulation)." *Maccabaean* 27, no. 3 (September 1915): 74–77.

The Key. Jerusalem: Azriel, 1925.

"The Mother." *Maccabaean* 31, no. 2 (February 1918): 35–36, 67.

"My School." *St. Nicholas Magazine*, May 1901, 638.

Nationalism and Universal Brotherhood. New York: Hadassah, 1914.

"Oasis." *Menorah* 8, no. 2 (April 1922): 87.

"Passover 5680." *Maccabaean* 33, no. 6 (June 1920): 172–74.

"Plow Deep." *Menorah* 8, no. 4 (August 1922): 213–25.

The Seekers. New York: Mitchell Kennerley, 1910.

Sefer ha-Goyim [Book of nations]. New York: E. P. Dutton, 1917.

"The Soap Bubble City." *Menorah* 9, no. 3 (August 1923): 238–40.

"Teacher." *Palestine Post*, November 13, 1936, 4.

"Three Hours." *Young Judean* 25, no. 4 (December 1936): 10.

"To the Jewish Teacher." *Maccabaean* 32, no. 8 (August 1919): 227.

"The War and the Jews." *Maccabaean* 25, no. 4 (October 1914): 124–25.

"Watchwomen." *Jewish Frontier*, November 1936, 45–54.

What Our History Means. New York: Judean Press, 1916.

Secondary Sources

Adams, Rachel. *Raising Henry: A Memoir of Motherhood, Disability, and Discovery*. New Haven, CT: Yale University Press, 2014.

Adler, Felix. *Creed and Deed: A Series of Discourses*. New York: G. P. Putnam's Sons, 1877.

Ahlstrom, Sydney E. *A Religious History of the American People*. New Haven, CT: Yale University Press, 1972.

Albanese, Catherine. *A Republic of Mind and Spirit: A Cultural History of American Metaphysical Religion*. New Haven, CT: Yale University Press, 2006.

Alofsin, Dorothy. *America's Triumph: Stories of American Jewish Heroes*. Cincinnati, OH: Riverdale, 1949.

Antin, Mary. *From Plotzk to Boston*. New York: Markus Wiener Publishers, 1986.

Antin, Mary. *The Promised Land*. Boston: Houghton Mifflin, 1912.

Antin, Mary. *Selected Letters of Mary Antin*. Syracuse, NY: Syracuse University Press, 2000.

Antler, Joyce. *The Journey Home: How Jewish Women Shaped Modern America*. New York: Schocken, 1998.

"Appeal on Behalf of the Yemenite Jews." *Maccabaean* 22, no. 5 (November 1912): 163.

Appel, John J. "Christian Science and the Jews." *Jewish Social Studies* 31, no. 2 (April 1969): 100–121.

Appiah, Kwame Anthony. *My Father's House: Africa in the Philosophy of Culture.* Oxford: Oxford University Press, 1992.

Ariel, Yaakov. "Christianity through Reform Eyes: Kaufmann Kohler's Scholarship on Christianity." *American Jewish History* 89, no. 2 (June 2001): 181–91.

Ariel, Yaakov. "Hasidism in the Age of Aquarius: The House of Love and Prayer in San Francisco, 1967–1977." *Religion and American Culture* 13, no. 2 (Summer 2003): 139–65.

Arthur, Julietta. "Child Welfare in the Holy Land: Hadassah's Network of Public Health across Palestine." *American Journal of Nursing* 40, no. 4 (April 1940): 410–14.

Asad, Talal. *Formations of the Secular: Christianity, Islam, Modernity.* Stanford, CA: Stanford University Press, 2003.

Babauta, Leo, and Frank Ra. *Zen Habits Handbook for Life.* N.p.: Zen Habits, 2011.

Badt-Strauss, Bertha. *Jüdinnen.* Berlin: J Goldstein, Jüdischer Buchverlag, 1937.

Badt-Strauss, Bertha. *White Fire: The Life and Works of Jessie Sampter.* New York: Reconstructionist Press, 1956.

Bar Adon, Dorothy Kahn. *Writing Palestine, 1933–1950: Dorothy Kahn Bar Adon,* edited by Esther Carmel-Hakim and Nancy Rosenfeld. Boston, MA: Academic Studies Press, 2016.

Bar Droma, Zipporah. "Comrade So-and-So's Wife." In *The Plough Woman: Memoirs of the Pioneer Women in Palestine,* edited by Rachel Katznelson Shazar, translated by Maurice Samuel, 182–84. 1932. New York: Herzl, 1975.

Barnes, Colin, and Geoff Mercer. "Disability Culture: Assimilation or Inclusion?" In *Handbook of Disability Studies,* edited by Gary L. Albrecht, Katherine D. Seelman, and Michael Bury, 515–34. Thousand Oaks, CA: Sage, 2001.

Baron, J. B. *Palestine: Report and General Abstracts of the Census of 1922.* Jerusalem: Greek Convent Press, 1922.

Baron, Joseph L. *A Treasury of Jewish Quotations.* New York: Crown Publishers, 1956.

Baynton, Douglas C. *Defectives in the Land: Disability and Immigration in the Age of Eugenics.* Chicago: University of Chicago Press, 2016.

Beaman, Lori G. "The Myth of Pluralism, Diversity, and Vigor: The Constitutional Privilege of Protestantism in the United States and Canada." *Journal for the Scientific Study of Religion* 42, no. 3 (September 2003): 311–25.

Bender, Courtney. *The New Metaphysicals: Spirituality and the American Religious Imagination.* Chicago: University of Chicago Press, 2010.

Bentwich, Herbert. *The Progress of Zionism.* New York: American Federation of Zionists, 1899.

Berkovitch, Nitza. "Motherhood as a National Mission: The Construction of Womanhood in the Legal Discourse in Israel." *Women's Studies International Forum* 20, nos. 5–6 (September–December 1997): 605–19.

Berlin, George L. *Defending the Faith: Nineteenth-Century Jewish Writings on Christianity and Jesus.* Albany: State University of New York Press, 1989.

Berlin, Leah. "Be-Kav HaYashar" [In a straight line]. In *Bet Yesha: 30 Shana* [Jessie's House: 30 Years], 21–30. Givat Brenner, 1965.

Best, Wallace D. *Langston's Salvation: American Religion and the Bard of Harlem.* New York: New York University Press, 2017.

Bet Yesha: 30 Shana [Jessie's House: 30 Years]. Givat Brenner, 1955/1956.

Bhattacharya, Rima. "The Transgendered Devotee: Ambiguity of Gender in Devotional Poetry." *Indian Journal of Gender Studies* 25, no. 2 (2018): 151–79.

Bone, Kirstin Marie. "Trapped behind the Glass: Crip Theory and Disability Identity." *Disability and Society* 32, no. 9 (2017): 1297–314.

Boni-Davidi, Dganit. "Haganah." In *The Shalvi/Hyman Encyclopedia of Jewish Women.* Jewish Women's Archive. December 31, 1999. https://jwa.org /encyclopedia/article/haganah.

Boyarin, Daniel. *Unheroic Conduct: The Rise of Heterosexuality and the Invention of the Jewish Man.* Berkeley: University of California Press, 2000.

Braude, Ann. *Radical Spirits: Spiritualism and Women's Rights in Nineteenth-Century America.* Bloomington: Indiana University Press, 2001.

Breckenridge, Carol A., and Candace Vogler. "The Critical Limits of Embodiment: Disability's Criticism." *Public Culture* 13, no. 3 (Fall 2001): 349–57.

Bremer, Thomas S. *Formed from This Soil: An Introduction to the Diverse History of Religion in America.* Chichester, UK: Wiley Blackwell, 2015.

Brinkmann, Tobias. *Sundays at Sinai: A Jewish Congregation in Chicago.* Chicago: University of Chicago Press, 2012.

Brown, Victoria Bissell. *The Education of Jane Addams.* Philadelphia: University of Pennsylvania Press, 2004.

Buhler-Wilkerson, Karen. "Bringing Care to the People: Lillian Wald's Legacy to Public Health Nursing." *American Journal of Public Health* 83, no. 12 (December 1993): 1778–86.

Carmel-Hakim, Esther, and Nancy Rosenfeld. "Biography of Dorothy Kahn Bar-Adon (1907–1950)." In *Writing Palestine*, edited by Esther Carmel-Hakim and Nancy Rosenfeld, 1–15. Boston, MA: Academic Studies Press, 2016.

Charmaz, Kathy. "Loss of Self: A Fundamental Form of Suffering in the Chronically Ill." *Sociology of Health and Illness* 5, no. 2 (July 1983): 168–95.

Chauncey, George. "From Sexual Inversion to Homosexuality: Medicine and the Changing Conceptualization of Female Deviance." *Salmagundi*, no. 58/59 (Fall 1982–Winter 1983): 114–46.

Chaves, Mark, and Philip S. Gorski. "Religious Pluralism and Religious Participation." *Annual Review of Sociology* 27, no. 1 (2001): 261–81.

Chazan, Meir. "The Wise Woman of Givat Brenner: Jessie Sampter on Kibbutz, War, and Peace, 1934–1938." In *The Individual in History: Essays in Honor of Jehuda Reinharz*, edited by ChaeRan Freeze, Sylvia Fuks Fried, and Eugene R. Sheppard, 83–96. Waltham, MA: Brandeis University Press, 2015.

Clare, Eli. *Exile and Pride: Disability, Queerness, and Liberation.* Cambridge, MA: South End, 2009.

Cleves, Rachel Hope. *Charity and Sylvia: A Same-Sex Marriage in Early America*. Oxford: Oxford University Press, 2014.

Coggins, Megan L. "Fake It Until You Make It (or Until You Find Your Place)." In *Barriers and Belongings: Narratives of Disability*, edited by Michelle Jarman, Leila Monaghan, and Alison Quaggin Harkin, 195–200. Philadelphia, PA: Temple University Press, 2017.

Cohen, Alice Eve. *What I Thought I Knew*. New York: Penguin, 2010.

Cohen, Naomi. "The Maccabaean's Message: A Study in American Zionism until World War I." *Jewish Social Studies* 18, no. 3 (July 1956): 163–78.

Cook, Blanche Wiesen. "The Historical Denial of Lesbianism." *Radical History Review*, no. 20 (Spring/Summer 1979): 60–65.

Cook, Michael. *Modern Jews Engage the New Testament*. Woodstock, VT: Jewish Lights, 2008.

Cressler, Matthew. *Authentically Black and Truly Catholic: The Rise of Black Catholicism in the Great Migration*. New York: New York University Press, 2017.

Crocker, Ruth. *Social Work and Social Order: The Settlement Movement in Two Industrial Cities, 1889–1930*. Urbana: University of Illinois Press, 1992.

Crosby, Christina. *A Body, Undone: Living On after Great Pain*. New York: New York University Press, 2016.

Danith, Rebecca. "A Kvutzah of Shepherds." In *The Plough Woman: Memoirs of the Pioneer Women in Palestine*, edited by Rachel Katznelson Shazar, translated by Maurice Samuel, 56–58. 1932. New York: Herzl, 1975.

Daudet, Alphonse. *In the Land of Pain*, edited and translated by Julian Barnes. New York: Vintage Classics, 2016.

Davis, Allen Freeman. *American Heroine: The Life and Legend of Jane Addams*. Chicago: Ivan R. Dee, 2000.

Davis, Lennard J. *The End of Normal: Identity in a Biocultural Era*. Ann Arbor: University of Michigan Press, 2013.

de Haas, Jacob. *Louis Dembitz Brandeis: A Biographical Sketch with Special Reference to His Contributions to Jewish and Zionist History*. New York: Bloch, 1929.

Diamond, Steven L. *Full Circle: A Physician's Life Lived with Polio*. Troy, NY: Troy Bookmakers, 2014. Kindle.

Dinshaw, Carolyn. *Getting Medieval: Sexuality and Communities, Pre- and Postmodern*. Durham, NC: Duke University Press, 1999.

Dolfi, Elizabeth. "Christian Domestic Discipline and Queer Religious Studies." *Scholar and Feminist* 14, no. 2 (2007). http://sfonline.barnard.edu/queer-religion/christian-domestic-discipline-and-queer-religious-studies/.

Doyle, Arthur Conan. *A History of Spiritualism*. New York: Arno, 1926.

Dushkin, Alexander. *Living Bridges*. Jerusalem: Keter, 1975.

Eck, Diana L. "Prospects for Pluralism: Voice and Vision in the Study of Religion." *Journal of the American Academy of Religion* 75, no. 4 (December 2007): 743–76.

Edelman, Judith. "In the War Years." In *The Plough Woman: Memoirs of the Pioneer Women in Palestine*, edited by Rachel Katznelson Shazar, translated by Maurice Samuel, 59–64. 1932. New York: Herzl, 1975

Edelman, Lee. *No Future: Queer Theory and the Death Drive.* Durham, NC: Duke University Press, 2004.

Eiesland, Nancy. "Barriers and Bridges: Relating the Disability Rights Movement and Religious Organizations." In *Human Disability and the Service of God*, edited by Nancy Eiesland and Don E. Saliers, 200–229. Nashville, TN: Abingdon, 1998.

Eiesland, Nancy. *The Disabled God: Toward a Liberatory Theology of Disability.* Nashville, TN: Abingdon, 1994.

Einstein, Albert. "Foreword." In *Modern Palestine: A Symposium*, edited by Jessie Sampter, v. New York: Hadassah, 1933.

Eulberg, Marny K. "What Having Polio Causes, Might Cause, and Does Not Cause." *Post-polio Health* 28, no. 2 (Spring 2012): 1–5.

Evans, Darrell. "Your Love Is Extravagant," track 9 on *Freedom*, Vertical Music, 1998.

"Fifteenth Annual Convention of the Federation of American Zionists." *Maccabaean* 22, no. 1 (June–July 1912): 1–35.

Fineman, Irving. *Woman of Valor: The Life of Henrietta Szold.* New York: Simon and Schuster, 1961.

Fishbayn Joffe, Lisa. Foreword to *Girls of Liberty: The Struggle for Suffrage in Mandatory Palestine*, by Margalit Shilo, ix–xi. Waltham, MA: Brandeis University Press, 2016.

Foucault, Michel. *History of Sexuality.* Vol. 1. Translated by Robert Hurley. New York: Vintage, 1990.

Frank, Lucy. "'Bought with a Price': Elizabeth Stuart Phelps and the Commodification of Heaven in Postbellum America." *ESQ: A Journal of the American Renaissance* 55, no. 2 (2009): 165–92.

Furey, Constance. "Body, Society, and Subjectivity in Religious Studies." *Journal of the American Academy of Religion* 80, no. 1 (March 2012): 7–33.

Furey, Constance. *Poetic Relations: Intimacy and Faith in the English Reformation.* Chicago: University of Chicago Press, 2017.

Gilder, Joseph. *Critic* 26 (1887): 293–94.

Gill, Carol. "A Psychological View of Disability Culture." In *Disability: The Social, Political, and Ethical Debate*, edited by Robert M. Baird, Stuart E. Rosenbaum, and S. Kay Toombs. Amherst, 163–67. New York: Prometheus Books, 2009.

Gmur, Priska. "'It Is Not Up to Us Women to Solve Great Problems': The Duty of the Zionist Woman in the Context of the First Ten Congresses." In *The First Zionist Congress in 1897—Causes, Significance, Topicality*, edited by Heiko Haumann, translated by Wayne van Dalsum and Vivian Kramer. Basel: Karger, 1997.

Gordon, Jael. "The Kvutzah of Twenty." In *The Plough Woman: Memoirs of the Pioneer Women in Palestine*, edited by Rachel Katznelson Shazar, translated by Maurice Samuel, 89–94. 1932. New York: Herzl, 1975.

Hagood, Taylor. *Secrecy, Magic, and the One-Act Plays of Harlem Renaissance Women Writers.* Columbus: Ohio State University Press, 2010.

Halberstam, Jack. *In a Queer Time and Place: Transgendered Bodies, Subcultural Lives*. New York: New York University Press, 2005.

Harriss, M. Cooper, and Sarah Imhoff. Editorial. *American Religion* 1, no. 1 (Fall 2019): 1–4.

Haskell, Ellen. *Suckling at My Mother's Breast: The Image of a Nursing God in Jewish Mysticism*. Albany: State University of New York Press, 2012.

Haskins, David Greene. *Ralph Waldo Emerson: His Maternal Ancestors, with Some Reminiscences of Him*. Boston: Cupples, Upham, 1886.

Hellner-Eshed Melila. *A River Flows from Eden: The Language of Mystical Experience in the Zohar*. Stanford, CA: Stanford University Press, 2005.

Hertzberg, Arthur, ed. *The Zionist Idea: A Historical Analysis and Reader*. Philadelphia: Jewish Publication Society, 1997.

Herzl, Theodor. *Old-New Land (Altneuland)*, translated by Lotta Levensohn. New York: Bloch, (1902) 1941.

Hochman, Leah. *The Ugliness of Moses Mendelssohn: Aesthetics, Religion and Morality in the Eighteenth Century*. New York: Routledge, 2014.

Hoffman, Matthew B. *From Rebel to Rabbi: Reclaiming Jesus and the Making of Modern Jewish Culture*. Stanford, CA: Stanford University Press, 2007.

Hoffman-Ladd, Valerie J. "Mysticism and Sexuality in Sufi Thought and Life." *Mystics Quarterly* 18, no. 3 (September 1992): 82–93.

Holloway, Julian. "Enchanted Spaces: The Séance, Affect, and Geographies of Religion." *Annals of the Association of American Geographers* 96, no. 1 (2006): 182–87.

Hollywood, Amy. *Sensible Ecstasy: Mysticism, Sexual Difference, and the Demands of History*. Chicago: University of Chicago Press, 2002.

Hume, Janice. *Obituaries in American Culture*. Jackson: University Press of Mississippi, 2000.

Hutchison, William R. *Religious Pluralism in America: The Contentious History of a Founding Ideal*. New Haven, CT: Yale University Press, 2004.

Imhoff, Sarah. *Masculinity and the Making of American Judaism*. Bloomington: Indiana University Press, 2017.

Imhoff, Sarah. "Race, Religion, and Jewish Sexuality in an Age of Immigration." In *Religion Is Raced: Understanding American Religion in the Twenty-First Century*, edited by Penny Edgell and Grace Yukich, 95–113. New York: New York University Press, 2020.

Imhoff, Sarah. "Why Disability Studies Needs to Take Religion Seriously." *Religions* 8, no. 9 (2017): 186 (1–12).

Imhoff, Sarah, and Hillary Kaell. "Lineage Matters: DNA, Race, and Gene Talk in Judaism and Messianic Judaism." *Religion and American Culture: A Journal of Interpretation* 27, no. 1 (Winter 2017): 95–127.

Ingall, Carol, ed. *The Women Who Reconstructed American Jewish Education, 1910–1965*. Waltham, MA: Brandeis University Press, 2010.

Ivry, Alfred L. *Maimonides' "Guide of the Perplexed": A Philosophical Guide*. Chicago: University of Chicago Press, 2016.

Izraeli, Dafna N. "The Zionist Women's Movement in Palestine, 1911–1927: A Sociological Analysis." *Signs: Journal of Women in Culture and Society* 7, no. 1 (Autumn 1981): 87–114.

Jacobson, Kerry. *Life before Post-polio Syndrome*. North Charleston, SC: CreateSpace, 2015.

Jain, Andrea R. *Peace Love Yoga: The Politics of Global Spirituality*. New York: Oxford University Press, 2020.

Jakobsen, Janet. "Queer Is? Queer Does? Normativity and the Problem of Resistance." *GLQ: A Journal of Lesbian and Gay Studies* 4, no. 4 (October 1998): 511–36.

James, Edmund. *The Immigrant Jew in America*. New York: B. F. Buck, 1906.

Janaith, Rachel. "Stages." In *The Plough Woman: Memoirs of the Pioneer Women in Palestine*, edited by Rachel Katznelson Shazar, translated by Maurice Samuel, 137–45. 1932. New York: Herzl, 1975.

Jenson, Scott. *The Simplicity Shift: Innovative Design Tactics in a Corporate World*. Cambridge: Cambridge University Press, 2002.

Kafer, Alison. *Feminist, Queer, Crip*. Bloomington: Indiana University Press, 2013.

Kahn, [Dorothy] Ruth. "Yesha Sampter." In *Yesha Sampter: Leyom Hashloshim* [Jessie Sampter: after 30 days], 29–31. Kibbutz Givat Brenner, 1939.

Kane, Paula M. "'She Offered Herself Up': The Victim Soul and Victim Spirituality in Catholicism." *Church History* 71, no. 1 (March 2002): 80–119.

Kaplan, Mordecai. *Communings of the Spirit: Journals of Mordecai Kaplan*. Vol. 2, *1934–1941*, edited by Mel Scult. Detroit: Wayne State University Press, 2016.

Kaplan, Mordecai. *Judaism as a Civilization: Toward a Reconstruction of American Jewish Life*. New York: Macmillan, 1934.

Kark, Ruth, Margalit Shilo, and Galit Hasan-Rokem, eds. *Jewish Women in Pre-state Israel: Life History, Politics, and Culture*. Waltham, MA: Brandeis University Press, 2008.

Keane, Webb. "On the Materiality of Religion." *Material Religion* 4, no. 2 (2008): 230–32.

Keller, Helen. *The World I Live In*. New York: Century, 1910.

Khazzoom, Aziza. "The Great Chain of Orientalism." *American Sociological Review* 68, no. 4 (August 2003): 481–510.

Kidd, Thomas. *America's Religious History*. Grand Rapids, MI: Zondervan, 2019.

Klapper, Melissa. *Ballots, Babies, and Banners of Peace*. New York: New York University Press, 2013.

Korn, Eugene. Foreword to *White Fire: The Life and Works of Jessie Sampter*, by Bertha Badt-Strauss. New York: Reconstructionist Press, 1956.

Kotzin, Daniel P. "An Attempt to Americanize the *Yishuv*: Judah L. Magnes in Mandatory Palestine." *Israel Studies* 5, no. 1 (Spring 2000): 1–23.

Kuppers, Petra. "Crip Time." *Tikkun* 29, no. 4 (Fall 2014): 29–30.

Laderman, Gary, and Luis León, eds. *Religion and American Cultures: Tradition, Diversity, and Popular Expression*. 4 vols. Santa Barbara, CA: ABC-CLIO, 2014.

Lakoff, George, and Mark Johnson. *Philosophy in the Flesh*. New York: Basic Books, 1999.

Lazarus, Josephine. *The Spirit of Judaism.* New York: Dodd, Mead, 1895.

Lazarus, Josephine. "Zionism and Americanism." *Menorah* 38, no. 5 (May 1905): 262–68.

Lelwica, Michelle Mary. *Shameful Bodies: Religion and the Culture of Physical Improvement.* London: Bloomsbury, 2017.

Lepore, Jill. "Historians Who Love Too Much: Reflections on Microhistory and Biography." *Journal of American History* 88, no. 1 (June 2001): 129–44.

Lerner, Gerda. "Women's History Sources: A Guide to Archives and Manuscript Collections in the United States. Vol. 2: Index." *Library Quarterly* 51, no. 1 (January 1981): 102–4.

Levensohn, Lotta. "The Book of Nations." *Menorah* 5, no. 5 (October–December 1919): 296.

Liberson, Techiah. "Those First Years." In *The Plough Woman: Memoirs of the Pioneer Women in Palestine*, edited by Rachel Katznelson Shazar, translated by Maurice Samuel, 27–31. 1932. New York: Herzl, 1975.

Linton, Simi. *My Body Politic: A Memoir.* Ann Arbor: University of Michigan Press, 2007.

Little, Ann. *The Many Captivities of Esther Wheelwright.* New Haven, CT: Yale University Press, 2016.

Lowenthal, Marvin. *Henrietta Szold: Life and Letters.* New York: Viking, 1942.

Lucia, Amanda. *White Utopias: The Religious Exoticism of Transformational Festivals.* Oakland: University of California Press, 2020.

Mackelprang, Romel W., and Richard O. Salsgiver. "People with Disabilities and Social Work: Historical and Contemporary Issues." *Social Work* 41, no. 1 (January 1996): 7–14.

Madmoni-Gerber, Shashona. *Israeli Media and the Framing of Internal Conflict: The Yemenite Babies Affair.* London: Palgrave, 2009.

Marcus, Jacob Rader. *The American Jewish Woman, 1654–1980.* New York: Ktav Publishing House, 1981.

Marcus, Jacob Rader, ed. *The American Jewish Woman: A Documentary History.* New York: Ktav Publishing House, 1981.

Margalit, Elkana. "Social and Intellectual Origins of the Hashomer Hatzair Youth Movement." In *Essential Papers on Jews and the Left*, edited by Ezra Mendelsohn, 145–65. New York: New York University Press, 1997.

Marques, Joan F. *Empower the Leader in You!* Self-published, AuthorHouse, 2004.

McCune, Mary. *The Whole Wide World without Limits: International Relief, Gender Politics, and American Jewish Women, 1893–1930.* Detroit: Wayne State University Press, 2005.

McGinity, Keren R. *Still Jewish: A History of Women and Intermarriage in America.* New York: New York University Press, 2009.

McKean, Lise. *Divine Enterprise: Gurus and the Hindu Nationalist Movement.* Chicago: University of Chicago Press, 1996.

Medoff, Rafael. *Zionism and the Arabs: An American Jewish Dilemma, 1898–1948.* Westport, CT: Praeger, 1997.

Mehta, Samira K. *Beyond Chrismukkah: The Christian-Jewish Interfaith Family in the United States*. Chapel Hill: University of North Carolina Press, 2018.

Mendelsohn, Leonard. "The Travail of Jewish Children's Literature." *Children's Literature* 3 (1974): 48–55.

Merleau-Ponty, Maurice. *Phenomenology of Perception*. New York: Routledge, 2012.

Mindra, Mihai. "Evangelical and Progressive Inscriptions in Mary Antin's Autobiographical Discourse." *Studies in American Jewish Literature* 37, no. 2 (2018): 173–99.

Morgan, David. "Materiality." In *The Oxford Handbook of the Study of Religion*, edited by Michael Stausberg and Steven Engler, 271–89. New York: Oxford University Press, 2016.

Muñoz, José Esteban. *Cruising Utopia: The There and Then of Queer Futurity*. New York: New York University Press, 2009.

Nabhan-Warren, Kristy. "Embodied Research and Writing: A Case for Phenomenologically Oriented Religious Studies Ethnographies." *Journal of the American Academy of Religion* 79, no. 2 (June 2011): 378–407.

Nadell, Pamela. Introduction to *From Plotzk to Boston*, by Mary Antin, v–xxi. New York: Markus Weiner, 1986.

Neis, R. *The Sense of Sight in Rabbinic Culture*. Cambridge: Cambridge University Press, 2013.

Neumann, Boaz. *Land and Desire in Early Zionism*. Waltham, MA: Brandeis University Press, 2011.

Nordau, Max. "Muscular Judaism." In *The Jew in the Modern World: A Documentary History*, edited by Paul Mendes-Flohr and Jehuda Reinharz, 547. New York: Oxford University Press, 1980. Originally published as "Muskeljudentum," *Juedische Turnzeitung*, June 1903.

Nordau, Max. "The Physical Intellectual and Economical Amelioration of the Jews." *Maccabaean* 2, no. 2 (February 1902): 56–64.

O'Neill, William. *Everyone Was Brave: Feminism in America*. San Antonio, TX: Quadrangle, 1969.

Orsi, Robert. "'Mildred, Is It Fun to Be a Cripple?' The Culture of Suffering in American Catholicism in the Middle Years of the 20th Century." *South Atlantic Quarterly* 93 (1994): 547–90.

Orsi, Robert. "The Problem of the Holy." In *Cambridge Companion to Religious Studies*, edited by Robert Orsi, 84–106. New York: Cambridge University Press, 2011.

Padden, Carol A., and Tom Humphries. *Deaf in America*. Cambridge, MA: Harvard University Press, 1988.

Parsons, William B. Introduction to *Being Spiritual but Not Religious: Past, Present, Future(s)*, edited by William B. Parsons, 1–11. New York: Routledge, 2018.

Partnow, Elaine. *The Quotable Jewish Woman*. Woodstock, VT: Jewish Lights, 2004.

Petro, Anthony. "Race, Gender, Sexuality, and Religion in North America." In *Oxford Research Encyclopedia of Religion*, published online February 27, 2017, https://doi.org/10.1093/acrefore/9780199340378.013.488.

Phelps, Elizabeth Stuart. *The Gate's Ajar*. London: George Routledge and Sons, 1863.

Pianko, Noam. *Jewish Peoplehood: An American Innovation*. New Brunswick, NJ: Rutgers University Press, 2015.

Pianko, Noam. *Zionism and the Roads Not Taken: Rawidowicz, Kaplan, Kohn*. Bloomington: Indiana University Press, 2010.

Porterfield, Amanda. "Religious Pluralism, the Study of Religion, and 'Postsecular' Culture." In *The American University in a Postsecular Age: Religion and the Academy*, edited by Douglas Jacobsen and Rhonda Hustedt Jacobsen, 187–201. Oxford: Oxford University Press, 2008.

Presner, Todd Samuel. "'Clear Heads, Solid Stomachs, and Hard Muscles': Max Nordau and the Aesthetics of Jewish Regeneration." *Modernism/Modernity* 10, no. 2 (April 2003): 269–96.

Presner, Todd Samuel. *Muscular Judaism*. New York: Routledge, 2007.

Puar, Jasbir. *Terrorist Assemblages*. Durham, NC: Duke University Press, 2007.

Qafisheh, Mutaz M. *The International Law Foundations of Palestinian Nationality: A Legal Examination of Nationality in Palestine under Britain's Rule*. Leiden: Martin Nijhoff, 2008.

Rabin, Shari. "Jews in Church: Rethinking Jewish-Christian Relations in Nineteenth-Century America." *Religions* 9, no. 8 (2018): 237.

Raider, Mark A. *The Emergence of American Zionism*. New York: New York University Press, 1998.

Rambuss, Richard. *Closet Devotions*. Durham, NC: Duke University Press, 1998.

Regev, Eliezer. "HaEsh HaLavanah" [White fire]. In *Bet Yesha: 30 Shana* [Jessie's House: 30 Years], 1–6. Givat Brenner, 1965.

Rock-Singer, Cara. "Hadassah and the Gender of Modern Jewish Thought: The Affective, Embodied Messianism of Jessie Sampter, Irma Lindheim, and Nima Adlerblum." *American Jewish History* 104, nos. 2/3 (April/July 2020): 423–56.

Rosenberg-Friedman, Lilach. "David Ben-Gurion and the 'Demographic Threat': His Dualistic Approach to Natalism, 1936–63." *Middle Eastern Studies* 51, no. 5 (2015): 742–66.

Royce, Josiah. "The Seekers: An Introductory Word." In *The Seekers*, by Jessie Sampter, v–xii. New York: Mitchell Kennerley, 1910.

Rubinstein, Marion. *Adventuring in Palestine*. New York: Alfred A. Knopf, 1936.

Sampter, Jessie, ed. *A Guide to Zionism*. New York: Zionist Organization of America, 1920.

Sampter, Jessie, ed. *Modern Palestine: A Symposium*. New York: Hadassah, 1933.

Samuel, Herbert. *Leisure in a Democracy*. Cambridge: Cambridge University Press, 1949.

Samuels, Ellen. "Six Ways of Looking at Crip Time." *Disability Studies Quarterly* 37, no. 3 (Summer 2017). https://dsq-sds.org/article/view/5824/4684.

Sanford, Matthew. *Waking: A Memoir of Trauma and Transcendence*. N.p.: Rodale Books, 2008.

Satter, Beryl. *Each Mind a Kingdom: Women, Sexual Purity, and the New Thought Movement*. Berkeley: University of California Press, 2001.

Scarry, Elaine. *The Body in Pain: The Making and Unmaking of the World*. New York: Oxford University Press, 1985.

Schaefer, Donovan O. *Religious Affects: Animality, Evolution, and Power*. Durham, NC: Duke University Press, 2015.

Schlimowitz, Miriam. "The Women's Farm in Nachlath Jehuda." In *The Plough Woman: Memoirs of the Pioneer Women in Palestine*, edited by Rachel Katznelson Shazar, translated by Maurice Samuel, 159–63. 1932. New York: Herzl, 1975.

Schmidt, Leigh Eric. *Restless Souls: The Making of American Spirituality*. Berkeley: University of California Press, 2012.

Schumm, Darla, and Julie Pfeiffer. "Disciplining Normalcy: *What Katy Did* and Nineteenth-Century Female Bodies." In *The Embodied Child: Readings in Children's Literature and Culture*, edited by Roxanne Harde and Lydia Kokkola, 99–112. New York: Routledge, 2017.

Schumm, Darla. "Misfitting as a Practice of Justice: Religion, Disability, and Community in the U.S." Presentation to the American Academy of Religion, November 2017, Boston, MA.

Scott, Joan Wallach. *Feminism and History*. Oxford: Oxford University Press, 2008.

Segal, Hyman. *The Book of Pain-Struggle, Called: The Prophecy of Fulfillment*. New York: Massada Publishing Company, 1911.

Segal, Hyman. *The Law of Struggle*. New York: Massada Publishing Company, 1918.

Selka, Stephen. "Cityscapes and Contact Zones: Christianity, Candomblé, and African Heritage Tourism in Brazil." *Religion* 43, no. 3 (2013): 403–20.

Shamir, Moshe. *Yona MeHatzer Zara* [From a different yard]. Tel Aviv: Am Oved, 1973.

Shapira, Anita. *Ha-halikha 'al kav ha-ofek* [Going toward the horizon]. Tel: Am Oved, 1989.

Sheskin, Ira M., and Arnold Dashefsky, "Jewish Population in the United States, 2012." In *American Jewish Year Book*, edited by Ira M. Sheskin and Arnold Dashefsky, 143–211. Dordrecht: Springer, 2012.

Shotwell, Alexis. *Against Purity: Living Ethically in Compromised Times*. Minneapolis: University of Minnesota Press, 2016.

Siebers, Tobin. *Disability Theory*. Ann Arbor: University of Michigan Press, 2008.

Silk, Mark. "Defining Religious Pluralism in America: A Regional Analysis." *Annals of the American Academy of Political and Social Science* 612, no. 1 (July 2007): 62–81.

Simmons, Erica. "Playgrounds and Penny Lunches in Palestine: American Social Welfare in the Yishuv." *American Jewish History* 92, no. 3 (September 2004): 263–97.

Smith, Bonnie. *The Gender of History: Men, Women, and Historical Practice*. Cambridge, MA: Harvard University Press, 2000.

Smith-Rosenberg, Carroll. "The Female World of Love and Ritual: Relations between Women in Nineteenth-Century America." *Signs: Journal of Women in Culture and Society* 1, no. 1 (Autumn 1975): 1–29.

Stanislawski, Michael. *Zionism and the Fin de Siecle: Cosmopolitanism and National-ism from Nordau to Jabotinsky*. Berkeley: University of California Press, 2001.

Steer, Martina. "Bertha Badt-Strauss." In *The Shalvi/Hyman Encylopedia of Jew-ish Women*. Jewish Women's Archive. December 31, 1999. https://jwa.org /encyclopedia/article/badt-strauss-bertha.

Steer, Martina. "Bertha Badt-Strauss (1885–1970), a Biography." *Leo Baeck Institute Year Book* 49, no. 1 (January 2004): 266–67.

Steer, Martina. *Bertha Badt-Strauss (1885–1970): Eine jüdische Publizistin*. Frankfurt: Campus, 2005.

Stevens, Patricia E., and Joanne M. Hall. "A Critical Historical Analysis of the Medical Construction of Lesbianism." *International Journal of Health Services* 21, no. 2 (April 1991): 291–307.

Stewart Diakité, Dianne M., and Tracey E. Hucks. "Africana Religious Studies: Toward a Transdisciplinary Agenda in an Emerging Field." *Journal of Africana Religions* 1, no. 1 (2013): 28–77.

St. John, Robert. *Shalom Means Peace*. Garden City, NY: Doubleday, 1949.

St. Pierre, Joshua. "Distending Straight-Masculine Time: A Phenomenology of the Disabled Speaking Body." *Hypatia* 30, no. 1 (Winter 2015): 49–65.

TallBear, Kim. *Native American DNA: Tribal Belonging and the False Promise of Gene-tic Science*. Minneapolis: University of Minnesota Press, 2013.

Taves, Ann. *Fits, Trances, and Visions: Experiencing Religion and Explaining Experi-ence from Wesley to James*. Princeton, NJ: Princeton University Press, 1999.

"Teaching Children to Become Philosophers." *Current Literature* 50, no. 6 (June 1911): 630–32.

Thandeka. *Learning to Be White: Money, Race, and God in America*. New York: Con-tinuum, 1999.

Thomson, Rosemarie Garland. "Eugenics." In *Keywords in Disability Studies*, edited by Rachel Adams, Benjamin Reiss, and David Serlin, 74–78. New York: New York University Press, 2015.

Thomson, Rosemarie Garland. *Extraordinary Bodies: Figuring Disability in American Culture and Literature*. New York: Columbia University Press, 1997.

Tolles, Frederick B. "Emerson and Quakerism." *American Literature* 10 (May 1930): 142–65.

"Tsiunei Derech" [Milestones: From diaries, minutes, and newspapers]. In *Bet Yesha: 30 Shana* [Jessie's House: 30 Years], 31–47. Givat Brenner, 1965.

Twain, Mark. *Innocents Abroad*. N.p.: American Publishing Company, 1896.

Tzemach, Moshe. "Brit HaHayyim SheNahtama" [Signed covenant of life]. In *Bet Yesha: 30 Shana* [Jessie's House: 30 Years], 6–7. Givat Brenner, 1965.

Urofsky, Melvin I. *American Zionism from Herzl to the Holocaust*. Garden City, NY: Anchor, 1975.

Wald, Lilian. *The House on Henry Street*. New York: Holt, 1915.

Weight Watchers Success Everyday. New York: John Wiley & Sons, 1995.

Weiner, Isaac. *Religion Out Loud: Religious Sound, Public Space, and American Plural-ism*. New York: New York University Press, 2014.

Weisenfeld, Judith. *New World A-Coming: Black Religion and Racial Identity during the Great Migration*. New York: New York University Press, 2017.

Weiss, Meira. *The Chosen Body: The Politics of the Body in Israeli Society*. Stanford, CA: Stanford University Press, 2004.

Wendell, Susan. *The Rejected Body: Feminist Philosophical Reflections on Disability*. New York: Routledge, 1996.

Wenger, Tisa. *Religious Freedom: The Contested History of an American Ideal*. Chapel Hill: University of North Carolina Press, 2017.

Weston, Kath. *Families We Choose: Lesbians, Gays, Kinship*. New York: Columbia University Press, 1991.

White, Heather. *Reforming Sodom: Protestants and the Rise of Gay Rights*. Chapel Hill: University of North Carolina Press, 2015.

Wilcock, Evelyn. *Pacifism and the Jews*. Stroud, UK: Hawthorn, 1994.

Wilson, Jeffrey R. "The Trouble with Disability in Shakespeare Studies." *Disability Studies Quarterly* 37, no. 2 (Spring 2017). https://dsq-sds.org/article/view/5430/4644.

"Without a Country." *Maccabaean* 24, no. 5 (May 1914): 131.

Wolf, Rebecca Boim. "Jessie Sampter and the Hadassah School of Zionism." In *The Women Who Reconstructed American Jewish Education, 1910–1965*, edited by Carol Ingall, 46–62. Waltham, MA: Brandeis University Press, 2010.

Wolfson, Elliot. *The Circle in the Square: Studies in the Use of Gender in Kabbalistic Symbolism*. Albany: State University of New York Press, 1995.

Woodhull, Victoria. "The Principles of Social Freedom." In *Women and Romance: A Reader*, edited by Susan Ostrov Weisser, 39–44. New York: New York University Press, 2001.

Young, Bette Roth. "Emma Lazarus and Her Jewish Problem." *American Jewish History* 84, no. 4 (December 1996): 291–313.

Yuknavitch, Lidia. *The Book of Joan*. New York: Harper Collins, 2017.

Zangwill, Israel. *Children of the Ghetto: A Study of a Peculiar People*. London: W. Heinemann, 1892.

Zangwill, Israel. *The Melting-Pot: Drama in Four Acts*. New York: Macmillan, 1910.

Zangwill, Israel. *The Voice of Jerusalem*. New York: Macmillan, 1921.

Zola, Irving. "The Language of Disability: Problems of Politics and Practice." *Australian Disability Review* 1, no. 3 (1988): 13–21.

Index

Berlin, Leah (Sampter's partner): as care-giver, 13, 92–94, 104, 132–33; family, 132; fictional character modeled on, 205; marriage and, 120; meeting Sampter, 126; photograph of, 127; Sampter's death and, 196, 200; Sampter's relationship with, 7–8, 83, 108, 119, 126–43, 171, 187; work, 130–31. *See also* Kibbutz Givat Brenner

Betar, 165–66

Bhagavad Gita, 37

Bible, 152, 155, 240n43; 1 Kings, 88; Job, 77; Leviticus, 88

Binyamini (physician), 16

biographical writing, 2–4; embodied method-ology, 4–14, 71, 146–47; partial knowledge and, 218; Sampter's reception history, 193–214; as stories, 194; time in, 19–25, 76–77. *See also* autobiographical writing; narrative histories

bisexuality: use of term, 109. *See also* queerness

Blackness, 30. *See also* African Americans; race

Bnai Brith Messenger, 195

B'nai Israel Bulletin, 170

bodies: awareness of, 71; idealized male bod-ies, 15–18, 124, 150; physical knowledge, 5; transcendence of, 70; Zionist ideal of strong healthy bodies, 1–2, 15–18, 67, 69, 92–93, 137–38, 150, 169–72, 187. *See also* disability; embodiment and embodied experience; mind-body-soul connection; pain; reproduction; suffering

Book of Pain-Struggle, The (Segal), 10, 149–50, 160

Border Roads Organisation, 214–17

Boyarin, Daniel, 16

Brandeis, Louis, 14, 15, 156, 157, 161

Braude, Ann, 57, 61

Breckenridge, Carol, 95

Brenner, Yosef Haim, 189

British Empire, 163, 192, 216

British Mandatory Palestine, 168, 181–83

Buber, Martin, 145

Buddhism, 35, 217

built environments, 9, 29–30; disability and, 83–84, 90

Bureau of Indian Affairs, 65

Butler, Judith, 11–12

Chazan, Meir, 164, 214

children: education for Yemenite Jews, 205–7; songs and verses for, 201–2; Zion-ism and, 175. *See also* family; reproduction

children's literature, 210–11

Christianity: disability as sin, 87–89; Jewish identity and, 43–45; Native Americans and, 65; religious recombination and, 61–62; Sampter's interest in, 27, 30, 36; sexuality and, 111–12; Spiritualism and, 53; theology, 151

Christian mysticism, 42

Christian Science, 49, 61, 66

chronic pain. *See* pain

Clare, Eli, 125, 234n12

Cohen, Hermann, 145, 208

collective living, 17–18, 186–87; work and, 137, 139–40, 189. *See also* Kibbutz Givat Brenner; kibbutzim; kvutza/kvutzot; moshavim

collectivist democracies, 158, 177, 182. *See also* democracy

colonialism, 15, 166, 182–83. *See also* imperialism

Commentary, 204

conversion, 28, 51, 59, 62, 148, 208

Cressler, Matthew, 62

crip and cripple: Sampter's cripping of Zion-ism, 145, 149–51, 154, 168–74; supercrips, 77; use of terms, 79–80. *See also* disability

crip theory, 142; religion and, 84–86. *See also* disability studies

crip time, 20–23, 82, 87, 229n1. *See also* time

Crosby, Christina, 108

crucifixion, 54, 151

cultural pluralism, 44, 152, 156

cultural Zionists, 15, 144, 208

Dalai Lama, 216–17

Danith, Rebecca, 186

Darwin, Charles, 33, 42

Daudet, Alphonse, 81

Davar HaPoelet, 196, 202

Davis, Allen Freeman, 234n9

Davis, Lennard, 84–85

deaf/Deaf education, 97–99, 170, 231n56

death: Sampter's, 8, 104, 137, 193, 195–202; theological reflection on, 31–32; time and, 82

democracy: collectivist, 158, 182; Zionism and, 144, 166–69, 177, 178–84

depression, 76, 131, 170–71, 173–74

de Sola Pool, David, 199

de Sola Pool, Tamar, 130

Deutsch, Gotthard, 161

Dinshaw, Carolyn, 109

disability, 68–105; built environments and, 83–84, 90; cultural assumptions about, 88, 231n54; cultural norms and, 83–84, 92–93; emotional aspects (*see* mental health); framing of, 22–23 (*see also* disability studies); gender norms and, 125; holiness and, 122; life cycle and, 83–84; meanings of, 84–105; medical model of, 70, 89–91, 98; as metaphor, 100–102; as metonym, 101–2; as obstacle in the world, 74–75, 80, 89–93, 103; political/relational model of, 91, 98; religion and, 70–71; sexuality and, 112, 115, 122, 125, 234n12; as sin, 87–89, 101; social model of, 23, 70, 90; terminology for, 79–80; time and, 81–84 (*see also* crip time); as way of engaging the world, 102–4; Zionism and, 16, 67, 93–100, 220. *See also* bodies; illnesses and physical weakness

disability studies, 9, 20; nationalism and, 95; personal narratives and, 85–86; relationships and, 108; religion and, 70–80, 84–86, 104; validity and, 103; victorious narratives and, 77–78

diversity. *See* religious diversity

Dolfi, Elizabeth, 142

Doniger, Margaret, 199

Droste-Hülshoff, Annette von, 207

Druze, 178

Dubnov, Arie, 244n209

Dushkin, Alexander, 56, 153, 200

Dushkin, Julia, 12, 56, 199–202

Dutton, E. P., 160

economic conditions: kinship and, 141; in Palestine, 167, 186; polio and, 72–73; religious recombination and, 63; sexuality and, 111

Eddy, Mary Baker, 61, 66

Edelman, Judith, 186

Edelman, Lee, 235n34

Eder, Edith, 92

education, 153; for deaf children, 97–99, 170, 231n56; for Yemenite Jewish children, 205–7

Eiesland, Nancy, 9

Einstein, Albert, 1, 8, 14, 158–59

embodied methods of research, 4–14, 71, 146–47

embodiment and embodied experience: ideologies and, 2–4, 14, 69–70, 102–5, 221–22; metaphysical ideals and, 56; political-religious writing and, 145–47; religious identity and, 34–37; thought processes and, 6–7; time and, 19–25; truth and, 47; understanding and, 45–48, 70–71, 103

Emerson, Ralph Waldo, 42, 47, 66

Enright, Ann, 220

Ethical Cultural Society, 30, 32–33, 40–41, 64

Ethiopian Hebrews, 65

ethnicity: religious identity and, 34–37, 156–57. *See also* race

Evelyn (Sampter's friend), 53, 56

faith, 46, 86

family: in American Jewish history, 212–13; chosen, 111, 117; nuclear, 117, 140, 142, 213; traditional, 115–20, 139–40, 142. *See also* children; heteronormativity; kinship; marriage; queer kinship; reproduction

Federation of American Zionists, 15, 17, 157, 242n128. *See also* Zionist Organization of America

Federation of Labor, 186

First Aliyah, 185

Fox sisters, 39, 61

free love, 139

Freud, Sigmund, 92, 129

ence of, 233n120; God and, 77; making sense of, 70; social model of disability and, 90–91; time and, 81–84; Zionism and, 10, 149–51, 170. *See also* suffering

Paine, Albert Bigelow, 41

Palestine: Balfour Declaration and, 192; under British Mandate, 168, 181–83; citizenship, 168, 181; economic conditions, 167, 186; gender norms in, 124, 141, 144, 165, 176, 184–90; non-Jewish Arabs in (*see* Arabs, non-Jewish); pacifism and, 158–66; population of, 144, 178, 192 (*see also* Arabs, non-Jewish; Yemenite Jews); Sampter's life in, 93–100, 124–42 (*see also* Kibbutz Givat Brenner); state building, 144, 158–66, 169, 210; women's suffrage, 181, 184–85; Zionism in, real and ideal, 158–90

Palestine Post, 195–96

Palestinian Citizenship Order, 168

palm readers, 54, 67, 89

pantheism, 46

Pawnee nation, 65

Peace Mission (Father Divine), 64–65

Peretz, Y. L., 211

personal narratives. *See* narrative histories

Petro, Anthony, 84

Phelps, Elizabeth Stuart, 61

Photoplay, 88

Pianko, Noam, 244n209

pluralism. *See* cultural pluralism; religious pluralism

Pluralism Project, Harvard University, 58

poetry, 13, 38, 54–55, 139–40, 160–61, 199, 210–11

polio: aftermath of (post-polio syndrome), 72–75, 80–84, 91–93, 131 (*see also* illnesses and physical weakness); effects of, 73–74, 199; pain caused by, 68–69, 72, 81; paralytic, 68–69; Sampter's religious thought and, 37–38; treatments for, 71–72, 78–79

Porterfield, Amanda, 59

productivity, 81–82, 172. *See also* work

Progressive Era politics, 40, 198

Promised Land, The (Antin), 41–42, 116

Quakers, 47, 61

queer, use of term, 106–8

queer desire, 108, 143; gender roles and, 112–13; Sampter and, 111–19, 124, 137; use of term, 111. *See also* friendships, female

queer kinship, 108, 143; Sampter's relationships and, 115, 119–24, 130; use of term, 111; Zionist ideals and, 120, 137–42

queerness, 106–43; disability and, 115; Sampter's queering of Zionism, 144–45, 154, 168, 221. *See also* homoeroticism; homosexuality; sexuality

queer theory, 20, 79–80, 118; religion and, 84–85, 142–43

queer time, 118, 143, 235n34

Rabin, Shari, 63–64

race, 30, 34–37, 63, 224n29; Jewish identity and, 34–37, 156–57, 230n17. *See also* ethnicity

racism, 13, 154, 156

Reconstructionist, 34, 140, 147

Reconstructionist Judaism, 55, 147–48

redemption, 77–78, 151

Reform Judaism, 30, 64, 211

Regev, Eliezer, 187

Rehovot, 7, 134, 174

Reich, Marcus, 99

Reinertsen, Sarah, 234nn13–14

relationships: disability studies and, 108; intimate, 108–11, 113, 124, 128, 136, 143, 200. *See also* family; friendships, female; marriage; queer desire; queer kinship; sexuality

religion: disability studies and, 70–80, 84–86, 104; heritage and, 35; innovation in, 27; religious desire as queer, 142; sexuality and, 111–12; as way to make sense of disability, 70–71. *See also* American religion; Christianity; God; Judaism; occult; religious recombination; Spiritualism

religious diversity, 27; American, 56–60, 66–67, 226n2; defined, 58

religious identity: as exclusive, 32; practices and, 57. *See also* Jewish identity